Strategies of Pu
Shaping a Can

Given declining budgets and uncertain political support, the environment for international co-operation in Canada and other industrial democracies has become exceptionally challenging. A collection of essays by experts in the field, *Strategies of Public Engagement* explores ways in which Canadian development organizations and non-governmental organizations (NGOs) can strengthen political and public support.

Development organizations need to reaffirm the Canadian consensus that international co-operation works and persuade the public and politicians that sustainable development is the key to human security and international order. The way to achieve this, contributors argue, is by demonstrating effectiveness and by systematically documenting, evaluating, and disseminating development successes through reasoned policy dialogue and strategic public engagement.

Strategies of Public Engagement contributes to the search for new ways to enhance the relevance and value of development organizations in the twenty-first century. It will be of interest to readers concerned with NGOs, Canadian development assistance, and North-South relations.

DAVID GILLIES is Manager, Development Policy and Research, Aga Khan Foundation Canada.

Strategies of Public Engagement

Shaping a Canadian Agenda for International Co-operation

EDITED BY DAVID GILLIES

McGill-Queen's University Press
Montreal & Kingston · London · Buffalo

Published under the auspices of the

 AGA KHAN FOUNDATION CANADA –
FONDATION AGA KHAN CANADA

Aga Khan Foundation Canada is a non-profit, private development agency that seeks fresh solutions to pressing social and environmental problems. The Aga Khan Foundation, which has units and affiliates on four continents, supports health, education, and rural and institutional development programmes in low income countries of Africa and Asia. The Foundation is part of the Aga Khan Development Network of social, economic, and cultural development institutions.

© McGill-Queen's University Press 1997
ISBN 0-7735-1677-8 (cloth)
ISBN 0-7735-1687-5 (paper)

Legal deposit fourth quarter 1997
Bibliothèque nationale du Québec

Printed in Canada on acid-free paper

McGill-Queen's University Press acknowledges the support received for its publishing program from the Canada Council's Block Grants program.

Canadian Cataloguing in Publication Data

Main entry under title:
 Strategies of public engagement: shaping a
 Canadian agenda for international co-operation
 Papers originally presented at the conference entitled
 Systematic learning, held in Ottawa, Ont. June
 22-23, 1996.
 Includes bibliographical references.
 ISBN 0-7735-1677-8 (bound) -
 ISBN 0-7735-1687-5 (pbk.)
 1. Economic assistance, Canadian – Developing
 countries. I. Gillies, David, 1952-
 HC60.S77 1997   338.91'7101724   C97-900687-2

This book was typeset by Typo Litho Composition Inc.
in 10/12 Baskerville.

Contents

Foreword / vii
NAZEER AZIZ LADHANI

Preface / ix

Introduction / 3
DAVID GILLIES

1 Trends in International Co-operation / 19
   ROGER C. RIDDELL

2 Becoming a Learning Organization, or, the Search for the Holy Grail / 63
   MICHAEL A. EDWARDS

3 Effective Policy Dialogue in the North: A View from Canada / 95
   TIM DRAIMIN & GERALD J. SCHMITZ

4 Effective Policy Dialogue in the South: Pakistan's National Conservation Strategy / 138
   ABAN MARKER KABRAJI

5 Strategies of Public Engagement / 155
   ERIC YOUNG

Future Directions / 173
DAVID GILLIES

Appendix One: Canadian Voluntary Organizations and CIDA: Framework for a Renewed Relationship / 189

Appendix Two: Global Citizenship: A New Way Forward / 201

Contributors / 221

Foreword

International co-operation to reduce global poverty has been an important part of international relations for more than four decades. The passing of the Cold War, growing demands for democracy and good governance, the acceleration of globalization, and the search for collective solutions to complex global problems should place development co-operation at the centre of the stage as a compelling public idea shared by all global citizens. Despite the opportunities presented by a more favourable international environment, however, support for development co-operation in many advanced industrial countries is more uncertain than in the past. This is reflected in a growing concern about the effectiveness of foreign aid and in reduced public spending for it.

Aga Khan Foundation Canada is a member of the wider Aga Khan Development Network, with strong roots in Canada and several developing countries. One of its priorities is public engagement activities that link Canadian values, such as self-reliance and equity, to our international co-operation programmes. Canada is not exempt from what some have called "compassion fatigue," but support for international co-operation remains a common value uniting Canadians from coast to coast. The lessons of the Foundation's public engagement experience underline the importance of appealing to the minds as well as the hearts of Canadians.

It was this knowledge that encouraged us to contribute to the debate that is under way about the future directions of Canada's foreign policy including its development policy. We chose to organize a round table whose theme would be the role of learning in divining a future path for development organizations – particularly those in the voluntary sector – and in promoting public support for international cooperation. Aga Khan Foundation Canada has found that by drawing on accurate development knowledge, and positive stories of self-reliance, community action, and improved well-being, it is possible to engage Canadians from all walks of life.

As a non-governmental organization promoting innovative social sector programmes in selected countries of East Africa and South and Central Asia, the Aga Khan Foundation fosters the cross-fertilization of ideas and know-how among sectoral development interventions and into national and international policy dialogue. Our specific learning objective is to contribute to the overall enhancement of the non-profit sector, both in the North and in the South.

Aga Khan Foundation Canada's research programme examines three strategic challenges facing the non-profit sector. These are strengthening the enabling environment for non-governmental organizations, enhancing institutional performance, and demonstrating that non-governmental organizations are effective development partners for governments and donor agencies.

Despite the more difficult national circumstances that currently prevail, Canada's development organizations are showing through their work in a myriad of international programmes that there are abundant reasons for hope and pride. I hope that this book will contribute to the rethinking under way as Canadian aid organizations seek new ways to enhance their relevance and value in the twenty-first century.

The Foundation wishes to thank the Partnership Branch of the Canadian International Development Agency for its generous assistance and each of the contributors for their expertise, insight, and commitment to this project. Special thanks are also due to Philip Cercone, executive director at McGill-Queen's University Press, for the prompt and professional approach to the publication, to Cranford Pratt for constructive advice, and to Marion Magee for able editorial assistance. Finally, Aga Khan Foundation Canada wishes to acknowledge the quality of ideas presented by all the participants at the 1996 round table. Their thinking is reflected throughout these pages.

                Nazeer Aziz Ladhani
                Chief Executive Officer, Aga Khan Foundation Canada

Preface

This volume examines the nature of the current "crisis" of confidence in international development and identifies some directions for renewing public support for Canadian international co-operation. The vantage point of the voluntary sector is prominent throughout, for it seems clear that non-governmental organizations (NGOs) in Canada and other developed countries face an identity crisis. In a setting of declining aid budgets and the growing importance, capacity, and direct funding of Southern NGOs, Northern NGOs must reinvent themselves to ensure their continued relevance – and hence public support for their work – as we move into the twenty-first century.

Most of the essays in this volume were originally presented as papers to a round table organized by Aga Khan Foundation Canada with assistance from the Canadian International Development Agency (CIDA) and held in Ottawa on 22 and 23 June 1996. The theme of the meeting was "Systematic Learning: Promoting Public Support for Canadian International Cooperation," and it brought together Canadian and international development professionals, journalists, scholars, public servants, and opinion leaders to discuss four sets of questions:

1 To what extent should development organizations adjust their vision and knowledge base from a narrow focus on aid to a broad mandate of international co-operation framed around interconnected global issues?
2 To what extent and how should development organizations invest in organizational learning?

3 What is the role of the voluntary sector in helping set agendas and in formulating public policy and how can NGOs strengthen their policy dialogue skills and messages?
4 What do Canadian development educators actually want people to do and what are the key messages to help strengthen support for international co-operation?

The contributors to this volume were selected for their expertise and for their ability to provide not just analysis but also practical suggestions on ways to strengthen public support for international co-operation. Particular attention was given to ensuring that a strong international voice was projected into the debate being played out in Canada. To enrich the discussion, we deliberately drew on a variety of expertise from research institutions, development practitioners, and social marketers.

In his introductory article, David Gillies sets out the Canadian context of the problems under discussion and offers an overview of systematic learning, policy dialogue, and public engagement. Roger Riddell analyses trends in international development and challenges the non-profit sector to deepen its understanding of how development co-operation fits into a more complex international system and a range of often interconnected global problems.

The volume moves on to address the institutional environment by examining strategies to enhance organizational learning and effective policy dialogue and the prospects for success in these pursuits. Michael Edwards provides a practitioner's assessment of the outlook for and limitations of organizational learning within development agencies. Taking issue with a lessons-learned approach, he maps out the more complex terrain that must be traversed before NGOs can approach the Holy Grail of the learning organization. And he argues that in seeking this goal, it is the journey and approach to knowledge rather than the destination that is key. Two essays illustrate the vicissitudes of NGO policy dialogue. Tim Draimin and Gerald Schmitz examine the efforts of Canadian NGOs to influence the recent foreign and development policy reviews undertaken by parliament and the government in Canada. They arrive at the ironical conclusion that in a policy setting that is increasingly constrained in its ability to respond to the kinds of claims advanced by NGOs, the voluntary sector has at least defended the focus on poverty of the international assistance envelope from systematic erosion. Aban Marker Kabraji takes an insider's look at the genesis of the National Conservation Strategy in Pakistan. Her account is important not just as a success story, but also because it was achieved in a dysfunctional political system.

Turning to the implications of more effective organizational learning and policy dialogue for public engagement strategies, Eric Young offers a social marketing perspective on public engagement. Recognizing that increasing public support has little influence on aid flows, Young cautions that effective public engagement first requires a clear understanding of the goal. If public support does not influence aid levels, why do it? One answer seems to be that the emphasis on process and consultation which are part and parcel of policy dialogue and public engagement add value by preserving trust, accountability, and participation in our public institutions.

The concluding essay draws on the findings of the Ottawa round table to provide a synthesis of and commentary on the main arguments. Two policy statements – one from CIDA and one from the Canadian Council for International Co-operation – complete the volume. They illustrate current thinking in Canada as the government sets out to "renew" its relations with the voluntary sector, and as some elements of the Canadian voluntary sector attempt to recast their public engagement strategies.

In its emphasis on learning, this book attempts to address in a Canadian context the call by the Organization for Economic Co-operation and Development (OECD) for a "reorientation of development education so that the challenges and obstacles, as well as the progress, are portrayed realistically rather than in sensational terms." The organizing premise is that development agencies, and NGOs in particular, can counter "compassion fatigue" by becoming more effective learning and influencing organizations. It is suggested that more systematic attention to demonstrating effectiveness by documenting and disseminating the lessons learned from development interventions will enhance the capacity of NGOs to improve their own practice, to influence development policies, and to strengthen public support for development. As several authors point out, this is by no means a simple, linear, or necessarily causal set of relationships. But while the linkages among learning, policy dialogue, and public engagement are complex and not easy to realize, it is surely clear that careful deliberation over ways to appeal more systematically to the minds as well as the hearts of Canadians is a worthwhile activity for development organizations.

The original round table and this volume form one strand in a host of deliberations on the future of Canadian international co-operation. In April 1996, the House of Commons Standing Committee on Foreign Affairs and International Trade organized a forum on "Promoting Greater Public Understanding of International Development Issues." This was followed by a cross-Canada consultation by the minister for international cooperation with major development stakeholders. CIDA subsequently tabled with the minister new public engagement priorities for its work which emphasize Canadian youth and the educational system. And in the autumn of 1996, after extensive consultations, the agency released its framework for a renewed relationship with the voluntary sector, and the Canadian Council for International Co-operation endorsed a strategy for public participation that will turn on the concept of global citizenship. Finally, in November 1996, a blue-chip task force chaired by Maurice Strong released its report, *Connecting with the World: Priorities for Canadian Internationalism in the 21st Century*. The report called for a doubling of Canadian aid spending on knowledge-based development activities, from 7.4 per cent to 15 per cent of official development assistance. This recommendation was based on an analysis that Canada's influence in world affairs is not guaranteed, that the traditional case for aid will not apply in the next century, and that learning and capacity development are areas in which Canada can add value and remain influential.

This book will be of interest to development professionals both in government and the voluntary sector. While the Canadian context is prominent, three essays by international experts tackle the generic themes of learning, dialogue, and public engagement in ways that should have resonance for the development communities in many OECD countries. Because the book offers the varied perspectives of development practitioners, researchers, and a social marketer it should appeal to practitioners, students, and informed citizens, and to opinion leaders and scholars of international relations, communications, and development co-operation.

The contents of this volume reflect the views and opinions of the individual authors alone and are not necessarily those of Aga Khan Foundation Canada, or those consulted in its preparation.

Strategies of Public Engagement

Introduction

DAVID GILLIES

For more than forty years, development co-operation to reduce global poverty has been a durable expression of moral vision in international relations (Lumsdaine 1993). Today, however, there is a marked erosion of confidence in and support for development co-operation in most rich countries. In the United States, for example, the public is generally poorly informed about foreign aid, and in the absence of a convincing rationale and in the face of pressing domestic priorities, both politicians and public are questioning the spending of money on overseas aid.[1] Unprecedented changes in the world economy and in international relations are restructuring the development business. Mounting pressures for fiscal probity across the industrialized North confront extraordinary global demands for development resources from those same nations.

Since the beginning of this decade the total amount of official development assistance (ODA) available to the developing world has declined significantly. Aid from the countries of the Organization for Economic Co-operation and Development (OECD) fell from US$60.85 billion in 1992 to US$55.96 billion in 1993. And although twenty-one OECD donors committed US$59 billion in official development assistance in 1995, in real terms this was a drop of 9.3 per cent. At 0.27 per cent of their combined gross national product (GNP), OECD donors are now giving less than at any time since 1970 (*Aidwatch* 1996). Moreover, assistance to the countries of the former Soviet world and aid for humanitarian crises driven by ethnic conflict offer strong competing claims for funds once focused on the poorest countries and on longer term development. In 1993, an estimated US$3.2 billion or nearly 6 per cent of total ODA was spent on managing complex humanitarian emergencies, and the share of the aid from the countries of the Development Assistance Committee of the OECD devoted to emergency relief rose from 1.5 per cent in 1991 to 8.4 per cent in 1994 (ICVA 1995, 1996).

Canada is no exception to the general trend. There, public support for ODA peaked in the mid-1980s and has since slipped. In a 1993 Angus Reid poll, respondents ranked ODA as the second most favoured area in which to cut government spending in order to reduce the deficit while more than 70 per cent of respondents believed trade rather than aid was a better way to help poorer countries (cited in ODI 1994). In a 1994 Ekos poll, Canadians placed foreign aid last in a list of 19 priorities for the federal government. Pollster Frank Graves interpreted this finding as evidence of a "general hardening of Canadians' compassionate arteries" as citizens show "increasing reluctance to endorse the more ... tolerant activities of government" such as aid, immigration, and wealth redistribution (Ekos 1995). These attitudes are most marked among the "comfortable" social classes and the governing élites for whom economic interests, such as deficit reduction and competitiveness, have increasingly trumped more humane values.

Government funding for development aid has also dropped sharply since the late 1980s. As a percentage of GNP, Canada's ODA has fallen from 0.49 per cent in 1988/9 to 0.35 per cent in 1996/7. In the 1996 federal budget, Canada's aid agency, the Canadian International Development Agency (CIDA), took another 15-per-cent budget reduction. Canada's aid budget is projected to fall to approximately Cdn$1.9 billion in 1998/9 with an ODA/GNP ratio of just 0.27 per cent (including refugee support). As a proportion of total federal government expenditures, ODA will have declined to 1.45 per cent in 1998/9 from a high of 2.1 per cent in 1991/2. This is a drop of almost one-third over seven years. Contrary to any notion of a post–Cold War "peace dividend" that would free up money for social purposes, cuts in spending on international co-operation have outpaced even those on defence (CCIC 1996). Moving towards the United Nations ODA target of 0.7 per cent of GNP is less and less likely, even though lip service is still paid to this goal in Canada as elsewhere.

What explains these trends? First, the passing of the Cold War has reduced the geopolitical significance of aid to the poorest countries. Secondly, governments of all stripes are now more fiscally conservative. Thirdly, political forces at odds with the basic assumptions underlying development assistance have risen to challenge the prevailing wisdom that international co-operation is a key element of Canada's foreign policy. Fourthly, and perhaps most importantly, politicians and publics doubt the effectiveness of development aid. In 1991 a poll commissioned by CIDA found that 81 per cent of Canadians agreed with the statement that most of the money sent to poor countries never gets to those most in need. And 1995 polling data by Environics Research revealed that 83 per cent of respondents agreed that foreign assistance does not reach the needy (cited in SCFAIT 1996).

In sum, the three pillars of a rationale for development aid – poverty reduction, wealth redistribution, and interdependence – are treated with increasing scepticism by those outside the sector. How can we turn this around?

RENEWING SUPPORT FOR FOREIGN AID

There are grounds for re-making the case for aid. First, development remains the most urgent challenge facing the human race. The basic elements of human well-being are still lacking for many people in large parts of Africa and South Asia. More than one billion people, a fifth of the world's population, live on less than a dollar a day. UNICEF (1993) has spoken of "the last great obscenity – the needless malnutrition, disease and illiteracy that casts a shadow over the lives and futures of the poorest quarter of the world's children."

A second reason for hope is that aid has often worked. Durable social progress has been made in many parts of the developing world since the end of World War II, prompted in part by sustained and well-targeted ODA. Infant mortality rates have been cut in half, fertility rates have been lowered by 40 per cent, malnutrition rates have fallen by 30 per cent, and life expectancy has increased by nearly a decade (Summers & Thomas 1993: 241). Almost 1.4 billion people gained access to clean water during the 1980s (OECD 1996). UNICEF data show that 25 developing countries have achieved substantial economic growth *with* significant and sustained reductions in poverty (cited in Jolly 1995). Moreover, aid offers good value for money, a public service message that needs to be driven home to global taxpayers. The US$6 billion that was cut from OECD country donations in 1993 saved taxpayers only 1.8 cents of every $1000 of public expenditures (ICVA 1996). That money could have funded universal access to safe family planning.

A third reason to maintain support for development co-operation is the global spread of democracy and civil societies. With these changes has come an expansion of non-governmental organizations (NGOs) and citizen initiatives in the developing world. In India, an estimated 15,000 to 20,000 NGOs and grassroots organizations are active in rural development (Robinson et al. 1993). In Pakistan, the Aga Khan Foundation found one community-based organization for every 5000 people in the slum areas of Karachi: two-thirds were established in the last decade (AKF 1991: 63). Some of these Southern NGOs and membership organizations reach significant numbers of people. Their achievements speak for themselves. In Bangladesh, the Grameen Bank has two million borrowers in 34,000 villages with a daily loan volume of US$1.5 million and a 98-per-cent repayment rate. The Bangladesh Rural Advancement Committee runs programmes in 35,000 Bangladeshi villages and reaches 1.2 million households; 40 per cent of its annual budget of US$65 million is self-financed. In Pakistan, the Orangi Pilot Project provides low-cost sanitation at US$33 per household, a cheaper unit cost than services from comparable government programmes. Turning to local resources, this project was able to mobilize 17 times the volume of donor assistance. In Sri Lanka, the Sanasa Savings and Credit Cooperative Federation has 750,000 members with US$40 million in savings (Knisha et al. 1997).

The principles of human rights, gender equity, and citizen participation in the OECD democracies provide a potent source of support for continuing assistance for development. And there is a growing body of opinion, particularly in the United States, that predicts and welcomes a post-welfare world in which key social tasks are undertaken by the voluntary sector, not the state (Drucker 1994; Salamon 1994). The voluntary sector has an opportunity to strengthen this view of the world in its development education activities.

THE CANADIAN VOLUNTARY SECTOR

Canada is among the leading OECD countries in the volume of ODA that it channels through the voluntary sector,[2] roughly 17 per cent annually. But the mid-1990s have been tough on Canadian NGOs. As part of a cut of Cdn$1.3 billion to be made over three years in its overall ODA budget, the government's 1995 budget inflicted cuts in the funds channelled to NGOs that averaged 20.5 per cent. Then the minister of foreign affairs announced that development agencies without an overseas programme would lose all their funds for development education, a decision which led to a loss of $13.4 million for development education in Canada and to the elimination of approximately 90 community-based education centres in Canada (Tomlinson 1996; Smillie et al. 1996). The competitive environment for Canadian NGOs has intensified in other ways as well. The government has put NGOs on notice that "preference will be given to those partners who demonstrate the most effectiveness and efficiency, and who provide programming that is complementary to the objectives of the Government in promoting sustainable development." In addition, "special attention will be paid to supporting partners who can contribute their own financial resources and the time of volunteers, or who allow young people to serve abroad" (Canada 1995: 70).

Effectiveness – and in particular cost-effectiveness – is becoming one of the litmus tests for sustaining donor support, and NGOs may pay the price if they do not meet the challenges of professionalism. Tim Brodhead predicted this trend several years ago: "As NGOs become more prominent they lose the 'security of obscurity' which has sometimes protected them in the past; the media, politicians, and others will be quick to identify mistakes and weaknesses, just as they have with official agencies. Demands for greater accountability and more thorough scrutiny will grow. Thus the key to the continuing health and vitality of the voluntary sector is in the constant effort to enhance agency effectiveness, rather than in promoting an appealing public image or cultivating government support" (Brodhead & Herbert-Copley 1988: 153–4).

That development agencies are no longer immune from public scrutiny is clear from private member's bills to restrict lobbying activities, and media stories of allegedly high overheads or of spending which does not reach the poor.[3] NGOs must be prepared to explain the complexity of doing development and take steps to be transparent. The code of ethics of the Canadian Council for International Co-operation (CCIC) sets out standards for governance, financial management, and fundraising and is a welcome signal that the sector does take the issue of accountability and transparency seriously.

Canada's non-profit organizations express some of the best values in Canadian society, such as commitments to freedom, justice, and equity at home and abroad and to voluntarism as a means to pursue these goals. They have a primary stake in re-making the case for international development in Canada. But in a setting of declining budgets, value-based appeals for continued support for foreign aid are no longer sufficient or fully compelling. Donors are demanding more empirical evidence of sustainable and cost-effective programmes (results-based management), but the research and learning that are prerequisites for such evidence may not be a funding priority when fiscal pressures are prompting donors to defend the fundamentals of programming for poverty alleviation.[4] NGOs are thus faced with difficult choices as they seek to adapt to challenges and transform themselves in response to the new funding realities (Marquardt 1994).

Roles and Responsibilities

Some Southern NGOs now say that Northern NGOs should get out of direct involvement in overseas operations and concentrate on attacking the causes rather than the symptoms of poverty. This would mean moving away from doing projects and towards educating public opinion and influencing national and international development policies (Malena 1995: 20). Southern NGOs have a growing capacity to implement projects themselves, and official donor agencies are beginning to bypass Northern NGOs and fund Southern NGOs directly (see, for example, Lewis et al. 1994). To the extent that Southern NGOs can strengthen their organizational capacity and deepen their links to grassroots constituencies, they look set to alter the power dynamic masked by notions of "partnership" in North-South NGO relations (Malena 1995).

But if Northern NGOs are not to implement or manage projects, what are they to do? A growing number are in fact turning their attention to enhancing the institutional capacity of their Southern partners. However, evidence from the United Kingdom questions the likelihood of a significant number of Northern NGOs moving away from projects and towards public education and advocacy (Dolan 1992). Investing in learning and in policy-influencing activities at home is expensive and may have no visible or immediate pay-off. As Ian Smillie notes (1995): "policy development is not an attractive fundraising tool, and so it is rarely if ever mentioned in NGO publicity material." And for NGOs that rely significantly on government grants, policy influencing and advocacy may run the risk of biting the hand that feeds them. Public engagement is made more difficult because some see development NGOs as publicly financed but unrepresentative "special interests" with "particular axes to grind" (quoted in Delacourt 1995).

This is not to suggest that sustaining public support for international co-operation is not a primary NGO objective. But in Canada a succession of public advocacy campaigns and lobbying in parliamentary committees and during government foreign policy reviews have yielded cold comfort to development NGOs (Pratt 1994). Development's star continues to fall in this country, and the way out of this impasse is not fully clear. It is likely that Canadian NGOs that have a strong project portfolio and that have invested in lessons-learned activities to demonstrate results will have a competitive edge in gaining funding for development education. But development NGOs will no longer be able to rely completely on government to underwrite their public engagement initiatives and will need to broker financial, managerial, and intellectual partnerships with other players including – potentially – the private corporate sector and domestic voluntary organizations.

In sum, the current environment for Canadian development NGOs is exceptionally challenging. The sector remains highly dependent on public funds, and only a handful of Canadian NGOs is directly operational. The North-South Institute's estimate of 350 Canadian NGOs in 1994 may have been the high-water mark for the sector, which is now experiencing a shakedown, including the demise of many development education organizations and the termination or radical restructuring of CIDA-created and regionally focused NGO alliances and funding mechanisms such as Partnership Africa Canada and South Asia Partnership (Smillie et al. 1996).

The search for ways to renew support for international development in Canada and for the Canadian development NGO sector in this challenging setting was the underlying premise of the papers in this book. This search included examination of the concepts of systematic learning, policy dialogue, and public engagement.

SYSTEMATIC LEARNING

Sustaining donor and government support is tied to the continuing capacity of NGOs to improve practice and demonstrate value. Rather than being something outsiders do, learning and remembering are core development skills that must be nurtured *within* NGOs.

Learning is today's metaphor for managing change and the concept of a learning organization is fashionable. Effective learning builds a professional culture skilled at creating, acquiring, and transferring knowledge. This knowledge is used to modify organizational behaviour in response to changes in the surrounding environment and to internalize and act on new thinking and insights.[5] The bottom line is to determine obstacles to the organization's continuing success and identify methods to improve the way it does business.

Learning principles have been widely applied in the private sector but much less so among development organizations, particularly those in the non-profit sector. This is surprising because development administration is an inexact science and practitioners grapple daily with imperfect information, uncertainty, and complexity. NGOs are difficult organizations to manage and lead. The uncertainty and diversity of the environments in which they operate mean that they face challenges that in some ways dwarf those in the public and private sectors. More effective learning can help development organizations cope with complexity and rapid change.

In principle, there is a continuum of learning in most development organizations linking key tasks, such as fundraising, development education, and programme management (see Figure 1). This virtuous circle begins when programme management generates information about field experiences. Research then distils lessons learned, which are fed back to improve programme management and communicated

Figure 1

to stakeholders and media through training, policy dialogue, and development education. The circle is completed when research and public engagement help to mobilize and sustain programme funding.

NGOs have at least two distinctive research niches. First, they are well placed to send messages from their "micro" experiences to inform "macro" development debates. Secondly, because development is about the human condition, NGOs are best placed to give what John Clark calls the "street view" of development, drawing on the narrative voice of the communities they work with (Clark 1992: 199, 128).

Recent work on the economic organizing strategies used by South Asian women tries to combine both approaches. Using case-studies to highlight the organizing strategies of seven NGOs, the researchers defined economic empowerment from the perspective of the women at the grassroots who are the project beneficiaries. Irrespective of the organizational form used by women's groups, whether a trade union, a co-operative, or a village organization, economic empowerment is being achieved by a mix of strategies, such as financial intervention, enterprise development, marketing, collective bargaining, and socio-political mobilization. Women reported that economic organizing increased their bargaining power in one or more spheres of their lives: in the household, the extended family, and the community, with local élites, and within markets. The research thus drew out the close linkages between economic and political empowerment by showing that economic organizing is perhaps the most effective entry point for enhancing women's overall empowerment. The research demonstrated that most economic transactions involve a power dynamic and most economic strategies involve challenging that dynamic. In effect, the economic is political (Carr et al. 1996).

Another approach is for NGOs to sponsor thematic research to help build an environment that will enable NGOs to concentrate effectively on a social agenda. Rapid growth and direct funding from abroad have made some Southern governments antagonistic towards the NGO sector, leading to a more restrictive or disabling environment. Close examination of the regulatory environment for NGOs can help identify the constraints on and opportunities for building a more healthy relationship between states and civil societies (see, for example, World Bank 1996). The challenge is to persuade government to acknowledge the voluntary sector as a free-standing and equal partner in development rather than as an irritant, an enemy, or a mere adjunct.

Why should operational NGOs invest in systematic learning? Management gurus answer that "knowledge-based" organizations are best equipped to meet the challenges of rapid change in the information age. Many private sector firms routinely invest in research and development to improve their products, to innovate, and to remain competitive, but, ironically, as NGOs move towards the centre of the development stage, there are few guides based on comparative analysis of the factors that make for their successes and failures. This lack can be costly because inadequate information "hampers an agency's capacity to place its work in the context of broader development" issues and may mean that opportunities to improve an NGO's effectiveness in delivering services and influencing governments and the public are lost (Brodhead & Herbert-Copley 1988: 149).

A few Southern service delivery NGOs, such as the Bangladesh Rural Advancement Committee, the Aga Khan Rural Support Program in Pakistan, and Proshika in Bangladesh, now have research and evaluation wings that undertake project-based, thematic, or advocacy-driven research. Research may sometimes be an integral part of NGO operations, as in the Intermediate Technology Development Group. And there are signs that a new generation of "support" NGOs is emerging. Some are organized around research or training, such as the NGO Resource Centre in Pakistan, Participatory Research in Asia (PRIA) in India, PACT (Private Agencies Collaborating Together) and the Institute for Development Research in the United States, and INTRAC (International NGO Training and Research Centre) in Britain. But these are still the exceptions rather than the rule. Think-tanks in both North and South, with little first-hand field experience to draw on, have not filled the gap. Nor have official donor agencies. Although donor-sponsored evaluations of NGO-supported projects abound, most are geared to providing accountability to taxpayers rather than to identifying lessons learned.

While some Northern NGOs are extending their roles as knowledge-based and policy-influencing organizations, their campaigning and advocacy work has too often been undermined by a lack of attention to building analytic capacity (see, for example, INTRAC 1994). In Canada, universities have not, by and large, built partnerships with NGOs to undertake joint research. Public sector research institutions, such as the International Development Research Centre in Ottawa, have tended to focus on strengthening Southern universities and think-tanks and are only now beginning to address the research capacity of Southern NGOs.

POLICY DIALOGUE

Policy dialogue is a process of reasoned and empirically based argument in which NGOs attempt to influence the major development policy directions of governments and donors. The process can be conceptualized as a pyramid in which operational NGOs at the base of the pyramid and research institutions in the centre of the pyramid collaborate to document and analyse field experiences, draw implications for public policy, and then communicate the lessons learned to decision-makers at the apex of the pyramid.[6]

A key issue in development management is whether social change can be achieved through services to the poor or whether poverty is "rooted in social structures which relegate the poor to conditions of dependency." If the former, "then the central problem may be one of increasing the effectiveness of service delivery." If the latter, "then the central problem may be to reduce dependency by measures which increase the potential of the poor to take ... political action on their own behalf" (Korten 1979).

The lesson learned by large Southern NGOs, like the Bangladesh Rural Advancement Committee, the Self Employed Women's Association, and Sarvodaya, is that both strategies have a place. The challenge for many other NGOs is to extend their traditional roles as implementers by adding influencing to doing. Developing this skill is particularly urgent for Northern NGOs as implementing capacity grows in the South and as official donors increasingly transfer funds directly to Southern NGOs. John Clark (1992) has underlined the leverage that influencing can bring: "whether NGOs seize the opportunities or not depends largely on whether they create the space to step back from their conventional work [and] discover the skills of analysis and persuasion needed to shape an alternative vision of development out of their experience of working with the poor. The challenge is to move from a tactical to a strategic approach. By doing this they have the chance to transform development."

Northern NGOs have campaigned to defend or increase development spending. They have addressed key development issues, such as structural adjustment and debt relief. Yet there has been little systematic analysis of the impact of NGO advocacy and policy research. NGOs are prone to base their critiques of adjustments on official reports rather than on their own research. Too often, they offer blanket and one-sided criticisms adrift from political verities, and few workable alternatives. As well, in many developing countries, the administrative and political culture resists public participation, consultation, and access, constitutional veneers notwithstanding. However, where opportunities for dialogue prevail, a spirit of pragmatism and the acknowledgment of legitimately differing interests is more likely to yield results and undermine those critics who regard NGOs as the voice of special rather than popular interests.

There are perhaps four markers of an NGO's capacity to engage in policy dialogue. First, can it influence the policy agenda? Secondly, can it influence the policy process? Thirdly, does it influence policy outcomes? Fourthly, is it able to collaborate with the state in service delivery or to persuade government to adopt or adapt successful NGO innovations?

As voices for the needs of the disadvantaged and marginalized, NGOs are an important but by no means a dominant segment of civil society. Their claims must be balanced with those of others, such as business, academia, and labour. NGOs may thus have to acknowledge that there are bound to be limits to dialogue and influence. For its part, government must distinguish between consultation and choice, because in the final analysis, it is government that decides.

PUBLIC ENGAGEMENT

NGO advocacy campaigns which are not founded on a well-researched and watertight argument will not be taken seriously by decision-makers. Equally, no matter how well NGOs document and demonstrate their case, research will not prompt significant policy change unless it is backed by public support for those changes.

The three pillars of a successful strategy to re-engage the public are: information, education, and advocacy. But strengthening support for development assistance in Canada is challenging in the context of a jobless recovery and a public that has become arguably more inward-looking and anxious about their economic future. Moreover, Canadians have a very limited understanding of what development is, and what the development community does. If the public lacks a reasonable grasp of the problems of development, it is ill equipped to comment on potential solutions. A 1992 Gallup poll found that less than 10 per cent of Canadians could define "sustainable development" in any way that remotely resembled the definition put forward by development professionals. This lack of knowledge is compounded by the print and electronic media which feed their publics on a steady diet of despair, disease, and disaster in the Third World. NGOs, for their part, have sometimes reinforced these images, relying on emotional and values-based appeals to obtain funding.

These messages have helped pay for emergency relief and may, over time, prompt donors to support longer term development projects. But the strategy carries risks. The Canadian Council for International Co-operation estimates that Canadians contributed Cdn$340 million to international aid groups in 1994 (cited in Lindgren 1995). The public (and media) perception is that NGOs spend almost *all* these aid dollars directly on the poor; yet the management of both emergency relief and long-term development is a complex business and money must be spent on the communications, administration, and technical tasks which are essential components of programmes to reach the poor. The public's unsophisticated perceptions could have repercussions on the image of Canadian NGOs. How can this view be turned around? Should Canadian NGOs reconfigure their fundraising appeals to accent – or at least include – more positive images of the Third World? Can NGOs get across to the public the complexity of delivering development assistance?

A 1995 poll sponsored by CIDA (1995) reveals a silver lining in the cloud that has settled on the Canadian development profession. A majority of respondents still want a Canadian aid programme. In a public ranking of the reasons to give aid, food and medicine for disaster relief had the highest priority. However, the poll also found that basic human needs, that is, support for longer term development, was accorded almost the same priority.[7] Supporting democracy and promoting women's rights were ranked third and fourth. Interestingly, infrastructure and business development were ranked lowest. These rankings affirm the importance of many of the niches Canadian NGOs and their Southern partners already occupy: basic human needs, disaster relief, and building strong, independent, durable, and open civil societies.

How can NGOs build on these findings and use applied research and policy dialogue to shift public attention from the costs to the benefits of official development assistance? The American pollster, Daniel Yankelovich, has shown that it can take decades to transform public judgments on complex issues from superficial to informed responses. Many Canadians have empathy for the concerns of other nations. But the results of a recent OECD survey of public opinion suggest that many citizens in OECD countries are "working through" their views on development. They may hold contradictory opinions and may find it difficult to move from resistance or superficial opinions to informed and consistent judgments (Foy & Helmich 1996). To help citizens to make an informed judgment on aid issues, Yankelovich calls for a new communications strategy for international co-operation. This strategy should emphasize positive messages, base appeals on both altruism and national interest, link aid with domestic concerns, demonstrate effectiveness, and use language with universal appeal (such as "development" or "empowerment") rather than abstractions (Yankelovich 1996). This strategy can be reinforced by Northern NGOs moving beyond their moral messages to the public to emphasize the practical concerns of impact, effectiveness, and sustainability.

CONCLUSION

Public support for development aid and international co-operation remains strong in Canada and across the OECD countries generally. It is political support that has withered. It is imperative to regain political support for official development assistance. One approach may be to use the growing recognition of the voluntary sector as a bulwark of democracy and deliverer of social goods to obtain larger investments in NGO grassroots poverty-reduction programmes. This approach can appeal to governing élites as is clear from the American experience where Vice-President Gore used an address to the United Nations Social Development Summit to announce a New Partnership Initiative "to channel up to 40 per cent of its assistance to poor countries through private aid and charity groups that have demonstrated greater efficiency than many international organizations" (*Washington Post*, 13 March 1995).

Successful public engagement in the 1990s requires strategies that go beyond values-based appeals and build messages which demonstrate impact, cost-effectiveness, and sustainability. The broader challenge is to restore a Canadian consensus that aid works, to persuade publics and power brokers that sustainable development is a key to human security and international order, and to underline that more than one billion people in poverty is an unacceptable start to the twenty-first century.

NOTES

1 In a University of Maryland poll, the median estimate by respondents of spending by the American government on official development assistance was 15 per cent of the budget. Attitudes changed when the true level of aid, less than 1 per cent of the government's budget, was understood: 33 per cent of respondents then said the actual level was too low. In 1995 the budget committee of the United States Senate proposed to halve its contri-

bution to the eleventh renewal of the World Bank's soft-loan facility (Stackhouse 1995).
2 Voluntary sector institutions are private in form, but primarily public in purpose, and are formally organized, self-governing, separate from government, do not distribute surplus income primarily to their members, and exhibit a meaningful degree of voluntarism.
3 A book that highlights the high costs of fundraising but is otherwise broadly sympathetic to the voluntary sector – Walter Stewart's *The Charity Game* (1996) – may be emblematic of what is in store from the less reflective media.
4 NGOs also complain that their access to generic (responsive) government funding is eroding and that CIDA is increasingly parcelling NGO funding into special "windows." The net effect is to reduce NGO autonomy and to add to their administrative load.
5 This section draws on Morgan (1995).
6 Recognizing the limitations of rationality and objectivity in policy analysis, a report from the International Development Research and Policy Taskforce (1996) suggests the term "policy inquiry" to denote the uncertainty of policy knowledge and the scope for a variety of legitimate views, and limits "policy dialogue" to discussing policy options among multiple stakeholders.
7 Respondents ranked the priorities in basic human needs as follows: clean water and sanitation, nutrition and primary health care, followed by basic education, family planning, and shelter.

REFERENCES

Aidwatch. 1996. May 1996.
AKF (Aga Khan Foundation). 1991. *International Strategy.* Geneva: AKF.
Brodhead, T., & B. Herbert-Copley. 1988. *Bridges of Hope? Canadian Voluntary Agencies and the Third World.* Ottawa: North-South Institute 1988.
Canada. 1995. *Government Response to the Recommendations of the Special Joint Parliamentary Committee Reviewing Canadian Foreign Policy.* Ottawa: Canada Communication Group.
Carr, M., M. Chen, and R. Jhabvala, eds. 1996. *Speaking Out: Women's Economic Empowerment in South Asia.* London: Intermediate Technology Publications on behalf of Aga Khan Foundation Canada and United Nations Development Fund for Women.
CCIC (Canadian Council for International Co-operation). 1996. "A Profile of Canadian Official Development Assistance." Ottawa: CCIC.
CIDA. 1995. "Canadian Opinions on Canadian Foreign Policy, Defence Policy and International Development Assistance." Paper prepared by Insight Research Canada for CIDA.
Clark, J. 1992. *Democratizing Development.* Hartford CT: Kumarian Press.

Delacourt, S. 1995. "Losing Interest." *Globe and Mail* (Toronto), 1 April.
Dolan, C. 1992. "British Development NGOs and Advocacy in the 1990s." In *Making a Difference: NGOs and Development in a Changing World*, edited by M. Edwards & D. Hulme. London: Earthscan.
Drucker, P.F. 1994. "The Age of Social Transformation." *Atlantic Monthly* (November): 53–80.
Ekos Research Associates. 1995. *Rethinking Government '94: An Overview and Synthesis.* Ottawa: Ekos.
Foy, C., & H. Helmich, eds. 1996. *Public Support for International Development.* Paris: OECD.
ICVA (International Council of Voluntary Agencies)/Eurostep. 1995. *The Reality of Aid 1995: An Independent Review of International Aid.* London: Earthscan.
– 1996. *The Reality of Aid 1996: An Independent Review of International Aid.* London: Earthscan.
International Development Research and Policy Taskforce. 1996. *Connecting with the World: Priorities for Canadian Internationalism in the 21st Century.* Ottawa: (International Development Research Centre/North-South Institute/International Institute for Sustainable Development.
INTRAC (International NGO Training and Research Centre). 1994. *A Survey of Research by UK NGOs.* Oxford: INTRAC.
Jolly, R. 1995. "Poverty Targeting: Policies and Strategies." Paper delivered to the Public Forum on Poverty Reduction Strategies for Development, Toronto, 13–14 June.
Knisha, A., N. Uphoff, and M.J. Esman. 1997. *Reasons for Hope: Instructive Experiences in Rural Development.* Hartford CT: Kumarian Press.
Korten, D.C. 1979. *Population and Social Development Management.* Caracas: Instituto de Estudios Superiores de Administración.
Lewis, D., B. Sobhan, and G. Jonsson. 1994. *Routes of Funding Routes of Trust? An Evaluation of Swedish Assistance to Non-Governmental Organizations in Bangladesh.* Stockholm: Swedish International Development Authority.
Lindgren, A. 1995. "Crisis in Confidence: Canada's Aid Agencies Combat a Public Relations Disaster." *Ottawa Citizen*, 24 June.
Lumsdaine, D.H. 1993. *Moral Vision in International Politics: The Foreign Aid Regime, 1949–1989.* Princeton NJ: Princeton University Press 1993.
Malena, C. 1995. "Relations between Northern and Southern Non-Governmental Development Organizations." *Canadian Journal of Development Studies* 16.
Marquardt, R. "The Voluntary Sector and the Federal Government: A Perspective in the Aftermath of the 1995 Federal Budget." Ottawa: Canadian Council for International Development.
Morgan, P. 1995. "Becoming a Learning Organization." Report to Aga Khan Foundation Canada.
ODI (Overseas Development Institute). 1994. *Crisis or Transition in Foreign Aid.* London: ODI.

OECD (Organization for Economic Co-operation and Development). 1996. *Shaping the 21st Century: The Contribution of Development Co-operation*. Paris: OECD.

Pratt, C. 1994. *Lessons from the Last Time Around*. Ottawa: North-South Institute.

Robinson, M., J. Farrington, and S. Satish. 1993. "NGO-Government Interaction in India: Overview." In *Non-Governmental Organizations and the State in Asia: Rethinking Roles in Sustainable Agricultural Development*, edited by J. Farrington & D. Lewis. London: Routledge.

Salamon, L.M. 1994. "The Rise of the Nonprofit Sector." *Foreign Affairs* (July/August).

SCFAIT (House of Commons Standing Committee on Foreign Affairs and International Trade, Canada). 1996. "Forum on Promoting Greater Public Understanding of International Development Issues." *Minutes of Proceedings and Evidence*. Issue 9 (18 April).

Smillie, I. 1995. *The Alms Bazaar: Altruism under Fire – Non-Profit Organizations and International Development*. London: Intermediate Technology Publications.

Smillie, I., F. Douxchamps, and Rebecca Sholes/Jane Covey. 1996. *Partners or Contractors?* Oxford: INTRAC.

Stackhouse, J. 1995. "Funding Cuts Threaten World Bank Aid Projects." *Globe and Mail* (Toronto), 5 June.

Stewart, W. 1996. *The Charity Game: Greed, Waste and Fraud in Canada's $86 Billion-A-Year Compassion Industry*. Vancouver: Douglas and McIntyre.

Summers, L.H., & V. Thomas. 1993. *World Bank Research Observer* 8 (2).

Tomlinson, B. 1996. In ICVA, *The Reality of Aid 1996*.

UNICEF (United Nations Children's Fund). 1993. *The State of the World's Children*. New York: UNICEF.

World Bank. 1996. *Pursuing Common Goals: Strengthening Relations between Government and Development NGOs*. Dhaka: University Press Ltd for the World Bank.

Yankelovich, D. 1996. "Public Judgement on Development Aid." In Foy & Helmich (1996).

1 Trends in International Co-operation

ROGER C. RIDDELL

This overview of trends in international development co-operation focuses in particular on those issues which influence, or are likely to influence, Northern non-governmental organizations (NGOs) and NGO activities especially in relation to enhancing their capacity as learning and influencing organizations. With such an extensive brief, I have aimed for breadth of analysis – trying to set out the wide range of issues which need to be brought into the analysis rather than to select a smaller number and cover them in greater depth.

The first of the paper's two major sections focuses on recent trends and new issues emerging in international development co-operation. Its first sub-section focuses on the contemporary "crisis" in aid, drawing together a number of ideas to explain current doubts and scepticism about aid and international development co-operation more widely. With this as background, the second sub-section addresses the themes of public support for aid and international development co-operation, and the issue of aid effectiveness. A number of questions are raised about the importance of public opinion and the analysis of the impact of aid (official and non-official) in both establishing and influencing the agenda on aid and development co-operation. The final sub-section discusses the complex issue of globalization, drawing out a number of different, though related, themes of importance to the nature of future aid and development co-operation, including support for development.

The second major section of the article reflects on what these recent trends and new issues in international development co-operation might mean for Northern NGOs. It considers the different ways that these trends are influencing, and should in the future influence, Northern NGOs especially in relation to their work domestically in the North. It starts by providing an analytic framework for locating different types of activities (such as advocacy, lobbying, service provision, and innovation) and different forms of engagement with governments (collaboration, confrontation, or complementarity), concluding that there is no a priori "best" way for Northern NGOs to act.

I go on to suggest, however, that there are important and increasing reasons for NGOs to focus their Northern-based activities well beyond aid issues and that in attempting to nurture support for international development co-operation, coalitions will need to be built with non-traditional partners. Indeed, it may be that the most effective way of building support for international development is to focus attention beyond international co-operation issues to the different elements which make up more general attitudes within the wider society of Northern donor countries. My analysis is critical of the way that supporters of aid have focused so much on the *supply* of aid and points to some features of an approach to promoting support for aid which would place far more emphasis on the needs and capabilities of recipients. Additionally, in the context of the evolving debate about the nature of future aid programmes, questions are raised about the relative (and even absolute) importance of traditional NGO activities. Finally, the discussion turns to a number of problems concerning the relationships among Northern NGOs and their interaction with Southern NGOs emanating from the rising support being given to the non-profit sector as a whole across the industrialized countries.

Overall, the discussion suggests that the role and importance of Northern NGOs in influencing development co-operation is likely to remain significant, and may well increase. However, I would argue that the growing importance of Northern NGOs in policy debate and discourse may well, and perversely, limit and dilute the role that Northern NGOs can and should play as NGOs in this discourse, especially if they focus more on trying to secure their funding base by responding to short time horizons and working on agendas which, in order to try to minimize conflicts among donors (and NGOs), tend also to reduce the impact of aid.

I conclude with a few brief comments on the link between NGO approaches to development and learning mechanisms within NGOs. While I argue that most NGOs need to improve their internal systems to gain a better understanding of how they perform, how to build on their strengths, and how to minimize recurrence of failed methods and approaches, I support the view that NGOs need to consider focusing on learning systems which are rooted less in the past and more on those strengths which characterize NGOs and distinguish them from other organizations working in the development field.

1 New Issues and Trends in International Development Co-operation

THE CRISIS IN AID AND DEVELOPMENT CO-OPERATION

During the 1990s, official aid agencies, NGOs, and development professionals have perceived a growing sense of uncertainty about the future of development co-operation. While few believe that the "end of aid" is in sight, fewer people are talking about temporary aid "fatigue" and more are speaking about a deeper and more far-reaching "crisis" in aid.[1] For supporters of aid and international development co-operation more generally, growing perceptions of a crisis stimulate discussion about ways to address that crisis. The round table which inspired this volume was built around a number of propositions and assumptions, based, inter alia, on the views that public support for development co-operation is important and that this support is being undermined by scepticism about the impact of aid. These views are linked in part to pressures to reduce government spending but fuelled also by a sense that the old arguments in favour of aid appear to cut little ice.[2] As (it is assumed) aid and development co-operation still have a role to play, ideas are being sought on ways to address these problems, weaknesses, and scepticism so as to breathe new vigour into aid and international development co-operation – ways which are appropriate to the needs of the end of this millennium and the beginning of the next and which might gain sufficient public support to make a difference.

Before looking more closely at the current crisis, it is important to emphasize that aid has always been under attack: crises in aid are not new. Since its origins in the late 1940s, development aid and co-operation have continually been disparaged as unhelpful, unnecessary, and even a major part of the problem of poverty and development failure. In what way, then, does the current crisis differ from the succession of crises which have influenced the aid debate for the previous fifty years? Four main factors can be identified:

1 the end of the Cold War and changing perceptions about security, and how to respond to these changes;
2 a substantive fall in aid volume which is likely to continue combined with less aid going to traditional low-income recipients;

3 the failure of aid's increasing and now multiple objectives either to maintain interest in aid and development co-operation issues or to stimulate new interest in them; and
4 a series of challenges to traditional notions of aid originating in debate within donor countries about approaches to welfare, the role of the market, and the nature of the state.

The End of the Cold War

The most superficial but quite widely held view about aid and the Cold War is founded on the belief that one of the main reasons that governments originally decided to provide aid was to secure and enhance their strategic interests in the East-West conflict. There is no longer a major East-West threat and thus a major reason for providing aid has fallen away. As a corollary, if it cannot be shown that aid has a positive impact on development, the raison d'être for providing it will have fallen away. There are two major problems with this view. First, the strategic argument for aid both was and continues today to be far wider and deeper than the East-West conflict. No better illustration exists than the United States which still provides billions of dollars in economic assistance (for instance, to Israel and Egypt) for non-developmental strategic and political reasons. Indeed, the world of today is probably a more insecure and volatile place politically than the world of the Cold War period, suggesting that if strategic and political interests were a major motive for providing aid before 1989, and aid levels were linked to preserving and furthering these interests, then current political and strategic concerns should be manifested in higher aid levels today. Thus, the deeper and more interesting question is why there has not been a rise in aid during this more volatile post-1989 period as one means of helping to address or contain these tensions. In part the answer lies in the influence of other factors which have been present (and growing) in the post–Cold War period.

Aid Volume and Its Proportionate Allocation

A second feature of the contemporary crisis revolves around the quantity of aid provided. There are three linked characteristics of aid volume trends. First, the overall quantity of aid provided by donors has fallen more sharply in the 1990s than over the previous quarter-century.[3] Secondly, the combined effect of rising allocations to emergencies and peacekeeping and new allocations to the former Soviet Union and Eastern Europe means that the amount of aid earmarked for traditional recipients has fallen more sharply than figures on aggregate aid levels would suggest. Thirdly, with very few exceptions, major donors are unlikely to increase aid levels substantially in the foreseeable future and a meaningful number will continue to lower aid levels if not absolutely then as a ratio of total government spending and/or gross national product (GNP). In 1997, Canada's ratio of official development assistance (ODA) to GNP is forecast to be 0.33 per cent, the lowest level in thirty years (ICVA 1996: 101).

This fall in volume is summarized in the following statistics. In 1989, the volume of aid fell by a marginal 0.5 per cent; in 1992, it fell by a larger 3.9 per cent. Then in 1993, overall aid volumes contracted by 5.4 per cent over the previous year, but the volume of aid provided by the donors from the Organization for Economic Co-operation and Development (OECD) fell – for the first time for a decade – by almost 6 per cent in real terms. In 1993, aid from the members of the OECD's Development Assistance Committee (DAC), as a share of their GNP, stood at its lowest level for two decades (OECD 1996a: 73). In June 1995, the OECD's aggregate figures for 1994 aid volume confirmed the trend: in 1994, total flows of ODA fell by an additional 1.3 per cent in real terms, with flows from OECD donors falling by 1.8 per cent and the ODA/GNP ratio falling to 0.29 per cent, the lowest for twenty-one years. Finally, in June 1996, the OECD published its 1995 aid figures which showed a further, and far sharper, annual fall in aggregate real aid flows of 5.4 per cent in 1995, and that aid from the leading OECD donors fell by a greater 9.3 per cent in the year (OECD 1996c: Table 2). In mid-1996, the OECD commented that aid provided by DAC members had fallen to 0.27 per cent of GNP, the lowest ratio recorded since the United Nations adopted the 0.7-per-cent target in 1970. In terms of destination and composition, recent figures show that the amount of official aid going to low-income countries fell from 52 per cent of the total in 1990 to 45 per cent by 1994, that aid going to the former Soviet Union and Eastern Europe accounted for 4 per cent of the total in 1990 but rose to 13 per cent by 1994, and that aid allocated for disaster relief and peacekeeping more than doubled from US$2.5 billion in 1990 to some US$6 billion in 1994–5 (World Bank 1996: chap. 2).

Overloading the Agenda

A third element of the contemporary crisis has been the failure to draw up new purposes for development aid ("add-on" factors) to increase, or even maintain, donor support. Throughout the history of aid giving, a notable feature of the development rationale and purpose of aid has been the manner in which it has continually changed. Originally, aid was given to accelerate the development process on condition that certain prerequisites about its potential beneficence were met – for example, to fill foreign exchange and savings gaps; in the 1970s, it was provided to help meet basic needs and address poverty problems directly; in the 1980s, aid was tied again, this time to a broader set of conditions linked to the implementation of structural adjustment programmes.

What is notable was not merely the flexibility with which the development purposes of aid changed and helped to sustain support for aid but the way in which new objectives were added to the old ones. In the early to mid-1980s the environment and gender were incorporated into the objectives for aid; in the late 1980s and early 1990s, democracy, good governance, and human rights; and, more recently, capacity-building. But what characterizes the most recent additional objectives for aid is that this time the add-ons have not stimulated the renewed interest in aid, manifested in the continued expansion in aid volume, which marked all the previous add-on initiatives. Does this mean that the flexibility of aid vis-à-vis its development purposes which for so long was clearly an asset has become a burden or a liability? Has the list of development priorities and purposes for aid become so long that nothing is a priority? Are people (and policy-makers) less and less convinced of aid's ability to make an impact in so many different ways?[4]

Revisiting the Nature and Purpose of Aid

Or is the crisis in aid more fundamental still, lying in the nature of aid in a world where development is market-based and market-driven? While differing perceptions about the nature and urgency of security and political issues have certainly influenced decisions within various donor countries about the size of their aid budgets, it is also apparent that the aid vote has been influenced by domestic debates and discussions, not least a concern with public sector finances. The relationship between the aid vote and these debates is evident at two different levels. At its simplest level, cuts to aid form part of a more widespread need to cut all public expenditure programmes because of the growing and unsustainable gap between (rising) recurrent expenditure programmes and a desire to reduce the rising tax burden. Thus, if cuts have to be made across the board, no vote – not even the aid vote – should be immune. A more complex argument has been voiced in some donor countries, especially in the United States and the United Kingdom: namely, that growing inequalities in wealth and in income distribution and deeper pockets of poverty at home – which ten to fifteen years of free market policies have exacerbated, if not caused – require governments to meet acute domestic needs first.

But domestic debates about intervention in social and economic life, about the best way to address welfare problems, and about the relationship between the state, the market, and civil society provide a growing and deeper set of challenges to traditional arguments for aid. Within donor countries today, there is little support for the view that the best way to help the poor at home is by direct state action; instead solutions are seen to lie more in the hands of the poor who, if they wish to improve their living standards, need to be encouraged to take personal action to respond to expanding market opportunities.

What this thinking is doing is to drive a wedge into the link which has so often been made automatically between *helping* and *providing aid*. Thus, even if it is agreed that donors should assist poorer, and less well endowed, countries to develop, the manner in which this help is to be provided is increasingly informed by these new perceptions of the role of the state and its resolution of poverty problems domestically. Three types of conditionality are gaining increased acceptance. It is argued, first, that development aid should be provided within the context of efforts to enhance and extend the role of the market in the development process.[5] Secondly, state-to-state aid to enhance and extend the market should not be provided if the recipient is able to obtain the resources which aid provides through the market. Thirdly, while aid can legitimately be provided to address needs resulting from the lack of markets, market failure, or market distortion, short-term aid needs to be provided in a context and manner which does not frustrate the goal of achieving longer term market-based solutions.

In their turn, these orientations towards "aid for the market" have increased awareness of, and in some quarters support for, the (quite old) view that aid and the aid relationship in general could be part of the problem rather than part of the solution. Thus it is argued not merely that some recipient countries have received such large quantities of aid for so long that they have become aid dependent but that aid dependence is caused, in part, by the aid relationship which has been set up, developed, and now become entrenched: that efforts to reduce dependence upon aid and to move towards a self-sustaining form of development are impeded by the actions and interests of influential groups within recipient countries who gain from the permanence of aid dependence (see, for example, Sobhan 1982, 1991, 1995; Riddell 1996a).

Another way that "new" thinking has influenced the aid debate and expectations of what aid can and should do is by drawing out the distinction between the motive for providing aid and the purpose of the aid provided. Traditionally, not only have aid's advocates based their argument for donors to provide aid on the poverty, need, and level of deprivation of recipients (the motive) but they have quickly gone on to argue that the success of the aid provided should be judged in relation to the extent to which poverty has been alleviated or eliminated, needs have been met, and deprivation eliminated. However, if the purpose of aid in the contemporary market-based context is to facilitate the ability of recipients to achieve the ends of development by themselves, then aid would be judged less in relation to immediate success in eliminating poverty or meeting other basic needs and more in relation to progress achieved as measured by indicators reflecting the ability, capability, and capacity of recipients to attain these objectives for themselves.

What is interesting about the four factors identified as key new elements contributing to the current crisis in aid and development co-operation is the absence of public opinion and support for aid or aid's development impact as influences on that crisis.

PUBLIC SUPPORT AND ITS LINK TO AID EFFECTIVENESS

Public Opinion

Historically, much has been made of the high level of public support for aid within and across donor countries. Most opinion surveys have indicated widespread public support for aid, and this finding has been used to argue that because public support has been high, aid levels should continue to be high. Based on this linkage, the preliminary documentation for the round table on which this volume is based suggested that increasing public support for aid and international development co-operation will be particularly important in influencing the future level, direction, and orientation of Canada's aid and development policy.

Some recent evidence suggests that one needs to be wary of drawing so strong a connection between public opinion, actual aid volumes, and government policy. Thus, summarizing the results of a study conducted across donor countries, Andrew Rice states that (despite recent sharp declines in aid flows): "the evidence ... suggested that on the whole – despite differences among countries – the level of support for development assistance in the abstract has not changed significantly in recent years. Almost everywhere a majority of citizens continues to favour development aid" (1996: 11). The evidence of another (unconnected) study undertaken across donor countries on public opinion, international civil society, and North-South policy since the Cold War leads to the view that "the influence of opinion on general development aid policy has been very limited ... and cannot be proved" and concludes that there are no "indications that public opinion, understood as mass opinion, has greater direct influence on foreign aid policy in the 1990s than it did during the Cold War" (Olsen 1996: 338, 351). These studies confirm what otherwise would be viewed as a strange phenomenon, namely, that in the 1990s a succession of donor countries has cut aid – some, like Finland, quite massively – even though public support for aid has remained high.[6] More perverse still is evidence from Norway and the Netherlands in the 1990s showing increasing support for aid at a time when aid flows were falling (Winter 1996: 5). What is more, the Olsen study argues that "the influence of the popular view will be reduced still further in future" (1996: 352).

A recent survey of American aid since the late 1940s (Ruttan 1996) builds on these views to make a number of more detailed (and for policy purposes perhaps more useful) comments. Vernon Ruttan's thesis is that in the United States aid and development policy is determined more by domestic forces than by what is happening in the developing world. On the matter of opinion and policy, Ruttan makes three points. First, public support for aid has been primarily linked to support for responding to humanitarian issues.[7] Secondly, there is rising public support for and concern with development in the context of global issues although, confirming the point made by Olsen for other donors, Ruttan argues that in the United States the increase in public support seems to have had little effect on actual aid flows. Thirdly, and perhaps most interestingly, public support for aid appears to be linked critically to its perceived effectiveness, and Ruttan uses this information to suggest that falling aid levels are not only bad in themselves but are likely to have a cumulatively bad effect because lower levels of aid will reduce the impact of aid and in so doing will lower levels of public support for continuance of even the reduced amount of aid.

Clearly these studies and surveys do not mean either that public views about aid and development policy are irrelevant to the aid and development policies which individual donors pursue or that it is unimportant to inform and expand public support for aid and international development policies. But they suggest two interlinked conclusions. First, one should be wary about the practical policy consequences of marginally increasing public awareness, information, and concern about development issues: it may well be that substantive resources and funds channelled into such activities will produce a minimal return. Secondly, potentially limited results from what may be quite costly programmes to improve and deepen public knowledge of aid and development co-operation efforts suggest that one needs to assess the potential benefits (and costs) of other methods of influencing aid and development policies.

On this second conclusion, the Olsen study points to a number of ideas of direct relevance to the theme of this volume. Thus, while Olsen downgrades the importance and influence of public opinion "in general," he highlights the importance of the media in influencing policies through the way they can (and do) capture the imagination of the public. On the one hand, this suggests that advocacy work ought to focus on ways to influence and alert the media to aid and international development issues. On the other hand, there are limits to the effect of such work for encouraging support for more substantive and complex development issues because media and specific-issue-focused public support tends to be support for humanitarian issues and be most influential when linked to immediate and very short term crises. Perversely, therefore, there is a danger that pursuing the popular media "stories" of development will further encourage the use of aid disproportionately for meeting immediate problems rather than for addressing longer term and more structural development problems.

More positively, however, Olsen sees the combined effect of the reduction of the influence of general public opinion in aid and development policies and the rise in the importance of NGOs as part of a virtuous circle. He argues that as this process evolves, policy-makers and decision-makers will be more open to the influence of and interaction with NGOs right at the heart of policy and decision-making. In other words, as public opinion becomes less crucial and influential, NGOs are likely to find that their ability to influence policy decisions on development more directly will increase.

The Growing Importance of Aid Effectiveness

To what extent is the current crisis in aid due to the failure of aid – or the failure to show that the aid provided is effective? And to what extent is aid's impact likely to be an increasingly important factor influencing the level and composition of aid provided? The picture is far less clear-cut than might initially be thought.

A number of strands and influences provide substantive evidence to conclude that aid effectiveness is of great and rising importance. First, as the World Bank has summarized it: "as aid budgets decline, aid effectiveness becomes a paramount concern" (1996: 26). This view has been articulated in policy statements, with donors both individually and as a group stressing the importance of impact and effectiveness as a key manifestation of and justification for their aid programmes. For instance, in their joint policy statement, "Development Partnerships in the New Global Context," DAC members stated that they would intensify their activities in evaluating aid effectiveness and the implementation of best practice: "Our co-operation must be effective and efficient ... Both bilateral and multilateral development assistance must be managed for maximum efficiency and effectiveness. We are confident that past achievements and lessons learned in development co-operation show clearly how best to reinforce current efforts of developing countries" (OECD 1996b).

Secondly, aid administrations are under more and more pressure from other government departments, especially treasuries and finance departments, to provide evidence of "value for money": defending aid budgets within government will increasingly require evidence that the funds have had an impact and have been used effectively. Thirdly, and following from the previous point, there is a growing interest in cost-effectiveness issues, in managing for results, in expanding the use of analyses such as the Logical Framework[8] to projects and programme aid, and in using a variety of market-based instruments (such as competitive bidding) for a range of different contracts, and a growing reluctance to fund research activities which are not linked to specific donor policy concerns. Fourthly, more and more donors are not merely placing major emphasis on the sustainability of the aid they provide, and on assessing the potential sustainability of projects and programmes at the earliest (appraisal) stage, but some (such as the United States Agency for International Development [USAID]) are beginning to use financial sustainability as a proxy for judging cost-effectiveness.

It is, however, important to place these statements and initiatives in a wider context. There is a range of other policies and practices of donors which tend to play down the apparent importance of aid effectiveness, at least in terms of development practice. The first point to make is that however much donors may desire to focus more rigorously on ways of analysing aid to ensure it is used effectively and efficiently (building on past achievements and lessons learned), current practice is pulling donors in precisely the opposite direction. Thus, donors' aid agendas are expanding rather than contracting, and as part of that growth the aid portfolio of all donors is embracing more initiatives and approaches at the "soft" rather than the "hard" end of development – away from economic and infrastructural projects towards social development projects including those focusing on capacity-building, institutional development, democracy and human rights initiatives, and, in general, more "process" projects. Not only are these areas for which past experience of impact is of limited relevance, but they are areas in which work still needs to be done to develop a consensus on output indicators, a basic prerequisite for cost-effectiveness analysis. And even then, there is doubt among donors whether it will be possible to analyse impact with rigour.[9] Moreover, as aid is increasingly being provided in the context of market failures and market inadequacies, the assumptions of, and predictions associated with, effectiveness analysis based on neo-classical theories, such as cost-benefit analysis, are going to be inappropriate tools to use in judging impact and effectiveness.

Another dimension of the impact/effectiveness debate concerns the stress many aid administrations now put on steps to enhance the administrative capacity and efficiency of aid management itself. For instance, although the approaches are somewhat different, both the British Overseas Development Administration and USAID are placing increased emphasis on "management for results." Two aspects of this trend are relevant to the current discussion. The first is the emphasis given to management rather than impact as at least one key element in obtaining "value for money." The second is that the catchphrase used is management "for" results not management "by" results. If results achieved were the dominant influence and feature of the new orientation, then major emphasis would be placed on assessing what those results are, with future resource allocations likely to be profoundly influenced by relative success and failure: this would be management "by" results. Managing "for" results suggests that although results are important, the emphasis is on strengthening management skills and capacities to work more effectively and efficiently. A consequence – noted already – is that donors are increasingly willing to state that they view the purpose of aid not so much in terms of achieving particular and more traditional and tangible development objectives as in terms of enhancing the capacity of recipients to manage and implement development for themselves "unaided." Accelerating donor interest in aid-dependency issues reinforces the emphasis given to this dimension of aid. This orientation again puts into perspective the assertion of donors that the aid they provide should be judged in relation to its "development" impact and results.

It is important, however, not to press the argument too far the other way. I am not saying that development impact is not important, or that donors are not taking steps to try to enhance the impact of the aid they provide – they clearly are doing this. But the combination of a declining quantity of aid with a large (and growing) set of tasks and objectives which now include aid interventions which embrace social, political, managerial, and administrative as well as more narrowly economic purposes, perceived within a process and more long-term perspective, necessarily means both that more is expected of aid and that the results of aid intervention are going to be more complex.

The conclusion that surely has to be drawn is that the expectations of what aid can do in this new setting are going to have to be lowered, and the ability to know accurately, objectively, and quantitatively what aid has achieved and is able to achieve is also likely to be reduced. Indeed, this is precisely the conclusion drawn by the World Bank's Wapenhans Report (1992). Noting that its own internal assessment of project performance indicated a significant decline in project portfolio performance, the report attributed this change to "the need for more complex and challenging undertakings in response to new development priorities." There are two possible outcomes. Either donors will acknowledge that the new agenda makes it less possible to draw accurate conclusions about aid's impact, leading them to be more cautious, indeed to backtrack on, the unrealistic expectations that they have helped to nurture, almost certainly to the detriment of building, deepening, and extending the case for aid. Or they will increasingly strain the credibility of their aid programmes by arguing more with political gusto than with evidence that it is their efforts which make the crucial difference to development.

GLOBALIZATION

Thus far my focus has been on trends in aid and the different elements which contribute to the current crisis in aid. Now I wish to look briefly at the phenomenon of globalization.[10] Put simply, the term refers to the process by which the economies of the world and economic agents, both locally and within emerging regional and national groupings, are being influenced by and influencing changes in the nature, intensity, and pace of change in financial flows, production and technology, international trade, migration, and employment. In a number of ways, globalization has already led to changes in the world of aid and development co-operation. The most striking of these changes has been the rise in interest in environmental issues beyond national boundaries, leading to the creation of different funds to address current problems, rising awareness of global problems, and decisions by national governments to implement specific policies within the framework of timetables agreed internationally. There is considerable evidence to suggest that in addition to continuing interest in more immediate humanitarian issues, there is significant and growing public support for addressing global issues.

These developments have stimulated interest in expanding the international agenda to other areas (three examples would be gender issues, security questions, and the management of emergency assistance) and in increasing the role and importance of international/ multilateral agencies, notably the United Nations, to address them. In turn, this has led to debate about the efficiency and effectiveness of the current array of multilateral agencies and the withdrawal of funds from some (such as the United Nations Educational, Scientific and Cultural Organization, the United Nations Industrial Development Organization, and the African Development Bank). As well, it has stimulated the commissioning of a series of studies on the comparative efficacy of bilateral and multilateral aid and aid institutions. In general, while bilateral donors (who, it needs always to be remembered, remain the main funders of multilateral organizations) continue to praise the notion of multilateralism, stagnant and falling aid budgets are leading them to seek ways of clawing back commitments to these agencies.

These developments are by no means the only, or perhaps even the most important, elements of the globalization process which have a bearing on aid and development co-operation issues. I will discuss (briefly) three others: the contextualization of aid; globalization and aid priorities; and longer term questions about the nature of development.

The Contextualization of Aid

At its best, development aid cannot solve the problems of poverty and underdevelopment but it can contribute to resolving them more quickly. Thus aid needs to be viewed as one element of a far wider set of policies contributing to the acceleration of the development process, policies both within developing countries and beyond their borders. Yet, usually from the best of motives – wanting aid to be as pure as possible and remain untainted by (often powerful) commercial, financial, and security interests – aid's supporters in donor countries may well have clouded this perception of aid's contribution to development by arguing the case for an aid ministry distinct and separate from finance, trade, and other departments which also interact with recipient economies. In many ways, too, aid's detractors and those with self-motivated interests in the aid vote have had a stake in advocating and arguing for the preservation of this institutional relationship.

Especially since the end of the Cold War, however, there has been growing evidence of a change in these institutional relationships in donor countries. In particular, a number of bilateral donors – Finland, Sweden, Norway, and Denmark – have moved their aid agencies entirely into their foreign affairs ministries, or have shifted some responsibilities (such as emergency aid in the case of Norway) to foreign affairs, or are actively discussing such changes. Such developments have usually been carried out with very little opposition from domestic aid lobbies, sometimes even with their active support. A major reason for such support (or lack of strong dissent) lies in the recognition that in the more globalized world economy there is an ever increasing need for aid and other policies not merely to be consistent but to be harmonized. Thus, the absorption of (small) aid agencies into (big) departments is not a sign of earlier principles being eclipsed by short-term political and security interests but an acknowledgment of the need for other departments to execute policies consistent with the donor's development co-operation principles. It is no accident that these institutional changes have taken place in donor countries where the moral and solidarity reasons for providing aid have been the strongest. Though the approach has been somewhat different, what has happened in Switzerland is in many ways even more radical. There, all government departments, including those which ostensibly deal exclusively with domestic issues (such as education and internal health), are required to carry out an audit to ensure that all their policies, purchasing arrangements, and the like are consistent with Swiss development policy principles.

Other donors have been actively debating changes in the institutional relationship between aid and other departments. The United States is a good example of a donor country in which the development lobby (USAID and private voluntary organizations) has been in the forefront of those expressing strong opposition to discussions about "absorbing" USAID more explicitly into the State Department than it is at present. Indeed, it is not uncommon for such advocates to view the institutional changes in other donor countries as detrimental and harmful to the development interests of recipient countries.[11]

The relevance of these moves and debates to the process of globalization is important. Increasingly, international transactions beyond the aid relationship are going to play a more prominent and influential part in determining the economic and development prospects of developing countries.[12] Even among the most aid-dependent economies of the world, only four (Mozambique, Nicaragua, Tanzania, and Uganda) had ODA/GNP ratios in excess of 25 per cent in 1992/3. As globalization proceeds, it will become comparatively less important to focus on ensuring that aid remains "pure and untainted" and more important to seek to ensure that the development-linked policies of donor countries are consistent with wider policies of individual donor countries and in harmony with developing country engagement with the increasingly globalized world economy. In such a context, moves to integrate aid agencies with other departments in donor countries ought to be seen as opportunities to focus on monitoring for transparency and consistency in all policies and relationships with poorer economies and regions. Conversely, initiatives aimed at isolating aid from wider international relationships will be increasingly detrimental to achieving aid's developmental purposes.

Globalization and Aid Priorities

Globalization trends are also likely to raise more specific questions about the content of aid programmes. Economies which are developing successfully in the new global economy are likely to exhibit two important attributes. The first will be the ability to be flexible: to respond to and to adjust domestically to change. The second will be the extent, quality, and level of skills, the knowledge base of the economy, and the ability to adopt "new learning processes" (learning to learn and learning new ways to learn).

To the extent that aid donors continue to focus on a sectoral approach to their aid portfolio, this suggests that they will need to raise the status they have traditionally given to education and training, even if, in part, this shift is dressed up as a particular (and particularly important) aspect of capacity-building. For the poorer countries in particular, it is not merely a matter of boosting educational capacity in order to catch up with others, or focusing on helping to provide basic education in the hope that development will create the resources for subsequent expansion into secondary and tertiary education. Such a response is likely to leave poorer countries condemned to falling farther and farther behind. Increasingly, what is likely to be required is assistance in promoting a rapid and accelerated expansion of education at all levels and in helping to inculcate and expand new ways of learning.[13] And, as the World Bank has recently argued, this is an area where non-market intervention is likely to be particularly relevant.[14]

Longer Term Questions about the Nature of Development

Pursuing aid and development co-operation policies to assist poor and disadvantaged countries, economies, and people to be better placed to gain from globalization is one thing. Assessing the prospects of success is quite another. Whether at the village, district, or national level, aid and development projects are enacted in the expectation that they will succeed, with risk analysis introduced to assess the veracity of these expectations. But what are the prospects for success?

Throughout the history of aid giving, the industrialized economies and the living standards within them have been an important model, or target, for the poorer aid-dependent economies to strive to emulate. In recent years, the (macro-economic) conditions which donors have increasingly applied to the aid given to poorer countries symbolized the way that donors have encouraged the replication of models of the North into and across countries and economies the South. Indeed, to the extent that a particularly prominent feature of the 1980s and

1990s continues – namely, faster average growth in the South than in the North – the South's journey to become like the North will be hastened. It is thus particularly important to consider some emerging and perverse characteristics of recent developments in the North.

First, there is growing evidence of post–World War II record high levels of unemployment across many leading OECD economies: the unemployment rate in the OECD stood at about 3 per cent in the mid-1970s; it rose to 5.1 per cent by the end of the 1970s, to 6.3 per cent by the end of the 1980s, and to 8.1 per cent by 1994. In some of the poorer OECD countries, such as Italy and Finland, unemployment levels have persistently been above 10 per cent for over a decade while in Spain the rate had grown to 24 per cent by 1994. Secondly, in some donor countries there is evidence of growing inequalities among citizens, rising levels of poverty, and a greater incidence of "permanent poverty": indeed, in Britain and the United States, the main cause of poverty is not so much a lack of work as low pay.[15] In Britain between 1979 and 1992/3, the number of people living in poverty rose from 9 per cent to one-quarter of the population, with the number of children living in poverty rising from 10 per cent to a third of all children. In the same period, while average incomes have risen by 37 per cent, the poorest 10 per cent of the population saw their real incomes fall by 17 per cent (CPAG 1996).

Most poor countries are characterized by higher levels of unemployment and underemployment and greater degrees of income and wealth inequalities than exist in contemporary donor, industrialized, economies. As the experience of "freer" market policies in the industrialized and increasingly globalized world point to examples of rising unemployment, growing inequalities, and deeper and more extensive poverty, there is clearly a danger that these characteristics and outcomes will be even more manifest across many countries of the South. The 1995 *World Development Report*, which focused on employment issues, looked at performance across developing countries and found varying trends. The best achievements were in East Asia where income distribution has become more equal as trade has expanded. But elsewhere, notably in Latin America and Africa, there has been an increase in both wage and income inequalities. Overall, the report expressed concern about the "substantial risk that inequalities between rich and poor will grow over the coming decades while poverty deepens," adding that unless (direct) action is taken within countries, poor groups in particular will not benefit from overall growth (World Bank 1995: 4, 8).

What questions do these trends raise about the future role of aid and (interventionist) development co-operation policy? Should aid be used to accelerate a development process based on market deepening and market expansion, fuelled and accelerated by the forces of globalization? The overriding consensus seems to be that overall there appears to be little alternative, as the recent "conversion" to such approaches by the United Nations Conference on Trade and Development (UNCTAD) would tend to confirm. However, if the outcome of such a process is likely to be not merely necessary higher growth but also continuing high unemployment, wide inequalities, and persistent widespread poverty, it surely points to the need for aid funds to be used to help address these problems directly – for example, by providing training and re-training to the unemployed to enhance incomes and by helping recipient countries to meet the basic needs of the poor.

Yet even this "corrective" approach fails to address all the questions which need to be faced, especially when development is examined at the micro-level. Those who view development as the process by which "people with nothing" are helped will perceive all efforts to improve the lives of these people as an achievement, even if the (unintended) result is continuing high levels of poverty, inequality, and unemployment: growth and the gains accruing to the those benefiting from growth are seen as sufficient achievement. But this more economistic view of development is increasingly being challenged because it is based on a false picture of the nature of poverty. In particular, it is argued that many communities of poor people possess a range of traditional mechanisms for coping, or trying to cope, with their economic poverty and vulnerability. These comprise their cultural, including religious, heritage and the structures and norms of society and social interaction arising from living in usually close-knit, and often geographically limited, communities. In such a perspective, poor people are certainly not "people with nothing." What then becomes of special concern is that the process of modernization, accelerated by the new forces of globalization, carries with it the risk that where attempts to incorporate the poor into a modern expanding and globally linked economy fail to provide productive employment and alleviate poverty, the process can erode, and even destroy, the cultural, religious, social, geographic, and structural supports that enabled individuals and communities to cope with their original deprivation. Thus the process can contribute to creating the "poor with nothing." To the extent that aid and development co-operation efforts in the globalized world economy fail to bring the development (economic) benefits anticipated, the risk is that those who fail to benefit will be left in a far worse state than when they were "living in poverty." Indeed, some writers maintain that these adverse effects are already evident. Johan Galtung (1996), for example, argues that culturelessness (anomie) and structurelessness (atomie) are spreading fast and maintains that "many societies (perhaps most) are in a state of advanced social disintegration at the close of the 20th century."[16]

To the extent that one is persuaded by such analysis and arguments, pressing questions arise about aid and development co-operation. It is no longer sufficient to ask whether aid to assist the process of globalization is complemented by direct measures to help those who fail to benefit much from the process. It becomes necessary to ask whether one is sure that, and on what basis one can judge whether, the aid provided today is not contributing to the creation of even bigger problems for the future, or making future problems more difficult to resolve. What is more, it becomes increasingly important for those working on micro-projects (and thus many NGOs) to raise these sorts of questions, asking not only what are the prospects for the aid provided to particular groups of people to contribute to a better long-term future for those people, but also what the consequences of benefiting these people are likely to be for the wider population beyond the narrow confines of specific projects.

2 Implications for and Responses by Northern NGOs

A CONCEPTUAL MAP OF NGO POLICY ROLES

What are the implications of these trends and developments for NGOs, and Northern NGOs especially? What opportunities and constraints do they face in trying to enhance support for aid and international development co-operation? To answer these questions at all adequately would require substantive discussion of the nature, role, strengths, and weaknesses of NGOs (Northern and Southern) in development and influencing policy. Though this is not my purpose here, it is probably helpful to begin with a few very general and contextual comments to orient subsequent discussion.

First, some more questions. How should Northern NGOs balance what they do in terms of what they are good at doing vis-à-vis working on priorities in the aid/development co-operation field that need to be addressed? How should NGOs balance the need to respond to the domestic development agenda, the international development agenda, the agenda of developing countries in general, and the agenda of Southern partners and the communities with which they work? To what extent should NGOs seek to expand and deepen support for the more general development co-operation agenda as opposed to seeking to strengthen the NGO movement in general and their own organization in particular? How should NGOs balance the necessity of securing their own funding base with the need to undertake activities which could erode or even threaten that funding base?

It is clearly difficult – probably impossible – to answer these questions adequately at the very general level. The work a Northern NGO chooses to do will depend not only on trends and crises "out there" but also, and perhaps more importantly, on the nature, strength, size, skills, resources, purpose, mission, and current and future commitments of that NGO. Clearly, a small technically focused organization linked solely to small grassroots organizations in only one country will bring different strengths and attributes to debates within Canada than will a small generalist NGO in a single province with a small outreach programme. These smaller organizations, in turn, will differ in their attributes and the potential audience they can influence from the few large NGOs equipped with the range of skills to launch detailed nation-wide and international campaigns. Both these groups will differ, in turn, from large specialized NGOs with roots in the teacher, co-operative, and trade union movements, and across different Christian (radical, fundamentalist, evangelical, conservative) and other religious bodies – some of these have a mission to be involved in broad advocacy work, some limit their advocacy work to their own immediate constituencies. This variety of organizations which make up the NGO sector – some at the grassroots, some based exclusively in the North with no direct links to the South, some membership, some non-membership – makes it difficult to define and pin down. As Esman and Uphoff wryly, but almost accurately, quipped more than ten years ago: "almost anything that one can say about NGOs is true – or false – in at least some instance, somewhere" (1984: 58).[17]

In part to address this diversity, efforts have been made to provide typologies of NGOs. The approach developed by Adil Najam (1995) in the United States is particularly useful for this discussion because it constructs a conceptual map of NGOs which focuses on NGOs in relation to their role in policy-related work. Najam divides NGOs into four groups in terms of their activities: as monitors (for instance, monitoring what governments do); as advocates (lobbying for preferred policy options); as innovators (developing and demonstrating different ways of doing things); and, lastly, as service providers.[18] He further divides them by the (three) types of activity they engage in: agenda setting, policy development, and policy implementation. He uses these building blocks to construct a 3 × 4 two-dimensional policy matrix. Table 1 both reproduces Najam's matrix and fills it in, providing his (initial and tentative) assessment of the role and strengths of NGOs in relation to the different cell-constructs of the matrix, based on a detailed survey of a wider literature of NGOs, their activities, their performance, and their impact.

Table 1
Matrix of Different Policy Roles of NGOs and Competencies

	Monitors	Advocates	Innovators	Service Providers
Agenda Setting	moderate	**strong**	moderate	*weak*
Policy Development	*weak*	**strong**	*weak*	moderate
Policy Implementation	**strong**	**strong**	**strong**	**strong**

Source: Najam (1995: 17 and 34).

Table 2
Most Likely NGO Attitude towards Government

	Monitors	Advocates	Innovators	Service Providers
Agenda Setting	???	???	complementary	collaborative
Policy Development	???	confrontational/ complementary	complementary/ collaborative	collaborative
Policy Implementation	confrontational	confrontational	complementary	complementary/ collaborative

Source: Najam (1995): 36
Note: ??? denotes situation where all attitudes seem equally prevalent.

Najam's analysis and classification reveals that in practice development NGOs are involved in public policy work in each of the cells of the matrix. In other words, they occupy the entire policy map, leading him to conclude that there is no a priori reason why they should be more involved in one cell of his matrix rather than another. Concerning the assessments made of NGO strengths and weaknesses and depicted in Table 1, Najam stresses that the labels allocated to the different cells of the matrix are meant to be descriptive rather than prescriptive, though clearly the assessment of current activities indicates particular strengths in advocacy on all three tiers of policy work and in all four types of action in terms of policy implementation.

Building in part on the work of John Clark (1991), Najam groups the types of way in which NGOs might seek to influence policy (and governments) into three different approaches: confrontational, collaborative, and complementary. Building upon his review of what NGOs do, Table 2 provides what Najam describes as a very tentative and subjective assessment of the type of relationship commonly found and used by NGOs in each of the cells of the matrix in terms of the relationship adopted vis-à-vis the government. On the one hand, it suggests that NGOs acting as monitors or as advocates at the policy implementation level are most likely to exhibit a confrontational attitude, opposing the path of implementation selected by the government. On the other hand, NGOs acting as service providers are likely to choose a complementary or outright collaborative relationship with the relevant government agencies. Perhaps more important for this discussion than this subjective assessment of current and past NGO actions is the way this sort of mapping exercise might be used for policy purposes and for helping NGOs reflect on initiatives they might take. Thus Najam concludes: "The picture presented [in Table 2] is hazy since the strategic decision that any particular NGO might make in this regard is influenced by so many outside factors that a general statement about the global NGO community becomes almost meaningless ... [Yet] whether by design or fault, NGOs which have influenced policy successfully have tended to exhibit a match between their attitude to governmental actors with the role they best play in the policy stream. However, even if research on this question might not yield a fully 'filled' and definitive version [of the matrix], the insights it could provide about what attitude towards government is most likely to result in the greatest impact in what roles under what conditions could be a valuable strategic device for NGO managers as well as a potentially explanatory device for scholars of the sector" (1995: 37).

There are three conclusions from the Najam study and typologies that I think are useful for our discussion. The first is that it is likely to be unhelpful to think in terms of all Northern NGOs engaging in, or expanding, the same type of activity in order to influence aid policy, public opinion, or the media with the object of enhancing support for aid and international development co-operation. The second is that because different NGOs engage variously, and with varying degrees of success, in policy discourse through collaborative, confrontational, and complementary modes of interaction with governments, it is also likely to be unhelpful to conceive of the future actions of Northern NGOs in terms of all pursuing paths which are more or less collaborative, more or less confrontational, or more or less complementary with government approaches and government policies. Thirdly, however, these (negative) conclusions should not be used as a justification for particular NGOs or groups of NGOs side-stepping or failing to assess carefully which strategies they should pursue (either individually or as a group) to address the current crisis in development, and what resources to devote to this task.

With this as background, I offer some suggestions on the way forward for Northern NGOs in dealing with the new trends in aid and development co-operation. In providing these ideas, and concrete suggestions, I would like to stress that I am focusing largely on the medium to longer term: as I hope will become apparent, in a number of cases it would be detrimental (and confusing to supporters of expanded and enhanced and more effective international development co-operation efforts) to seek to make sudden changes in more traditional ways of presenting the case for international development co-operation.

MOVING TO A MORE HOLISTIC APPROACH

Both because of the way that short-term commercial and strategic interests have "corrupted" the development purpose of aid and because the hands-on experience of most Northern NGOs with development has been through (their own) aid projects, many NGOs have been in the forefront of efforts to increase aid and to keep it "developmentally pure." Both these objectives need to remain on NGO agendas. However, the post–Cold War changes and especially the accelerating forces of globalization point to the need to pursue an approach to international development co-operation which is more all-embracing, encompassing national, regional, and global security and financial and commercial interests and relating all of these to the problems of development. Thus, the new orientation ought to be less one of trying to isolate aid – to keep it pure – and more one of attempting to use government statements on aid and development co-operation to influence all other aspects of policy which touch on international development co-operation efforts. Efforts directed at "purification" need to be pitched far more widely than merely at aid issues. In relation to security and political concerns, the biggest task is surely not to dismiss these as irrelevant to the development debate but to try to increase consistency between longer term goals and objectives (which tend usually to be more consistent with articulated donor development policy statements) and short-term statements and action (which often tend to be inconsistent with these objectives).[19]

An important way in which this can be done is by building bridges, coalitions, and alliances among different interest groups, both those which have been traditional allies of aid advocates and those which have historically been seen as part of the process of "corrupting" aid. In terms of Najam's matrix (Table 1), the methods to be used are likely to involve monitoring and advocacy in terms of agenda setting and policy development. Thus, while one type of activity is likely to focus on issues linked to overall policy "transparency," another important element is likely to need to focus on the building and extending of coalitions and alliances among a range of different interest groups. Historically, it has been a common pattern for most Northern NGOs to be cautious about building coalitions even with official aid agencies and their personnel, and even more cautious of establishing links with security/military and commercial interest groups. Already in many donor countries, however, the drop in aid volumes is leading to less antagonism and stronger links between official aid agencies and NGOs. Though building coalitions first with government departments and then with a range of other interest groups carries risks (see below), there is a need to reassess past practice which has often tended to view relationships in terms of a simple either/or perspective: either one confronts or one co-operates with it (for example, the World Bank).

Though I am arguing, primarily, for the need to focus beyond aid on international development co-operation more generally, there are also grounds for asking whether one should stop there. There is some evidence to support the view that the best way to encourage support for international development co-operation lies not so much in stimulating awareness and consciousness of these issues within the donor population as in attempting (far more ambitiously) to address more all-embracing aspects of society in the donor country, especially its value systems. At the level of theory, the Norwegian aid analyst, Olaf Stokke, articulates this view by arguing that the prospects for aid increasingly will depend "on the way basic values in donor societies develop in the years to come – towards a society with a high welfare profile (where the indicators may be ... a policy geared towards social justice) or towards a society with a low welfare profile ... to indicate two poles. It is assumed that donor societies close to the former will produce an international commitment in the direction of humane internationalism and, accordingly, a high ODA volume, while donor societies close to the latter will produce an international commitment in the direction of 'international realism' and, accordingly, a low volume ODA" (1996a: 111).

What is particularly interesting is that a recent study of trends in aid giving by donor from 1970 to 1993 provides support for the view that this is precisely what has happened in that period. The study (Rao 1996) shows that there has been a negative relationship between external aid effort and the nature of donor societies: donor countries which have greater inequalities within their societies and a greater incidence of poverty tend to be less generous in terms of the aid given than those which are more egalitarian and have fewer problems of poverty. It concludes that "there is support for the hypothesis that generosity and equity in aid giving are negatively related to the degree of domestic inequality within donor nations" (1996: 23). As well, Rao finds that there is more stability in aid flows among the latter group of countries which are also characterized as providing aid to recipients based more on the needs of those recipients.[20] The conclusion is not necessarily that NGOs and aid's supporters should extend their own work into these new areas or activities, but that, minimally, they should be aware of the linkage between gaining support for their more narrow agenda and its roots in a more complex set of domestic agendas.[21]

AID VOLUME, AID NEEDS, AND INDIVIDUAL DONOR EFFORT

A major thrust of NGO lobbying activity over the years has been the supply of aid coming from individual donor countries. Efforts to increase supply have focused, variously, on reaching the target of 0.7 per cent of GNP; on increasing, then holding steady, the prevailing ratio; and on increasing, then holding steady, the amount of aid provided in real terms. There is a range of problems, weaknesses, and dangers in placing so much emphasis on a supply-led perspective.

- Focusing on volume gives the impression that development occurs as a result not merely of external injections of resources, but of aid per se: more aid means more development. In turn, this nourishes the view that it is relatively simple to assess whether aid is effective or not.
- Focusing on the 0.7-per-cent target can give the impression that this is the amount of aid required for development to occur.
- Focusing on what happens within a single donor country (one's own) gives the impression that it is solely or mainly aid from this country which makes the difference, encouraging the (false) views that co-operation with other donors is a secondary issue and that every donor ought to try to "cover the world." Recent OECD figures for bilateral aid provided by Canada to its top five recipients in 1993/4 (China, India, Egypt, Jamaica, and Bangladesh) show that Canada's contributions amounted to less than 3 per cent of total aid given to these countries in that period (1996a: Tables 33 and 42).[22]
- Focusing on aid supply reinforces the false belief that aid should continue indefinitely and fails completely to raise the question of targeting aid to meet a variety of interim objectives.
- Focusing on aid supply plays down the important point that aid requirements are based on need and that needs, and thus the nature

and composition of the aid provided, will vary depending upon the nature of the problems. For some recipients, peace and security will be a prerequisite for aid to have a chance of being effective; for others, inefficiency, corruption, and the lack of concern among domestic élites to work to eliminate the need for aid erodes its potential efficacy; for yet others, aid inflows are severely reduced, and in some cases wiped out, by outflows such as debt repayments; and for others still, effective aid is likely to require a highly complex process of trying to find a balance between meeting emergency needs and working on longer term structural problems of dependency.

These dangers and weaknesses are not pointed out to argue that aid volume and aid supply, and the contributions of individual (even middle-ranking) donors, are unimportant. Not only does need require aid to be supplied, and almost certainly in higher volumes than current flows, but as discussed above, there is some evidence that the (growing) gap between aid supplied and aid required not only contributes to the failure of aid to "make a difference" but also undermines support for aid within donor countries. Nevertheless, I would argue that the supply-side arguments have usually been overdone, in particular that they have (inadvertently) contributed to creating or deepening false or partial notions of aid's impact and expectations of its likely success. Consequently, efforts to encourage support for aid ought to change their goals:

- to focus far more on the (often very different) needs of different recipients;
- to be based more on putting forward realistic expectations of what aid can achieve;
- to lay bare the limited contributions made in so many countries and the limitations of what individual donors can do on their own and, as a practical consequence, to encourage domestic media coverage of what other donors and aid organizations are doing;[23]
- to encourage exposure to and analysis of the importance of recipients as essential parts of the aid relationship.

Reorienting the emphasis from aid supply to aid need, to the importance of different types of aid, and to the significance of contextual issues may sound like a good idea, but the consequences are unlikely to be entirely to the immediate liking of all development-focused aid lobbyists. Thus such an orientation could encourage support for multilateral over bilateral aid, encourage donors to withdraw aid (or particular forms of aid) from countries where there is little likelihood of it being used effectively, encourage bilateral donors to provide aid to far fewer recipient countries, and add fuel to the (unresolved) debate about the extent to which aid should be used to meet needs and address poverty directly rather than for capacity-building objectives. It is also likely that some of these outcomes could weaken rather than strengthen domestic support for aid, at least in the short term. But isn't this response due, in part, to the fact that some of the support which aid has enjoyed has been built on false or partial notions of its likely efficacy?

THE NEED TO WORK TO ENHANCE IMPACT — AND THE DANGERS

Despite the expansion of NGO activities in advocacy and monitoring, most of the work of Northern NGOs involves either implementing or funding Southern NGOs to implement discrete development projects and programmes. Indeed, apart from allocating more funds to emergency assistance, most of the additional funds from donors to NGOs have been channelled into these discrete NGO-initiated development initiatives. Yet successive studies in different donor countries over the past ten years have drawn attention not merely to the absence of data on the development impact of these projects and programmes but to the absence of mechanisms with which to appraise, monitor, assess, and evaluate their impact and to incorporate experience into the next project cycle (see ODI 1996).

The relative absence of a substantial body of non-partisan material on the impact of NGO projects and programmes leaves NGOs vulnerable on at least two fronts. First, it provides a greater opportunity for critics of aid in general and NGOs in particular to cite examples of poor-to-disastrous projects in support of a generalized view about the failure of aid and the foolishness of contributing financially to NGO work. Secondly, it encourages NGOs themselves to make extreme claims and generalizations about the impact of what they do, as a number of writers have pointed out. Although this practice can have a short-term positive effect on fundraising, it is dubious ethically and in the long term likely to damage the case for both aid in general and NGO aid in particular (Winter 1996: 16ff). Recently, however, there has been a marked eagerness among a large number of NGOs to know more about the impact of the development initiatives they implement or fund, to know how they can enhance the impact of what they do, and to learn from others. The reason has been simply, but powerfully, put by a leading British NGO thus: "if we don't know what works we can't disseminate it; if we don't know what doesn't work we might disseminate it. And in either case, we need to know why" (Barnett & Bush 1995).

In the United Kingdom and across a number of European countries, a growing number of NGOs (mostly larger and medium-sized ones) are themselves not only monitoring and undertaking impact evaluations well beyond traditional "problem projects," but are trying out and beginning to implement a variety of methods and approaches to analyse impact and thus to improve performance. Though there is little doubt that one stimulus for the NGO focus on these issues lies in the urging of donors, these activities are also related to an increasing recognition that the NGOs themselves need to know more about impact, not least in order to maintain, and indeed expand, support both for the work which they do as NGOs and for development co-operation initiatives more widely.[24]

There is, therefore, growing agreement both within NGOs and between NGOs and official donors that more attention needs to be given to appraisal, monitoring, and evaluation methods as well as broad support for the view that as these methods are used by more and more NGOs for longer periods they should help to strengthen the case for aid. But there are dangers, for NGOs and international development co-operation efforts more widely, in journeying too far along this particular path. The key issue revolves around the priority which should be given to "management by or for results" and the extent to which one should try to deepen support for aid and international development co-operation on the basis of their impact. The development work of NGOs involves a wide range of activities and modes of engagement. At one extreme are a cluster of activities in which NGOs act (and only wish to act) as service providers: this work consists largely of filling gaps and of extending the reach of, and in general supplementing, activities similar to those of the government and official donors. It is in fulfilling these roles that NGOs are likely to be most receptive to adopting methods of assessment and focusing on approaches which place particular emphasis on evaluating and enhancing the cost-effectiveness of what they do.[25]

What is potentially of great concern is if pressure is put on NGOs to judge *all* their work and development interventions in terms of the development results achieved, especially if this means that the funds given to NGOs by donors come to be based solely on the results achieved. While some NGO projects are, and are intended solely to be, gap-filling service-focused initiatives, others are undertaken because they are experimental, because they are risky, and because they test new and different approaches. Indeed in many ways it is the encouragement and pursuit of this type of work which distinguishes NGO initiatives from those of official donors and host governments (although this is not to argue that it is only NGO projects which are risky and innovative). Thus, some projects are executed not so much to achieve the "best" outcomes as to learn more about the appropriateness (and cost-effectiveness) of particular, and differing, approaches in specific, and often difficult, contexts. When linked to the uncertain and sometimes hostile environments in which NGO interventions are sometimes attempted, high risk is often an accepted part of the exercise. Indeed, risk minimization is frequently not the chosen path. In such circumstances, it will *usually* be misplaced to judge, and to strive to judge, the NGO intervention in terms of impact and results achieved.

With respect to these risky/experimental/innovative types of initiative, NGOs have three tasks. One is to continue to work in these often difficult areas. A second is to continue to exert pressure on official funders to provide funds to carry out these activities. And the third is to ensure that the support the general public gives them is informed (not least by the NGOs concerned) by this essential dimension of their work. Thus, the public needs to know and understand why NGOs will continue to experiment, take risks, and not try (always) to pursue the least risky, most cost-effective approach to development.

It is therefore particularly worrying that though donors often acknowledge the role and importance of NGOs as experimenters, risk-takers, and innovators, they continue to raise the status and importance of effectiveness and impact in general and of cost-effectiveness more particularly in their expanding relationships with NGOs.[26] In light of this tension, it is of some interest to the wider debate about enhancing support for international development co-operation within donor countries that there is evidence of aid departments sometimes being out of step with other domestic departments in the importance given to impact and results versus that given to encouraging innovative, risky, and experimental activities of NGOs. In particular, the recent study of cost-effectiveness undertaken for the British Overseas Development Administration compared the approaches and attitudes of the administration to the British NGOs it funded with those of other (domestic) government departments towards the voluntary sector within the United Kingdom. In contrast to trends occurring or under active discussion within the aid administration, it found the following views (see Riddell 1996b: 150ff):

- That impact assessment ought to use qualitative as well as quantitative criteria.
- That monitoring and impact assessment need to take account of the expected long-term benefits of projects even when government funding is only short term.
- That one should be extremely wary of trying to compare the costs of delivering services by different organizations, especially by using simple indicators, such as costs per client. Thus it is argued: "it is rarely possible to produce all-embracing measures of performance or out-

put, and some activities cannot be described by numerical measures. This should be recognised by Departments, but should not prevent monitoring of what can be measured or described."
- That government funds should be judged against the "customers' needs."
- That once government has decided that an organization ought to be funded, strict criteria should not be imposed on the voluntary organization, and there should not be a link between the money provided and the service funded.
- That even if there are no immediate prospects for projects to be financially sustainable, this is not, on its own, sufficient grounds for government not to agree to start funding a project: "There is value in testing innovative ideas on a short-term funding basis without getting locked into longer term support. Funding test or demonstration projects for limited periods allows Departments to assess their possible worth."
- That specific funds are and should continue to be set aside and allocated to voluntary organizations specifically to encourage them to undertake innovative work.
- And that the priority in evaluating innovative work is not to ensure that funds have been well spent (though this is clearly important) but to scrutinize these projects for the lessons to be learned for the future.

What this suggests for Britain – and for other countries where the evidence confirms growing government pressures for NGOs to conform to a more quantitative, narrowly cost-effective, and results-focused basis for funding – is that NGOs might focus more on carefully analysing existing domestic relations among the voluntary sector, government, and civil society more widely and, where appropriate, build upon this information to develop relations and linkages with relevant domestic government departments and interest groups.

NORTHERN AND SOUTHERN NGOS: POVERTY, CAPACITY-BUILDING, AND FINANCIAL SUSTAINABILITY

Working to enhance the impact of development initiatives presupposes agreement about the nature of those activities and initiatives. But is there agreement among NGOs about the way they should be helping the development process in poor countries? As noted, appreciation of differences between the motive for aid and the purpose of the aid provided, often linked to growing interest in capacity-building, has meant that many Northern NGOs are giving more attention to ways of strengthening Southern NGOs. At the same time many Northern donors have been expanding their direct funding of Southern NGOs.[27]

Nevertheless, many (if not most) Northern NGOs still see addressing/ alleviating/eradicating poverty as a central purpose of aid and a major part of their work. Indeed, the role of NGOs in involving themselves directly in helping particular groups of poor people has been influencing official donor approaches to aid in recent years, and it is not uncommon for papers on the future of aid to give pride of place to poverty as its prime focus and purpose.[28]

It is not my purpose to evaluate such perspectives or to discuss them in any great depth. What I do wish to do is to draw attention to the fact that discussions among NGOs and development practitioners in some countries are giving so much emphasis to capacity-building that it is being proposed that Northern NGOs should withdraw from funding direct poverty-focused work in the South. The most interesting, and possibly the most extreme, example comes from Norway. Thus, the report of the Royal Commission on North-South and Aid Policies (1995) is "sceptical about the idea that Norwegian or other international donor organisations should fund, and provide aid directly to the poorest parts of the population or special target groups in countries in the South. The role of aid ... must be to support countries' own development policies and institutions so that they can fulfil essential functions." For Northern NGOs in particular it is argued that: "Fewer NGOs should be involved in practical development aid ... The most important contribution for a majority of voluntary organisations will ... be cooperation with similar organisations in the South on the basis of common values and interests, in order to strengthen their ability and capacity to promote their goals. This is a task that cannot be carried out by official bodies. The majority of NGOs should concentrate on organisational cooperation with partners in the South."

The commission then extends this argument by suggesting both that the range of voluntary organizations which the government supports should extend well beyond those which have traditionally been involved in development and should be more reflective of Norwegian society as a whole, and that more emphasis should be placed on supporting those Norwegian voluntary bodies which are membership organizations: "The Commission suggests that Norwegian voluntary organisations be encouraged to further develop their organisational efforts and cooperation with like-minded organisations in the South, and that this should have an important place on the aid budget ... The Commission wishes to emphasise that the organisations which are to receive such support must clearly be based on voluntary support and efforts in Norway. Genuine organisational cooperation is conditional upon the organisations being based in Norwegian society and having a membership or support groups that are working to promote the same interests and values in Norway."

Should this type of thinking come to permeate other donor countries, it suggests that governments would be likely to lower (drastically) the funds allocated to Northern NGOs for direct poverty-alleviating initiatives. Clearly such a move would raise questions about both how both official donors and Northern NGOs might/should judge the impact of the indirect development work they do and how evidence of success in this area might be linked to the objective of nurturing and deepening support for international development co-operation efforts at home.

The rise in the prominence of the non-profit sector in the industrialized countries has been associated with growing attention to the impact of services provided by non-profit organizations, itself linked to questions of cost-effectiveness and value for money. In some countries, such as the United States and, more recently, the United Kingdom, there is clear evidence of a contraction in funds provided by the government to the domestic voluntary sector. This, in turn, is leading non-profit organizations to look for new/alternative sources of funds. The most prominent of these are solicitation of the corporate sector and charging clients for services (user fees) (see, for the United States, Salamon 1995; for the United Kingdom, Kendall & Knapp 1996). These trends within donor countries have influenced non-profit organizations working in developing countries in a number of ways. With growing fears of a contraction in funds from both the Northern public and from donors, and in common with their counterparts in the domestic voluntary sector, development NGOs, too, have been examining ways in which new sources of funding can be tapped, and some have been involved in introducing user fees in some of the programmes they implement in the South.[29]

For their part, official donors have commonly seen a virtuous link between wishing to ensure that they are getting value for money in the funds allocated to NGOs for development projects and rising concern in the literature with the sustainability of projects. In turn, these developments have had an influence on the direct poverty alleviation versus capacity-building debate taking place among Northern NGOs. Two types of arguments have been heard which reinforce each other. First, it is argued that efforts should be focused increasingly on capacity-building within and among Southern NGOs because the ultimate test of the "worth" of aid lies in the continuation of its positive effects after Northern donors/funders withdraw. But, secondly, it is argued that because Northern aid money provided for Southern NGO projects by Northern NGOs (from their own funds and from donor money) is going to run out, and may run out far sooner than envisaged even five years ago, it is essential for Southern NGOs to set about examining ways in which they can raise funds domestically to continue their activities. Indeed, the argument is increasingly heard that Southern NGOs should be judged in relation to the trend in the percentage of total income they are able to raise domestically.[30]

These arguments raise two major concerns for NGO development efforts in the South, and thus for relations between Northern and Southern NGOs. The first relates to the impact of user fees on the nature of programmes which introduce them. Most research on this issue has been done in the United States, particularly by Lester Salamon's studies (reviewed in his 1995 publication). They point to three trends. First, and not surprisingly, user-fee income contributes proportionately far less to a programme's total income in non-profit programmes for the poor than in non-profit programmes for the less poor or for the wealthy. Secondly, trends in sources of income over time show both a relative and an absolute rise in total non-profit income going towards non-profit programmes serving the more wealthy rather than the less wealthy. Salamon concludes that in the decade to 1989, there was a "shift from services targeted toward the poor to those targeted toward customers able to pay" in the social services field (1995: 229). Thirdly, however, and less self-evident, the contribution of government funds to the non-profit sector contributes directly to the expansion, and even the maintenance, of non-profit programmes which benefit the poor: "the greater the government support the more likely an agency is to focus primarily on the poor ... far from distorting agency missions, government support thus seems to have enabled nonprofit agencies to carry out their charitable responsibilities more fully" (Salamon 1995: 8).

The second major concern arising from these new views on the work of Northern development NGOs relates to perceptions about new sources of funding within the South, with Southern NGOs being encouraged to look for new/alternative sources of income from within developing countries to add to user-fee income. Private donations, corporate giving, or other commercially linked, income-raising initiatives are proposed, such as charity shops and sponsorships – in most cases mirroring developments within the voluntary sector in industrialized countries. What is worrying is not the investigation and pursuit of new sources of income for Southern NGO development initiatives (in general this is to be welcomed), and not even the notion that Northern funding will eventually run out, dramatic though the implications of this happening would be. What is most worrying is the assumption that so often lies behind the discussion of new funding initiatives, namely, that NGO development projects and programmes will eventually be able to be run and be supported by, indeed that they will *need* to be run and supported by, various combinations of private and corporate support, and thus *without* public sector support. This assumption is troubling because if there is one piece of firm evidence arising from the analysis of voluntary sector activity in the industrialized, and more affluent, world and of sources of income to carry out such activities, especially in the social sector, it is that such an assumption is an illusion. As Salamon argues for the United States, a country with the greatest degree of both private and corporate support for the non-profit sector, "government has emerged as the single most important source of nonprofit human service agency income, outdistancing private giving and service charges as sources of support" (1995: 34). And outside the United States, comparative data on sources of non-profit income in other leading industrialized countries indicate an even greater contribution by the public sector to total non-profit income (Salamon & Anheier 1995).

The phenomenal rise in the importance of NGOs in development activities in the South has been made possible financially largely by funds from the North: initially largely from Northern NGOs, but supplemented increasingly by official donor funds. In few, if any, of the poorest countries of the world, does the latter constitute less than 85 per cent of the total funds. The analysis of funding sources across the voluntary sector within industrialized countries indicates that any attempt by Southern NGOs to replace Northern funding of their development programmes and projects solely with a mix of domestic private and corporate donations and user fees is doomed to failure. It is doomed not only because of the experience of the industrialized world, but because the lower levels of wealth within poorer developing countries – one of the defining characteristics of underdevelopment – means that there is far less individual and corporate wealth in these countries to meet the income requirements of voluntary sector initiatives. If (as seems increasingly likely) funds from the North are set to decline, and if voluntary sector programmes for the poor within developing countries are to continue expanding, then it is going to be increasingly important for Southern NGOs to look to their governments as critical sources of income for their work. And it then becomes incumbent on Northern NGOs to incorporate this dimension of the funding problem into the work they do aimed at strengthening the capacity of Southern NGOs.

CONCLUDING COMMENTS

I will not attempt to summarize the issues covered in this paper – indeed, most of them have only been presented in summary form, giving, perhaps, one indication of the scope and complexity of the agenda facing Northern NGOs in the years ahead. However, a recurrent theme has been the emphasis placed on the need for NGOs to focus increasingly on broader contextual issues: to look beyond what their own organization is doing to NGOs in general; to look beyond NGOs to aid more generally; to look beyond aid to a complex set of different aspects of international development co-operation and to try to forge new, and what might seem at first sight unlikely, alliances; and even to look beyond international development issues to core issues of civil society in the North.

It is important, however, to draw attention to the dangers of such an "opening up," of a widening of perspectives, and potential involvement in more, and some very different, types of new activities. Clearly an immediate danger is that broadening the agenda runs the risk of reducing the impact of each discrete effort, especially as resources are likely to be stretched, although the stress on alliance-building is meant, in some ways, to address this particular problem. This risk is likely to be heightened to the extent that each NGO, and especially each larger NGO, perceives its role as requiring it to undertake each and every task and pursue every issue raised.

But the dangers/problems could be deeper. In a recent analysis of the politics of aid which focused especially on the weaknesses of aid, Engberg-Pedersen combines three notions which, he argues, have together had a devastating and perverse effect on aid's impact and on support for aid. These are, first, the wish of each and every donor to incorporate each new idea, each new fashion, and each new insight from the development agenda into their own programmes, and, secondly, the large and growing gap among donors articulating verbally the importance of collaboration and co-operation to maximize the development advantages of each and minimize the corruption of aid by non-developmental influences. He goes on to argue, thirdly, that this in turn encourages donors to compromise what they genuinely believe in so as not to undermine the overall "aid effort": aid politics has driven the art of compromise to the extreme of jeopardizing the craft of good aid delivery. All major donors have compromised themselves into the muddy waters in the middle: "The institutionalized search for compromise ... has found its most extreme form in the declarations and plans of action of the U[nited] N[ations] summits and conferences. Instead of using these platforms as an opportunity to recognize political differences as a foundation for future dialogue and cooperation, the UN has turned into a linguistic get-together, where government representatives and international bureaucrats collaborate in the *cover-up of conflict*" (Engberg-Pedersen 1996: 128, emphasis added). Although he was largely discussing official donors in an international context, Engberg-Pedersen's words provide a warning for the increasingly influential Northern NGOs seeking to devise national strategies of public support for international development co-operation to the millennium and beyond.

My final task in this paper is to shift gear to offer some practical ideas about how Northern NGOs might enhance their capacity as learning organizations. I have already alluded to a threefold range of capabilities which NGOs need to develop and deepen. To summarize:

- Most, if not all, Northern NGOs need to increase their professional competence in order to enhance the impact of what they do, and to expand into new areas of work and activities, at the same time paying attention to the increasing need (and demand for) greater transparency in their different activities.
- Most need to continue to maintain a creative tension between pursuing activities built on their strengths, building support on the basis of showing their successes, and ensuring especially that successes built on service delivery and replication are matched with experimental and innovative approaches.
- Most need to understand both individually and as a group when and if and how to act in a collaborative way with donors, government departments, and other interest groups, when and if to act in a complementary fashion, and when and if to take a confrontational stance.

Clearly one way to develop skills in these areas will be to continue to learn more about their strengths and weaknesses as NGOs individually and as groups and sub-groups. Precisely how they might do this is not really within my area of competence: other contributors to this volume have the skills and the knowledge to make a more profound contribution here. However I would like to end by sharing some of the ideas which the largest British NGO, Oxfam-UK, is addressing, discussing, and developing (see Roche 1995a, 1995b, 1996).

While placing a high priority on the need to enhance their capacity and ability to learn, it is argued that learning within the organization is limited in part because of the nature of activities undertaken. In recent years, NGOs, especially larger ones, have given increasing attention to appraisal, monitoring, and evaluation techniques for a variety of reasons: to understand what works and what does not, to increase transparency, to meet criticisms, and to build up a knowledge base which can be used to improve and enhance the impact of future programmes. However questions are now being raised about the usefulness of this accumulated knowledge to organizations for which many activities tend to be non-routine, and when the comparative advantage of the organization needs to be based not merely on what was done well in the past but in trying out what might work in the future.

Should this latter emphasis lead to a radical re-thinking, and in effect to a downgrading, of the need to learn at all? Christopher Roche argues not for a downgrading of learning but for a change of emphasis in the methods of learning and the approach used. More specifically, he asserts that efforts should be centred on methods of learning by deviation, meaning a focus on why plans have changed and on post-hoc accountability – thus giving more emphasis to internal learning systems and less to (ritualistic) external evaluations of impact.

What becomes particularly important is to seek a better understanding of those features of the organization which impede the development and acceptance of learning systems and which limit the extent to which lessons in one part of the organization are known to and shared with other parts of the organization – and influence them. For Oxfam, three impediments to learning have been pinpointed: weak structures and systems for extracting and disseminating learning and information; the low priority given to learning, and therefore the little space or time devoted to learning, and the lack of rewards for learning; and the existence of an unfavourable climate for learning within the organization, related to job insecurity, short-term contracts, and difficulties of working across the line management system. The combined impact of these influences is that it is very difficult for errors to be admitted and for good ideas to flow within and across the organization. To try to address some of these problems, in 1995 Oxfam set up the Cross-Programme Learning Fund to encourage lateral learning at all levels, but most especially across different field programmes. By early 1996, a substantial sum of £96,000 had been spent on a variety of cross-learning initiatives. Most involved bringing people together, but they included improving the organization's electronic communications hardware and software.

I will end with a final word of caution from Oxfam's Roche which links quite well the theme of learning and the wider attempts of this paper to gaze hazily into the uncertain future of international development co-operation: "The most striking thing about development practice over the last 30 years is how wrong people have been when they were convinced they were right, and how systems of mis-information become self-sustaining" (Roche 1995a: 4).

NOTES

1 The word "crisis" implies something fundamental is occurring and thus carries with it some notion of permanence, whereas the word "fatigue" means weariness (not malady or illness), suggesting that what is being de-

scribed is temporary in nature. This would appear to imply that the term "aid fatigue" is used to describe a temporary problem or difficulty with aid, while the term "aid crisis" describes something far more deep-seated and fundamental.

2 "Growing scepticism about the effectiveness of aid, coupled with pressures to reduce government spending are undermining public support for official development assistance (ODA). Traditional arguments in support of ODA, such as poverty reduction, redistribution, and interdependence, are viewed with increasing scepticism by those outside the profession ... Development professionals acknowledge the need for sustained and strategic action to renew public confidence in ODA" (AKF Canada 1995).

3 What is new is the fall in aggregate aid, the number of donors who have reduced aid volumes at much the same time, and contractions in aid by what the Organization for Economic Co-operation and Development calls the "front runners," largely the Scandinavian donors. Major contractions in aid by individual donors (such as the United Kingdom, the United States, Italy, and Ireland) or by blocks of donors (such as Arab donors) have been a feature of aid flows for at least the past fifteen years.

4 The notion of "add-ons" is taken up by Olaf Stokke in his recent overview of the future of foreign aid. He argues that the new priorities do "not necessarily exclude the traditional objectives set for aid but add to them" (1996a: 92).

5 An indication of the importance of the influence of market-based solutions to development problems comes from the 1996 annual report on the least developed countries produced by the United Nations Conference on Trade and Development (1996). Historically, UNCTAD, more than any other United Nations agency, has been associated with approaches to development designed to curb market excesses. However, this report argues that interventionist efforts to achieve economic autonomy have been rendered ineffective by changes in the global economy: "as a consequence, governments have few options other than to pursue market-oriented economic policies."

6 For instance, between 1992 and 1995 Germany's aid commitments were stagnant and the ratio of ODA to GNP fell from 0.38 per cent to 0.33. Yet in a 1994 survey, 75 per cent of former West Germans and 69 per cent of former East Germans expressed support for development co-operation, with one-fifth expressing very strong support, compared with 75-per-cent support recorded in a 1987 survey (Taake & Wiemann 1995).

7 The conventional wisdom is that there is minimal support for foreign aid in the United States. Vernon Ruttan (1996: 141) argues that the majority of Americans support programmes that focus on humanitarian issues. This support for humanitarian issues is confirmed for Canada and other donor countries by Ian Smillie (1995: 124).

8 Logical Framework Analysis was developed in the late 1960s as a way for donor agencies to test the logic of a plan of action by analysing it in terms of ends and means.
9 Thus technical notes from Britain's Overseas Development Administration (1992, 1995b) and the administration's publication (1995a) entitled *A Guide to Social Analysis for Projects in Developing Countries* comment thus: "Many projects now funded by [the administration] are based on a process, rather than blueprint design – a recognition that greater sustainability is achieved with flexible iterative planning, involving as far as possible all those with an interest in the project outcome ... For process projects, as inputs and outputs cannot be quantified at the outset and as relevant net benefits (e.g. in research and extension projects) are dependent on action external to the project itself, normal cost-benefit analysis or cost effectiveness is difficult to apply."
10 The alternate view that globalization is neither particularly new, nor irreversible, nor irresistible is argued in Hirst & Thompson (1996).
11 For instance, the Washington-based *News and Notices* comments: "we see some countries (the Netherlands, the US, Canada and Sweden) putting development funds more firmly in the hands of Finance, Commerce and Foreign Ministries" (January 1996: 2).
12 According to World Bank data, in the past five years total financial flows to developing countries tripled, growing by 11.5 per cent in 1995 alone. As a share of total flows, ODA rose from 15 per cent in 1980 to 29 per cent in 1990, but subsequently fell back to 14 per cent by 1995. In contrast, international trade rose from under 30 per cent of the total gross domestic product of developing countries in 1980 to over 40 per cent by 1994 (Qureshi 1996: 32).
13 A recent study for the International Monetary Fund draws attention to the need to re-think education methods: "Addressing wage dispersion in the long run, however, may require addressing skill levels at a much earlier stage (than vocational skills training programs). Rethinking curriculums in primary and secondary schools could potentially produce graduates with better labor force skills, irrespective of whether these might be trade skills or communication and analytic skills" (Buckberg & Thomas 1995: 19).
14 "If training is in the interests of both workers and employers and in market economies takes place in response to underlying economic circumstances, should governments get involved? Governments should intervene in the market for training if there are particular market failures or imperfections" (World Bank 1995: 38).
15 Those in work in Britain but paid low wages accounted for a full 40 per cent of those in poverty at the end of the 1980s. Similarly more than half of all Americans whose incomes fell below the official poverty line lived in house-

holds in which at least one person worked, and among full-time workers the numbers in poverty rose by 43 per cent between 1977 and 1987.
16 Galtung does not romanticize traditional life or poverty. Thus he argues: "Some very poor Third World countries have been ravaged by unspeakable violence between classes, nations and clans ... Some of this violence may be attributable to atomie/anomie and there are signs that it has reached the micro level of organization, with family members butchering each other – in other words, total violence" (1996: 412).
17 I am grateful to Adil Najam for this quotation which is cited in his paper (1995: 7).
18 Monitoring involves being the eyes and ears of citizen's interests, advocacy involves being their mouthpiece (Najam 1995: 20).
19 The same sorts of arguments can be made in relation to commercial, corporate, and defence issues, some of which are discussed by Draimin & Schmitz (1997).
20 Rao (1996) acknowledges that the indicators he has used to derive these conclusions have been fairly crude and simplistic and that the analysis has suffered from some data limitations. Yet he argues that the data are robust enough to conclude that generous donors tend to be fairer donors.
21 I do not suggest that this is going to be easy. For a discussion of both the complexities and of some interesting ways forward, see Yankelovich (1996).
22 Canada's real contribution is probably even less than this ratio indicates, as these tables compare gross disbursements (for Canada) with overall net disbursements.
23 During the Ethiopian crisis in the mid-1980s I travelled to four European donor countries in the space of a few weeks. In each country, television coverage focused solely on the activities of agencies (official and NGO) of that country, conveying the message that it was solely through the efforts of one's own national organizations that the problems of Ethiopia were going to be solved.
24 As the introduction to an international research programme (Oxfam and the Netherlands Organization for International Development Cooperation) on impact assessment which began in 1994 puts it: "There is an increasing recognition among development NGOs, both in North and South, of their need to be able unambiguously to demonstrate the value of their work, both in qualitative and quantitative terms. The pressure for them to be able to do so comes primarily from northern donors but is also driven by their own perceived need to be in a position to improve institutional learning and thus practice."
25 Working to enhance impact and to achieve greater cost-effectiveness does not mean that even for these types of activity, NGOs should be encouraged or forced to use methods of appraisal and analysis, such as orthodox cost-benefit analysis, which are more relevant to economic and infrastructural

projects than to social development and process-type projects. However, though many NGOs are fearful that donors will push them in this direction, recent developments across many donor agencies suggest that donors themselves are moving away from such narrow and limited methods. The issue is not so much whether these sorts of projects should be implemented with the view to enhancing their impact and improving their cost-effectiveness but precisely which methods to use. A study for the British Overseas Development Administration on cost-effectiveness concludes that the best way for donors to help enhance the impact of NGO development programmes is not to try to enhance the impact of discrete projects but to help NGOs address key weaknesses at the organizational level. More specifically, attention could helpfully be grouped into four sorts of initiatives:
- enhancing the capability and capacity of these NGOs to understand better the development problems of the communities they choose to work with, including the nature, appropriateness, size, duration, and cost-effectiveness of discrete projects they may wish to implement and promote;
- strengthening the management, institutional capacity, and skills of the NGOs implementing particular projects and programmes;
- facilitating greater networking of NGOs with like-minded organizations, especially NGOs of similar size and capabilities and working in the same sectors or with the same methods; and
- strengthening internal learning systems within those organizations. (Riddell 1996b: 188)

26 In Canada a 1995 draft policy paper mentioned the strengths of NGO interventions in terms of their "innovative responses to new development challenges, flexibility in programming, a long term commitment to partners in developing countries, building public awareness and support for international development." But it also stated that the Canadian International Development Agency (CIDA) will continue to make use of NGOs in implementing its programmes "in a cost-effective manner," not least by using competitive bidding procedures (1995: 7).

27 This is not a particularly new phenomenon: the Norwegian government has been funding Southern NGOs directly since the late 1960s. For a discussion of debates around the current expansion of such activities, and the dangers, see Riddell & Bebbington (1995).

28 For instance a paper written on the African perspective for the July 1995 United Nations University and WIDER conference entitled "Reorienting International Development Cooperation in the 21st Century for a Sustained Growth, Equity, Environment, and Human Development: Alternative Approaches to International Development" argued that ODA needs to be reoriented so both its objectives and its purposes favour sustainable human development: poverty reduction, sustainable livelihood, environment, popular participation, good governance.

29 An example of introducing user fees in hospital in Nepal is given in Riddell (1994).
30 This phenomenon is still most widespread for NGOs working on micro-enterprise projects, especially in relation to financial services. But it is also being extended well beyond these types of intervention. See Otero & Rhyne (1994).

REFERENCES

AKF (Aga Khan Foundation) Canada. 1995. "Systematic Learning: Promoting Public Support for Canadian International Cooperation." Ottawa: AKF Canada.

Barnett, A., & A. Bush. 1995. *Case Proven? A Review of the Impact of ITDG's Work as Evidenced in Evaluation and Reports to Major Donors, 1993–95.* Rugby UK: Intermediate Technology Development Group (ITDG).

Buckberg, E., & A. Thomas. 1995. "Wage Dispersion and Job Growth in the United States." *Finance and Development* (June).

CIDA (Canadian International Development Agency). 1995. "The Role of the Voluntary Sector in Development and CIDA's Relationship with Canadian Voluntary Organizations: CIDA Framework." Draft. Ottawa: CIDA.

Clark, J. 1991. *Democratising Development: The Role of Voluntary Organizations.* London: Earthscan.

CPAG (Child Poverty Action Group). 1996. *Poverty; The Facts.* London: CPAG.

Draimin, T., & G. Schmitz. 1997. "Effective Policy Dialogue in the North: A View from Canada." In *Strategies of Public Engagement: Shaping a Canadian Agenda for International Co-operation* edited by D. Gillies. Montreal & Kingston: McGill-Queen's University Press 1997.

Engberg-Pedersen, P. 1996. "The Politics of Good Development Aid: Behind the Clash of Aid Rationales." In *Domination or Dialogue? Experiences and Prospects for African Development Cooperation,* edited by K. Havnevik & B. van Arkadie. Uppsala: Nordic African Institute.

Esman, M.J., & N.T. Uphoff. 1984. *Local Organizations: Intermediaries in Rural Development.* Ithaca NY: Cornell University Press.

Foy, C., & H. Helmich, eds. 1996. *Public Support for International Development.* Paris: OECD.

Galtung, J. 1996. "On the Social Costs of Modernization: Social Disintegration, Atomie/Anomie and Social Development." *Development and Change* 27: 379–413.

Hirst, P., & G. Thompson. 1996. *Globalization in Question.* Oxford: Basil Blackwell.

ICVA (International Council of Voluntary Agencies)/Eurostep. *The Reality of Aid 1996: An Independent Review of International Aid.* London: Earthscan.

Kendall, J., & M. Knapp. 1996. *The Voluntary Sector in the United Kingdom.* Manchester: Manchester University Press.

Najam, A. 1995. "Nongovernmental Organizations as Policy Entrepreneurs: In Pursuit of Sustainable Development." Draft. Cambridge MA: Department of Urban Studies and Planning, Massachusetts Institute of Technology.

ODI (Overseas Development Institute). 1996. *The Impact of NGO Development Projects.* London: ODI.

OECD (Organization for Economic Co-operation and Development). 1996a. *Development Assistance Committee Report 1995.* Paris: OECD.

– 1996b. "Development Partnerships in the New Global Context." Annex to *Shaping the 21st Century: The Contribution of Development Co-operation.* Paris: OECD.

– 1996c. "Financial Flows to Developing Countries in 1995: Sharp Decline in Official Aid; Private Flows Rise." Paris: OECD news release, 11 June.

Olsen, G.R. 1996. "Public Opinion, International Civil Society and North-South Policy since the Cold War." In Stokke (1996b).

Otero, M., & E. Rhyne. 1994. *The New World of Microenterprise Finance: Building Healthy Financial Institutions for the Poor.* London: Intermediate Technology Publications.

Overseas Development Administration (United Kingdom). 1992. *The Process Approach to Projects.* London: ODA.

– 1994. *The Management of Risk in ODA Activities.* London: ODA.

– 1995a. *A Guide to Social Analysis for Projects in Developing Countries.* London: Her Majesty's Stationery Office.

– 1995b. *Technical Note on Institutional Development.* London: ODA.

Qureshi, Z. 1996. "Globalization: New Opportunities, Tough Challenges." *Finance and Development* (March).

Rao, L.M. 1996. *Ranking Foreign Donors: An Index Combining the Scale and Equity of Aid Giving.* New York: Office of Development Studies, United Nations Development Programme.

Rice, A. 1996. "Summary Report of the Consultation on Public Knowledge and Attitudes towards International Development." In Foy & Helmich (1996).

Riddell, R.C. 1994. *Evaluation of the Finnish NGO Support Programme: Country Case Study – NEPAL.* Helsinki: FINNIDA.

– 1996a. "Aid Dependency." Paper prepared for Project 2015. Stockholm: Swedish International Development Authority.

– 1996b. *Linking Costs and Benefits in NGO Development Projects: A Study Commissioned by the Overseas Development Administration.* London: ODI.

– 1996c. *Aid in the 21st Century.* New York: Office of Development Studies, United Nations Development Programme.

Riddell, R.C., & A. Bebbington. 1995. *Developing Country NGOs and Donor Governments.* Report to the Overseas Development Administration. London: Overseas Development Institute.

Roche, C. 1995a. "Basic Rights and Sustainable Livelihoods: The Learning Dimension." Oxford: Oxfam, Programme Development Team, Policy Department.

- 1995b. "Institutional Learning in Oxfam: Some Thoughts." Oxford: Oxfam, Programme Development Team, Policy Department.
- 1996. "Oxfam's Cross-Programme Learning Fund: An Update Report." Oxford: Oxfam, Programme Development Team, Policy Department.

Royal Commission on North-South and Aid Policies. 1995. *Norwegian South Policy for a Changing World.* Oslo: Royal Norwegian Ministry of Foreign Affairs.

Ruttan, V.W. 1996. *United States Development Assistance Policy: The Domestic Politics of Economic Aid.* Baltimore MD/London: Johns Hopkins University Press.

Salamon, L. 1995. *Partners in Public Service: Government-Nonprofit Relations in the Modern Welfare State.* London/Baltimore MD: Johns Hopkins University Press.

Salamon, L.M., & H.K. Anheier. 1995. "The Emerging Sector: The Nonprofit Sector in Comparative Perspective – An Overview." In *Dimensions of the Voluntary Sector – How is the Voluntary Sector Changing?* edited by J. Kendall & S. Saxon-Harrold. Tonbridge, Kent: Charities Aid Foundation 1995.

Smillie, I. 1995. *The Alms Bazaar: Altruism under Fire – Non-Profit Organizations and International Development.* London: Intermediate Technology Publications.

- 1996. "Mixed Messages: Public Opinion and Development Assistance in the 1990s." In Foy & Helmich (1996).

Sobhan, R. 1982. *The Crisis of External Dependence – The Political Economy of Foreign Aid to Bangladesh.* Dhaka: University Press Ltd.

- 1991. "External Dependence and the Governance of Bangladesh." National Professor Atwar Hussain Memorial Lecture, mimeo.
- 1995. "Aid Dependence and Donor Policy: The Case of Tanzania with Lessons from Bangladesh." Paper prepared for Project 2015. Stockholm: Swedish International Development Authority.

Stokke, O. 1996a. "Foreign Aid: What Now?" In Stokke (1996b).

- ed. 1996b. *Foreign Aid towards the Year 2000: Experiences and Challenges.* London: Frank Cass.

Taake, H., & J. Wiemann. 1995. *German Aid Policy.* Berlin: German Development Institute.

UNCTAD (United Nations Conference on Trade and Development). 1996. *The Least-Developed Countries 1996 Report.* Geneva: UNCTAD.

Winter, A. 1996. *Is Anyone Listening? Communicating Development in Donor Countries.* Geneva: United Nations Non-Governmental Liaison Service.

World Bank. 1992. *Effective Implementation: Key to Development Impact: Report of the World Bank's Portfolio Management Task Force.* Washington: World Bank. (Wapenhans Report)

- 1995. *World Development Report 1995.* Washington: World Bank.
- 1996. *World Debt Tables 1996.* Washington: World Bank.

Yankelovich, D. 1996. "Public Judgement on Development Aid." In Foy & Helmich (1996).

2 Becoming a Learning Organization, or, the Search for the Holy Grail?

MICHAEL A. EDWARDS

In 1988 I was commissioned by Oxfam-UK to write a report on institutional learning based on my experience as one of its field representatives in Africa (Edwards 1989a). Since then I have been engaged in my own quest for the "Holy Grail" of the "learning organization," both as a practitioner and manager in Save the Children Fund-UK and as an observer and analyst of the wider scene as more and more non-governmental organizations (NGOs) have embarked on the same journey. To equate institutional learning with the Grail is not to suggest that the learning organization is an unattainable goal, though undoubtedly it is much more elusive and the search more difficult than many realize – there are definitely no magic bullets. Rather, as in the real Grail story, it is to emphasize that the quest is every bit as important as the prize itself. Indeed, I would argue that by defining learning as a journey rather than a destination, we are likely to achieve much better results.

My focus is learning in development NGOs based in the industrialized world but working internationally – Northern NGOs like Oxfam and Save the Children Fund (SCF). This is not to diminish the central importance of learning in Southern NGOs; it simply reflects the bias of my own experiences working for a range of NGOs in the North. Many of the points I raise may carry resonance for NGOs elsewhere. They certainly have important implications for the future of North-South NGO relations – especially the issue of legitimacy (whose knowledge counts, and who speaks for whom) – but these questions are not within my mandate.

The first of the five sections of this paper summarizes what both theory and experience have to teach us about organizational learning. The rationale for learning, the sort of learning NGOs require, the barriers that stand in the way of learning, and how NGOs have overcome these barriers are each addressed in turn. Section 2 looks at what NGOs have actually learned over the last twenty years – about development, about their role in promoting it, and about the learning process itself. In Section 3 the focus turns to the future, considering what kinds of learning might be most important for NGOs against the backdrop of a rapidly changing environment for development assistance and non-state action. One conclusion is that NGOs would benefit from stronger links with other institutions which are also engaged in learning about development but have different skills and perspectives. Section 4 therefore examines the case for co-operation between NGOs and universities, research institutes, and those who finance development research. Both the opportunities and dangers of closer collaboration are explored. The final section tries to link the foregoing analysis of learning with promoting public support for Canadian international co-operation. This is difficult to do because there are no necessary or linear relationships between learning, policy influence, and public support; there may well be a link, but it is probably not the one identified by the Aga Khan Foundation in its proposal for this volume. By way of conclusion, I return to the Grail analogy, emphasizing that the spirit in which the quest is undertaken may be what distinguishes learning in NGOs from that in other types of institution and may also underlie the relative success or failure of attempts by NGOs to transform themselves into learning organizations.

1 LEARNING IN NGOS:
THEORY AND PRACTICE

Learning from Experience about Learning from Experience

What do theory and experience tell us about learning in NGOs? A great deal, in my view, and certainly enough to provide a solid foundation for our quest. Everyone, it seems, has come to believe in the centrality of learning for the success of the NGO mission, whatever the difficulties of turning principle into practice. Wave upon wave of management gurus reminds us that learning is the key to results in any organization, whether it be an NGO, a corporation, or a public agency. Continuous learning about NGO activity on the ground is essential to identify what works and what doesn't, more or less cost-effectively. Learning about the impact of wider forces (such as macro-economic policy) is crucial if NGOs are to advocate for change successfully at national and international levels. Learning is the foundation for accountability, dissemination, and influence – all matters of increasing importance to NGOs as they move away from a reliance on small-scale project interventions and engage in the broader processes of development. Learning about changes in the external environment (donor policy and development ideology, for example) is essential if NGOs are to anticipate threats and opportunities, and prepare for them. Learning is a key component of staff development and effectiveness. Learning from the ideas and experiences of others is vital if NGOs are to remain alive to innovation and challenge. And, finally, there *may be* a link between learning and support from the public or government. In the past, NGOs have been insulated from the costs of not learning by a loyal but relatively uninformed donor base and by their ideological popularity with government funding agencies. But in a future dominated by increasing competition, by closer scrutiny of the NGO world by its critics, by demands from donors for "results," and by the need for more transparency and greater accountability, this state of affairs is unlikely to continue (see Riddell 1997; Edwards & Hulme 1995; Hulme & Edwards 1996). As in the private (corporate) sector, organizations which fail to learn and adapt will go to the wall. This much is self-evident.

Does this mean that learning in NGOs is the same as learning in other organizations? Or is there something distinctive about the learning NGOs require which is linked to the type of work they do and the world in which they do it? I believe that there are at least four things which influence the nature and shape of learning in NGOs rather more than in other organizations (though at root they affect these other organizations as well). These characteristics make it even more imperative for NGOs to develop their capacity to learn while also making learning more complex and difficult. They are:

- the nature of development,
- the nurturing of wisdom rather than knowledge,
- the accommodation of error and failure, and
- the tension between belief and knowledge.

The nature of development. James Gleick (1987: 24) likens living in the world to walking through a maze whose walls rearrange themselves with each step one takes. NGOs know from their experience (especially in participatory development work) that this is a true description of the world they inhabit. Development situations are inherently unstable, uncertain, contingent, complex, and diverse (see Uphoff 1992; Booth 1994; Angelides & Caiden 1994; Roche 1995). Problems are caused by a multitude of interrelated factors that change as they interact with the proposal in play and with each other. Communities and institutions are fractured by different interest groups and varying perceptions of the same matter, so there is no single "reality" to be had – for example, the results of a project evaluation may be interpreted very differently by donor and partner, men and women. "Externalities" (unintended consequences) and second- or third-order effects of interventions are highly influential, yet rarely intentional, predictable, or measurable (Uphoff 1995). Connections are often more important than static facts (Hills 1994). Development processes are non-linear "open" systems which are extremely fluid and in which continuous learning is the sine qua non for being able to respond and intervene effectively. Even if we understand what led to sustainable change in one location, we cannot assume that the same course will lead to the same outcome in another. Knowledge advances through the observation and analysis of unexpected phenomena as well as by reflection on what is familiar.

This fluidity means that NGO learning (especially at ground level) must adapt to the characteristics of the environment in which intervention takes place. "Double-loop" learning, in which connections are made continuously between learning and decision-making throughout an organization, takes precedence over "single-loop" learning or simple error correction (Argyris & Schon 1978). Problem-solving gives way to preventing problems from shifting or spreading, anticipating unintended consequences, and living with diversity and non-standardization (Angelides & Caiden 1994). Building the capacity of people to learn and make connections becomes more important than accumulating information about lessons learned in the past – retained knowledge decays and may block the entry of new knowledge into the system. Interesting (positive or negative) experiences are targeted for learning instead of "averaging" experience across the board (Davies 1995). Patterns and generalizations may still be drawn out, but this is done not by aggregating diverse experiences but by identifying common elements, deviations from what is expected (Roche 1995), or the "edges of experience" (Davies 1995). In the messy, complex, and unpredictable world NGOs inhabit, it is the *process* of learning that really matters. Of course, the world is not completely messy or entirely unpredictable, so NGOs need not abandon their search for static lessons learned (guidelines or models of good practice, repositories of knowledge and experience, and so on). The important point is that in NGOs, even more than in other organizations, learning must adapt to the characteristics of dynamic, open systems, with "lessons learned and documented" being only one component of the process.

Information, knowledge, and wisdom. It is common for individuals and institutions to confuse and conflate different components of learning: *in-*

formation is the raw material that enters the learning system; *knowledge* implies the systematization of information through the various stages of filtering, testing, comparing, analysing, and generalizing; *wisdom* involves the ability to use knowledge (and experience, insight, and common sense) in action. These three components of learning are all important because they grow out of each other, but wisdom is the most crucial because learning that is not utilized effectively in practice is of little value, especially to NGOs with their activist traditions. The explicit linking of knowledge to action is what distinguishes the NGO approach to learning from the academic approach. Indeed, recent advances in the theory and epistemology of knowledge support what NGOs have always known intuitively – that "we cannot understand the world fully unless we are involved in some way with the processes that change it" (Edwards 1989b: 125).[1] For NGOs, the goal is not to store up information about the world but to change the world (or to help others to do so). Information and knowledge are important in that they can help us to be more effective in this task, but: "there is so much written and written so well that another effort always seems redundant. We quote from each other and generally say the same things. *When we act it is different, because it is a discovery*" (Roy et al. 1994: i; emphasis added). Learning also requires action because many of the mechanisms responsible for poverty and violence are invisible until they are activated by attempts at change – hidden interests or power relations in a community, for example.

Because of these necessary linkages, learning in an NGO may best be described as a process of reflection in action or learning by doing (Schon 1987); though, as we shall see, this is less true of those aspects of learning which are linked to policy and wider system changes. In this process, coaching is more important than training, dialogue replaces teaching, and technical problem-solving is placed in a wider context of reflective enquiry. "Know-how" is more important than "know-what" (Edwards 1996a). NGOs must therefore support their staff (and partners) in a process of structured learning from experience so that learning skills and abilities are developed continuously and lessons are genuinely learned and used. Strong feedback mechanisms at different levels of the organization are essential to connect information, knowledge, and action. Because NGOs are embedded simultaneously in the worlds of action and understanding, have a presence which crosses national boundaries, and possess a value system which (in theory) promotes learning and communication, they have a strong set of comparative advantages in the pursuit of learning. Although few have fully exploited these advantages, NGOs do have the potential to make a fundamental contribution to learning about development which probably cannot be replicated by other development organizations.

Accommodating error and failure. If (heaven forbid!) I were to try to write a bestseller on institutional learning, it would have to be called "Seven Easy Steps to Learn" or some such title reminiscent of all those self-help books that sell millions of copies on both sides of the Atlantic. Any scheme which gives the illusion of success without pain is bound to be popular. But real learning is never easy or comfortable; it implies change and challenge, doing away with some things as well as bringing in others. Superficial learning is very common in organizations, with lessons learned stored away, lost on the shelves, or accepted by management with rhetoric which "supports these conclusions completely" only to be quietly ignored in practice. Selective learning is also frequent: certain lessons are embraced (usually those which coincide with what is acceptable to those in power at the time) while others are discounted (usually those which contradict or conflict with an agency's "sacred cows"). In such circumstances, identifying the lessons of experience will not be sufficient to induce organizational change; there must also be a strategy to address these political blockages (strong leadership or external pressure, for example), unless circumstances change and what was once unacceptable suddenly becomes welcome. (An example of this kind of situation from SCF's experience is given in Section 2.) The reason for such reactions is straightforward – none of us likes to admit failure or ignorance, or risk personal discomfort and organizational destabilization, by facing up to the need to change, especially if the changes required run counter to deeply held beliefs about what works in development.

Yet, even more than in other areas of work, development is inherently as much about failure as about success. Even calling one experience a failure and another a success runs counter to the reality of development processes which are dynamic and unpredictable – farther down the line, we may find that what was once thought a failure has had unanticipated beneficial effects, while what earlier appeared a success may in time turn out not to be sustainable. There are as many (if not more) examples of failure in NGO work as of success, and learning from failure is every bit as important as learning from success – indeed, is essential if the same problems are to be avoided in future. To see NGOs acknowledge their failures is good; it only becomes bad if the same failures are repeated (Smillie 1995). The fact that NGO development work is often unsuccessful and ineffective is one reason why there is no simple connection between learning and public support; but this circumstance supports the case for changing public perceptions of success, not for ignoring the need to learn from failure.

Belief versus knowledge. It is, perhaps, a truism that only people learn, not institutions. Organizational systems and structures can help or hinder individual learning, and it is therefore important to get them right. However, the bottom line for learning lies within each individual. It is particularly important that NGOs recognize this fact because (by and large) NGOs are populated by people who have strong beliefs, values, and commitments to the work they are doing. They may therefore be driven more by what they believe in than by what they know or learn; or they may confuse the two, given that beliefs often stem from knowledge acquired many years ago during formal education. (The continuing hold of neo-classical equilibrium analysis over many economists, even though the underlying assumptions of this approach have been questioned and disproved many times over, is a case in point.) At the very least, those who work for NGOs need to be clear about the difference between things that they learn (implying some sort of rigorous methodology and analysis), things that they believe they have learned (without such rigour), and things they believe regardless of learning (their basic values and principles). All three are valid and valuable, but they are *different.*

To take a case from my own experience, SCF now insists on a "child-centred" approach to development which recognizes children as "social actors" who have the right to participate in decisions which affect them (SCF 1995).[2] The case for such an approach can be made on both moral grounds (children's rights) and practical grounds (society will benefit), but at present we certainly lack the information to prove the practical case. SCF made its decision to adopt this approach because it believes that it is the correct one. In time, proper learning will show whether this is true or not. As value-led organizations, NGOs inevitably confront many such dilemmas, which means that the place of learning and the interpretation of lessons learned will often be contested by different people within an agency or by the NGO and its partners. Is it the case that "seeing is believing" or that "believing is seeing"? Whose reality counts? As Dorothy Rowe says (cited in Chambers 1993): "Power is the right to have your definition of reality prevail over other people's." This is why a culture of honesty and openness is essential if NGOs are to learn, especially when information and knowledge are discordant – that is, when lessons learned run counter to deeply held institutional assumptions. For example, how would the Aga Khan Foundation react if research suggested that its Rural Support Programs had failed to build strong grassroots institutions and had, instead, substituted for government in ways which had made it more difficult for citizens to influence the state? However clear the theory of institutional learning, the personal, practical, and political dilemmas of learning remain.

Barriers to Learning

Learning in NGOs is, in practice, very difficult. Often, the characteristics and behaviour of NGOs are not favourable to the requirements for learning set out above. After all, there is nothing magical about NGOs as institutions which enables them to solve such complex learning dilemmas, however many comparative advantages they may possess in theory. In addressing barriers to learning in NGOs, the first step is to identify what they are, and we are fortunate in having a good deal of useful information about NGOs in general (Brown 1994, Edwards & Hulme 1995) as well as in Canada (Smillie 1995) and in the United Kingdom (Edwards 1994b, Slim 1993, Roche 1995). These different analyses point to strikingly similar conclusions:

- An activist culture may see learning as a luxury, separate from and secondary to "real work"; time and space for learning may be difficult to find and protect; differences in learning styles and languages are an inevitable feature of a large, dispersed, multicultural staff.
- Hierarchical, centralized, control-oriented structures are inimical to learning; the "tunnel vision of the project system" (Smillie 1995) restricts learning as time scales are compressed and experimentation discouraged; different parts of the organization (and different individuals within it) may guard information jealously rather than exchange it freely.
- Incentives and rewards for learning are weak and diffuse; failures are disguised or punished; inertia, defensiveness, complacency, and territoriality may override the NGO value of openness; risk aversion is commonplace; and job insecurity and short-term contracts make staff less amenable to learning.
- Systems for accessing, storing, transferring, and disseminating learning are underdeveloped, under-resourced, and inefficient. Information overload is common: there is a huge amount of information around, but insufficient structure to ensure that the right people get what they need at the right time. Indeed, there is too much information generally, and not enough learning – that is, information that is systematized into knowledge in action.
- The perceived need to provide an endless stream of uncomplicated success stories to the public undermines the depth of self-criticism and analysis required if NGOs are to be serious about learning; rising competition for public funds leads NGOs to give public relations priority over genuine learning – that is, to highlight the good and to bury the bad; and the pressure to demonstrate low overheads to donors curtails the investments required to learn effectively, even

though it is clear that learning is essential to achieve leverage and impact (and ought not therefore to be classified as overhead at all!).
- NGOs are not very good at dealing with discordant information – that is, learning that challenges the organizational consensus or threatens short-term institutional interests, particularly about roles and responsibilities, especially if (as an NGO based in the North) it is wedded to an operational role in the South. NGOs are never immune to the learning disabilities that plague all bureaucracies.

These conclusions are not meant to suggest that NGOs currently do not learn; only that they face considerable barriers in doing so. In consequence, learning tends to be concentrated in particular parts of the organization (especially at field level) and in particular areas of work (usually those which are less contentious).

Potential Solutions

What, then, do research and experience tell us about how such barriers to learning in NGOs might be overcome? Here again there are some common conclusions. Let me highlight seven: culture, capacity, incentives, structure, vision, balance, and process.

Culture. Changing the culture of any institution is always exceptionally difficult, but by instituting the right incentives and structures it is possible over the long term to introduce more of a learning orientation to NGOs and to encourage the people in them, especially managers, to favour enquiry, experimentation, and risk-taking as much as problem-solving and bureaucratic imperatives. Cultural change is an amalgam of changes in other areas and occurs when members of an institution or community begin to see themselves, and judge each other, in different ways. What is important is to start the process, however imperfectly, so that others can follow.

Capacity. Learning requires that the capacities of NGO staff to be self-critical, honest, and open be well developed. It is often said that "humility is the threshold of insight" (Edwards 1989a: 62) because it places individuals in a state of readiness to learn. In similar vein, Eric Dudley (1996: 191) concludes that a recognition of one's own ignorance is the absolute foundation for learning and success among field workers. Learning organizations welcome error and failure as opportunities to move forward rather than as mistakes to be concealed. But this implies that NGO staff are secure enough in themselves to admit to error and ignorance and to respond to them positively and creatively. I know of no easy ways to develop these capacities in people, short of some sort of inner experience, but as with the matter of culture there are certain things that can encourage openness and humility and others that can hinder their development – for example, overly hierarchical management structures, disbursement pressures, and fear of failure.

Incentives. NGOs, especially the larger ones, possess many of the characteristics of bureaucracies in general. In bureaucracies, the right incentives and rewards must be in place to stimulate organizational (or individual) change. For NGOs, the essential stimulus is to convince or reassure staff (especially those in the field) that their opinions and experience are valued by the organization. It is surprising how often this basic advice is ignored, especially in centralized management structures. More widely, NGO staff need to feel secure that they are not going to be penalized for making time and space for reflection and learning; learning has to be legitimized by senior managers and the necessary resources have to be protected. (Oxfam-UK's Cross-Programme Learning Fund is a good example of how more space for learning can be created with relatively few resources: Roche 1995.) Learning has to be built into job descriptions (for senior managers as well as for front-line staff), and rewards for experimentation and inquiry should be built into staff appraisal systems rather than (as is common today) action being taken to rid the organization of those who are seen as disruptive or subversive. It is unlikely that staff will invest time and energy in learning if they know they cannot influence the outcome of events, or if they lack a stake in the long-term future of the organization. (Short-term contracts may therefore act as a disincentive to learning.) Donors can assist in the provision of incentives by including additional resources for learning in grants and by holding NGOs accountable for what they learn (or do not learn). External pressure may be essential to induce change: one cannot "pull oneself out of a swamp by one's own hair" (Wierdsma & Swieringha 1992: 59)! But pressure from the top of organizations can also be vital: telling trustees more of the truth, for example, might stimulate learning in the rest of the organization by creating more of an incentive for change.

Structure. If there is one conclusion from the management literature which is well-nigh universal, it is that hierarchical and centralized management structures are fatal to institutional learning. Learning organizations are decentralized, organically structured, and task-oriented, with flexible units and teams built around pieces of work for which they are jointly accountable (Wierdsma & Swieringha 1992). Boundaries between departments are pragmatic, often temporary, and designed to facilitate co-operation through mutual interdependence. Horizontal linkages are deliberately fostered and professional distinctions blurred (for example, between programme and research staff). Planning is "hypothesis-led" (Dudley 1996: 190) so that projects are designed to be experimental. Different views and approaches coexist (at least until proved deficient). Hierarchy and centralization distance decision-makers from the "sharp end," compromising the link between learning and action and making it impossible for the agency to adapt rapidly enough to a dynamic and uncertain world. They also encourage distrust and stagnation because "rationality" in such systems requires that staff compete with each other and disguise their mistakes (Brown 1994). By contrast, in flatter and more democratic structures it becomes rational to co-operate. Buchanan-Smith et al. (1994) show how the highly decentralized early-warning system in Turkana (Kenya) enabled decisions to be taken quickly in 1990–1 because information and lessons learned could very quickly be transmuted into the right response. Strong feedback loops between learning, action, and decisions over resources are therefore essential. In NGOs which exist to transfer financial resources to projects or partners, there must be an explicit link between learning and resources received if incentives for learning are to be made concrete.

Vision. Peter Senge (1990: 209), one of the most influential management gurus, makes the point that in any organization a clear and shared vision is important if learning is to occur; otherwise the status quo will always predominate over innovation. There has to be leadership from the top of the NGO to legitimize the changes necessary for learning and to confront the inevitable barriers that arise along the way. If NGO leaders do not demonstrate their own readiness to learn, there is little prospect of learning spreading throughout the rest of the organization.

Balance. The need to inject an appropriate degree of structure into the learning process is explored in Section 3. Suffice it to say here that there must be a balance between different kinds of learning (or learning for different purposes), and particularly between internal and external learning, formal and informal learning processes, and the need to achieve coherence while respecting diversity (Kelleher & McLaren 1996: 20). The learning process can be likened to an iceberg, with a huge underwater mass representing all the learning that goes on in the field and the small tip emerging above the surface representing the formalization of lessons learned in policy statements, good practice manuals, and so on. If the balance shifts too far towards the formal, local initiative may be stifled and the process can become academic – after all, people learn best in their own milieu. If it moves too far in the other direction, mistakes may be repeated and opportunities for wider learning lost because people are only learning from their own, limited, experience.

Process. A preoccupation with documented knowledge and information storage is common in NGOs (a throwback to conventional concepts of education in which the purpose of learning is to accumulate facts). But such knowledge may quickly become obsolete and may serve to block the entry of new knowledge into the system. Real learning is a continuous process in which information and knowledge appear, disappear, and reappear. This requires all NGOs to support their staff in a deliberate, continuing, and structured process of action and reflection. Formal training should be placed within a wider framework of learning opportunities of different kinds which marry theory with practice. Building learning capacities should take precedence over building costly structures for information storage and retrieval. This is clear from SCF's own experience, which is recounted below.

2 LEARNING IN NGOS: WHAT HAVE WE LEARNED?

So much for the broad lessons of research and experience about how NGOs learn and how they can learn more effectively. What is the evidence that NGOs *have* learned anything significant over the past two decades? At the most general of levels, I think it is incontrovertible that NGOs are significantly more thoughtful, analytical, and mature in their self-criticism than they were twenty years ago. The production of materials on and about NGOs and their work has risen considerably, especially over the past five years, and much of it has come from within the NGO community itself. Learning and sharing has taken place at the broad level of NGO roles, identities, effectiveness, and accountabilities; at the detailed level of sectoral interventions and innovations (health, credit, agriculture, and so on); and in terms of methodologies of development work such as Participatory Rural Appraisal. There is an acknowledged reverse flow of ideas and influence from NGOs to official agencies in areas such as participation and the process approach to development work, gender, and sustainability.

In addition, nearly all NGOs have recognized that an exclusive concentration on small-scale projects is unlikely to bring sustainable change. Discussion and debate about how to scale up the impact of

NGOs is commonplace nowadays (Edwards & Hulme 1992) and has led NGOs to give renewed attention to learning and influencing, linking grassroots institutions with higher levels of the national and international system, working with governments, and international advocacy and campaigning. At a deeper level, NGOs are reconsidering their roles in international trade, in domestic development work in the North, and in nurturing alternative values and life styles among their supporters. All these are signs of a learning culture.

But there are at least three more fundamental tests of institutional learning among NGOs:

- Are such changes related to learning or to other influences? This is a test of learning overall.
- How have NGOs responded to learning which throws up conclusions and implications which challenge internal orthodoxies? This is a test of learning at that most difficult level of discordant information.
- Are NGOs now in a better position to anticipate changes in their environment and act accordingly? This is a test of NGOs' capacity to learn on a continuous basis.

How do NGOs measure up to each of these tests?

Learning and Change

There is not much evidence that most NGOs have transformed themselves into anything approaching learning organizations, or that learning is now organically connected to action on a day-to-day basis, or that changes in NGO policy and practice derive solely from learning (rather than other influences), though it is impossible to disaggregate internal and external influences in any scientific way. This is the result one would expect, given the complexity of institutional learning and the range of constraints acting on NGOs in the real world. But if we are to progress in this difficult terrain, it is important to assess the real impact of learning and to see where it is that NGOs need to do better. Two observations are worth making here.

First, at least some of the changes in NGO activity over the last decade do seem to be related to external pressures, influences, and fashions rather than to genuine learning. For example, nearly all NGOs are still preoccupied with formalistic strategic planning models which were abandoned some years ago by those in the corporate sector from whom NGOs have borrowed. In the next few years at least some NGOs will probably move away from such models back towards an approach to planning more in tune with the realities of the environment in which they work – iterative, dynamic, decentralized, and so on. NGOs do sometimes share the tendency (identified by Roger Riddell 1997) to add on themes and issues to their work rather than to integrate them properly. A good example is the current obsession of many organizations with micro-finance, which may have started as a response to poverty and the lessons of previous NGO programmes but which threatens to displace other equally important aspects of NGO work such as institutional development and popular education (Hulme & Edwards 1996). The availability of donor funding for some activities rather than others is obviously an important factor here, but learning organizations do not simply go where the money is; they are driven by, and remain loyal to, the lessons of their experience in the field.

A similar question could be raised about the prominence of certain forms of project appraisal and monitoring methodologies such as the Logical Framework and its derivatives. Are an increasing number of NGOs adopting these models because their experience demonstrates that they are superior, or because they are fashionable and/or are a requirement of certain bilateral donors? A need for better ways of measuring and accounting for performance has long been perceived among NGOs (as shown by research programmes in the Aga Khan Foundation, SCF, Oxfam, Actionaid, and others); but the Logical Framework is only one of many possibilities and arguably not the best (Edwards & Hulme 1995). All NGOs should therefore ask themselves why they take up certain activities, approaches, and methods and cease using others: what is the connection with learning? If there is none, why do it?

My second observation relates to the fundamental relationship between understanding and action that was raised earlier. Is it the case that NGOs do not learn, or is it that they do not put into practice what they do learn? Is more research needed, or just more action to implement what is already known? At the most basic level, NGOs surely already know how to facilitate effective grassroots development work: take your time, understand the situation, build on local knowledge and understandings, combat discrimination, maximize participation, develop strong local institutions, let things develop organically, and so on. Often, however, it is difficult to persevere in what they know to be the correct course, for all sorts of reasons – funding constraints, supporter attitudes, pressures of time, and so on. But unless NGOs have the strength and courage to apply the lessons they learn, learning becomes meaningless; without explicit links to action and accountability, learning from experience can simply mean the freedom to repeat the same mistakes.

Dealing with Discordant Information

The second test of institutional learning is whether NGOs learn the most difficult lessons of all: those which conflict with deeply held views about what the agency should be doing, and which imply more fundamental change, and perhaps even sacrifice, in the short term. Clearly, the answer will depend on agency and circumstance. A practical example from my own experience may shed some light on this difficult question. In Save the Children-UK, there has been a debate over the last five years on the issue of "approaches to work," a shorthand phrase for the different ways in which the agency sees its role: as an operational agency in the field, as a funding agency of Southern partners, as an advocacy and campaigning organization, as a think-tank, and so on. For the first four years of this debate it proved impossible to make much progress; different individuals within the organization held strongly divergent views on which approach offered a more effective use of resources and which worked best in practice. No amount of learning (whether in the form of internal evaluations or external literature reviews) seemed to affect these positions; people's beliefs were paramount. Information which collided with these beliefs was dismissed as biased; the debate did not move forward.

In 1995, two things happened: first, there were staff changes in key positions inside the agency which resulted in a strategic review of SCF's work; second, I undertook a study in India and Bangladesh which provided more information on the relative costs and benefits of different approaches to work and seemed to show that more impact could be achieved if SCF supported partners in the process of local institutional development (Edwards 1996c). This work coincided with other research which examined weaknesses in NGO legitimacy and accountability and assessed the implications of gradual de-operationalization for NGOs in the North (Smillie 1995; Edwards & Hulme 1995; Hulme & Edwards 1996; Edwards 1996d). These studies confirmed what was already known from the literature, but the coincidence of new learning and a more receptive environment for the lessons learned meant that the debate at last began to move. The challenge now will be to see how the rest of the organization (including staff in non-programme divisions, trustees, and supporters) reacts to a set of conclusions which has important implications for the future size, shape, and mode of operation of the agency as a whole.

One can, of course, read this story in two ways: as a success story, with the feedback loop between learning and action taking less than ten years to operate; or as a sign that SCF moves too slowly to adapt to a rapidly changing environment. Either way, it is clear that responding to discordant information is a difficult task and one which takes time. All NGOs based in the North face a similar set of questions about their future role: lessons learned from field experience suggest that traditional roles, relationships, and accountabilities are going to have to change in fundamental ways as Northern NGOs move away from donor-recipient relationships towards alliances and coalitions of equal partners working synergistically to achieve common goals. Will NGOs respond creatively to learning of this sort?

Anticipating Change

The third test of NGOs as learning organizations is whether they are any better prepared now to anticipate and respond to the changes occurring in the world of development assistance which Roger Riddell has outlined (1997) and to which I have already alluded. Are NGOs more secure and sustainable now than a decade ago? Can they overcome constraints which might formerly have crippled them? Are they clear about their future roles, and are they positioning themselves in good time to play them effectively? Is morale inside NGOs improving (often one of the best signs of a learning organization)?

At first sight the answers to such questions are not encouraging. The "new policy agenda" that is sweeping through the NGO world was largely unanticipated by most NGOs, and consequently they are struggling to come to terms with it (Edwards & Hulme 1995). Financial dependence on government grants is increasing and public support in many countries seems to have reached a plateau. Northern NGOs are experiencing an unprecedented period of self-questioning which manifests itself in more or less continuous strategic reviews, restructurings, new mission statements, and research projects aimed at clarifying the future of aid and the role of NGOs in it. Criticisms of NGO performance and accountability are mounting, even though thus far official support for NGOs remains strong. Though welcomed on the surface, the growing prominence of Southern NGOs on the world stage has thrown many Northern NGOs into defensive mode. My own (subjective) experience suggests that morale is declining in some of the largest Northern NGOs and that there appears to be little consensus on the way forward, or if there is a consensus it has yet to manifest itself in much practical action.

Perhaps, however, these judgments are too harsh. There can scarcely have been a time (if ever) when NGOs were subject to so many forces and influences at once, so much official support and critical attention simultaneously. Change is certainly afoot. It may simply be that NGOs need more time to absorb the lessons of the last twenty years and to manage what is undeniably a difficult transition between the old and the new. If so, this confirms the underlying conclusion of this part of my paper – that courage and vision are required if lessons learned are to be put into practice.

3 WHICH KINDS OF LEARNING SHOULD NGOS INVEST IN?

In large, multilayered, complex, diffuse systems (which is what international NGOs are), the learning process must be carefully structured if it is to be successful. It is not possible for everyone to learn everything, all the time; this leads to learning which is aimless, amorphous, and fragmented, in which information and knowledge disappear into organizational black holes (often located in the headquarters!) or remain lodged in the head of one or two individuals. There needs to be a balance between different types of learning, between learning in different parts of the organization, and between learning for different purposes. But this equilibrium must be achieved without sacrificing the freedom and flexibility which I earlier emphasized was the hallmark of successful learning in open systems. In addition, different types of learning carry different implications for the NGO in terms of skills, structures, systems, and resources, and there may be trade-offs between them and choices to be made. For example, an NGO which gives priority to participatory learning in the field may look very different to one that is primarily concerned with scientific research or with campaigning in the North. Indeed, the balance between participatory, field-based learning and learning which feeds into wider policy- and advocacy-related work is probably the most difficult one for NGOs to strike. Let us look at the different kinds of learning which NGOs might choose to emphasize, and the implications of each choice.

Participatory Learning in the Field

"The things we need to learn because, *for our own reasons*, we really need to know them, we don't forget" (J. Holt in Dudley 1993: 67). Direct, experiential learning among field workers and participants in development programmes is often the most powerful form of learning. It is certainly the most important – the foundation for sustainable development, genuine empowerment, and other forms of learning linked to good practice, policy, and advocacy work in NGOs. If learning is not taking place at the grassroots level, other layers in the learning system will be defective. Encouraging action and reflection and learning from experience on a continuous basis among field staff, partners, and people in projects must therefore be the first priority for all NGOs. Experience shows that people are unlikely to use or value learning if they see learning as someone else's responsibility (as is traditional in societies which divide those who think from those who act). So NGOs need to pay special attention to fostering learning among those who traditionally have not been encouraged to see themselves in this light. In addition, people are not going to use information which they consider irrelevant to immediate needs, whether by virtue of language, jargon, accessibility, length, format, or timeliness. NGOs tend to be excessively dependent on the (often badly) written word, but converting information into knowledge and knowledge into learning in a multicultural environment requires a much more imaginative approach, using visual communication (such as video), face-to-face encounters, and informal dialogue. Learning formats at the grassroots level and in an NGO's headquarters may have to be completely different.

This view of learning also raises questions of ethics and power. Learning at the higher levels in NGOs relies on the extraction of information and knowledge from the grassroots: who benefits from this knowledge? A case can obviously be made that policy and advocacy work can change systems and structures in ways which ultimately enable poor people to have more control over their lives, but this pay-off is always uncertain (Edwards 1989b). Therefore the prime purpose of learning at the grassroots level must be to promote self-development and social and economic change at that level, not to unearth interesting insights for consumption at headquarters. Learning is a process of personal growth and discovery, not just the accumulation of knowledge. This does not mean that information from the grassroots cannot be used by NGOs to lobby for change (though it almost certainly means that more attention should be given to supporting research, policy, and advocacy work undertaken directly by communities, partners, and field teams). Such information is fundamental if NGOs are to operate as an effective "reality check" on the impact of official policy or propaganda from governments (or from NGOs themselves!). We would, for example, know little of the actual horrors of the Gulf War had people on the ground not spoken out and documented the truth about laser-misguided weapons and such.

Facilitating learning at this level is a matter of adjusting the project development process so that there is enough time, space, and flexibility for those involved to learn; introducing incentives and rewards for learning along the lines spelled out earlier; and changing agency culture so that people want to learn rather than seeing learning as something which is unimportant. All these things are more difficult to provide in emergency situations, or where programmes are subject to complex bureaucratic requirements for timebound results and heavy reporting. The experience of SCF suggests that there is no substitute for strong leadership in encouraging learning of this sort; where senior field managers encourage their staff and protect the necessary space and resources, learning can find its proper place in the organization's activities. Conversely, blueprint approaches to planning, haste, and the imposition of external agendas mean that there is no space to reflect, let alone to learn.

Project-Based Learning

Most formal learning in NGOs is focused at the project or programme level because projects are still the core of most NGO activity (directly or indirectly). NGOs obviously need to learn about their performance, cost-effectiveness, and practice. They need to monitor and evaluate their work (or join with others in doing so) and develop stronger accountability systems both downwards (to the grassroots) and upwards (to trustees and donors). And they need to develop their own interpretations of good practice. "Always ask how we can do what we already do better" is Drucker's (1990) advice, to which one might add: "always ask whether we could be doing other things as well or instead."

Encouraging project workers to do these assessments for themselves is key and requires the same conditions as participatory learning: time, space, support, resources, incentives, and rewards. As one NGO worker in Palestine put it to me, "we need to tell our own stories" – to have the opportunity to stand back, reflect on experience, analyse it from the local perspective (which may differ from that of the outsider), and document it as a basis for organizational development more widely. This process is often second nature to many expatriates and other well-educated cadres, but it requires deliberate nurturing and structured support among others.

There is a copious literature on project-level research, monitoring, and evaluation among NGOs, so these matters need not detain us here. But a few pointers from SCF's experience may be useful in considering how to build the results of project-level learning into the wider institutional context of good practice and eventually into agency policy. Over the past six years, SCF has developed a wide range of good practice guides and manuals; a computerized global information system which provides access to "grey" material on all projects (retrieved through subject and geographical keywords); incentives for exchange visits, workshops, contract extensions, and short sabbaticals to write up project experiences; more systematic induction procedures linked to the outputs of the project monitoring and evaluation system; and revised job descriptions which emphasize learning as well as doing. These experiences are summarized in Slim (1993) and Edwards (1994b).

One of the most important conclusions to emerge from reviewing these innovations is that SCF overestimated the degree to which busy project staff would access written information and, more generally, would put time and effort into using sophisticated systems that store lessons learned on electronic media. The global information system is a superb resource, but unfortunately few people actually use it! A second conclusion is that the depth of analysis required to pull together the lessons of project experience and synthesize them into a usable form is significantly greater than most of our field staff possess, at least without considerable investments in additional training and support. (This has become a particular issue with sabbaticals and end-of-contract write-ups.) It seems that lighter, more decentralized systems are required, based less on the written word and more on supporting people in the field to "tell their own stories."

Policy-Related Learning

Project experience and the lessons of practice are the building blocks of NGO operational policy, but they must be generalized if policy is to have meaning. It is only at the level of policy that findings achieve a sufficient level of generality to be of interest and relevance to wider audiences. Senge (1990: 94) calls the search for these "systems archetypes" or "generic structures" (that is, patterns that recur over time and space) the key to learning and action. Yet herein lies a dilemma. As I pointed out earlier, the reality of the situations in which NGOs intervene is complex, diverse, uncertain, and contingent. If every situation is different and every experience unique, how is generalization possible? And if development is such a dynamic process, how can generalizations made at one moment in time be useful in another?

NGOs need to give a lot more consideration to addressing this challenging dilemma. A number of avenues suggest themselves. First, it is better to generalize by identifying key common elements in patterns of experience than by trying to aggregate the experiences themselves (as in "the average community in Africa is ..."). Such elements might concern the gender implications of projects, issues of participation, or successful local institutional development. Secondly, focus on experiences that seem especially interesting or different (positively or negatively): Davies (1995) calls this the "principle of sampling the edges of experience"; Roche (1995) "learning by deviation." Thirdly, look for differences in interpretation of the same experience among stakeholders and explore them, because such differences indicate that something important is happening. Fourthly, experiment with "purposive sampling" or the strategic selection of project-level experiences to try and reduce bias. Fifthly, build on long-term project experience and local research to give a richer picture of trends and pool the resulting information with other projects (or NGOs) in the same area.[3]

These are all ways of distilling the lessons of experience into policy without over-generalizing. Another is to approach this issue from the opposite direction (that is, top down), by deciding what area of policy an NGO wishes to learn about and then setting out to gather information to satisfy this objective through systematic research. SCF has a great deal of experience in this area of learning (which is analysed further – in terms of links with research institutions – in the next section). Although such an approach carries within itself the obvious dangers of bias (selecting information that proves the case while discounting other evidence), some of the research conducted over the past five years is acknowledged to have been both innovative and influential – for example, the work with Manchester University on NGOs, with the Institute for Development Studies on early-warning systems, and a five-country study on sustainability in the health sector. However, though credible intellectually and influential in policy terms, this research was too disconnected from field realities to elicit much of a sense of interest or ownership from inside the organization. In consequence, the results of the research have been used outside SCF, but not inside. The feedback loop to internal action was not strong enough. A major reason for this outcome was the way in which the research was carried out – by separate teams based in SCF's headquarters with weak links to the field. The guidelines for learning laid out in Section 1 were not followed, and the challenge remains to find ways of marrying internationally credible research with the requirements of participatory learning.

Advocacy-Related Learning

When an NGO wishes to use lessons from its experience in advocacy and campaigning work, it must address the same difficulties (of generalization) highlighted above in relation to policy. But there is an additional danger that arises because such activities are intended to promote a particular stance, namely, that information from the field will be distorted or used selectively to support a predetermined position. The diverse reality and dynamic nature of all development situations and the range of views of any particular event which NGOs will encounter mean that this use of information is bound to be an issue.

In advocacy work it is particularly important that NGOs learn from sources outside the agency as well as internal contacts and experience because this helps to challenge what can become too cosy a consensus. The increasingly ritualistic quality of much NGO advocacy on economic adjustment is a case in point. Again, one has to ask whose reality counts? This is particularly important when judgments are being made about ambiguous information because the temptation will be to select the interpretation of the centre (the NGO headquarters in the North). What originates as learning specific to a particular context (for example, the impact of user fees on access to a hospital) may be transposed into a general statement for lobbying the World Bank ("user fees are bad"). The general statement may still be true, or at least may be an accurate description of what the NGO believes to be true, but unless the method by which it has been reached is made transparent, the result can be both flawed and misleading. In addition, there are real question marks over the legitimacy of Northern NGO campaigning and lobbying work since few Northern NGOs can claim to be genuinely representative of grassroots views. Far better to support NGOs and others in the South to speak – and lobby – for themselves.

Scientific Research and Visionary Thinking

At the top of the learning tree (or the bottom, depending on one's point of view!) are activities which are related only tangentially to project work or grassroots realities, but which may nevertheless be extremely important in the longer term. Clearly, some NGOs may be uncomfortable with this sort of learning and may not see it as part of their remit at all. One example is scientific research which has (and must retain if it is to be credible) its own particular set of methodological standards and notions of rigour.

But there is another area of learning which is important for NGOs, if indeed it can be called learning at all. This is what Kelleher and McLaren (1996) call "possibility-creating" and what others might see as "envisioning" the future – dreaming of new worlds, thinking the unthinkable, and learning outside the normal parameters of NGO roles, interests, and agendas. Is this a luxury in an era when hundreds of millions of people still live in absolute poverty? I don't think so (though it can only be a minor component of NGO learning as a whole), and indeed Roger Riddell (1997) offers us some clues as to why this sort of thinking may actually be extremely important to NGO effectiveness in the future. Riddell's case is that conventional development assistance may well form only a small part of efforts to promote development in the years to come because there are other areas for action which are going to be as or more influential. These include "values of interconnectedness, humility and service; relationships of respect and equality;

and lifestyles which promote sustainable development over short-term gain," to use Hulme and Edwards' words (1996), not to mention alternative trading, international alliances for advocacy, and development work in the North. If the system for development assistance (or action) is changing, as it undoubtedly is, then clearly NGO roles within it will change, and as they change NGOs will need to sort out the priorities to be given to different forms of learning and learning in new areas. NGOs will have to spend more time and resources in unfamiliar territory: learning about alternatives to current economic orthodoxies and value systems; making links with churches, spiritual movements, and other non-development networks; and being open to influence from unexpected directions. The characteristics of the learning organization will serve NGOs well in this respect, but the lessons learned may well be surprising ones. Of course, there are question marks over the ability of NGOs to extend into these areas (do they have the intellectual skills?) and, perhaps more importantly, about whether they have any legitimacy to dream up alternative futures on behalf of other peoples, but the possibility is a fascinating one.

There are, then, many different types of learning, and each has its own requirements. It may not be feasible or desirable for every NGO to incorporate all types into its portfolio of learning activities, and it is certainly advisable for NGOs to make a conscious decision about which forms of learning they wish to emphasize, so that they can ensure that they learn effectively in key areas (rather than allow learning overall to become amorphous). In particular, NGOs need to strike the right balance between participatory learning among staff, partners, and others at grassroots and project levels and learning which is intended to feed into wider policy, advocacy, and campaigning activities at the national and international levels. These two large areas of learning have very different implications in terms of time scales, resourcing, and methods; although they can be married together successfully, there will always be tensions in doing so.

Participatory learning is the key to all learning and is (I would argue) the bedrock of any NGO learning system. If people have the capacity to learn and are encouraged to use it, then a solid foundation for institutional learning will be created. But because of the characteristics of development work (dynamic/contingent) and the requirements of individual learning (action/reflection), participatory learning cannot be forced onto organizational tramlines or predetermined agendas. Conversely, if other people and institutions are to learn, lessons must be made available in some sort of generalized form; and if learning is to be generalized without too much loss of rigour, NGOs need the help of others who are more experienced in how this might be done. Section 4 considers these linkages in detail. There will always be a tension between local ownership of learning and information (that is, the need to respect diversity and flexibility) and the need for NGOs to achieve some degree of coherence, quality control, and methodological standardization if they are to carry on a sensible dialogue with anyone else.

4 HOW CAN NGOS BUILD STRONGER LINKAGES FOR LEARNING?

NGOs have a clear comparative advantage over formal research institutions when it comes to participatory learning and action research in the field. They are closer to and are in continuous contact with the subjects of research, are able to put learning into action, and usually (though not always) have the necessary participatory skills. However, as the need to generalize increases, different skills are required: a knowledge of formal research methods, analytical rigour, an overview of the literature and who is doing what in the same field, and independence from internal (institutional) agendas which may ignore discordant information. Information must be transformed into knowledge – that is, systematized, synthesized, analysed, and interpreted. A knowledge of theory is important, however much practitioners may distrust it, because theory is what underlies policy: "practical men in authority who believe themselves to be quite exempt from any intellectual influences are usually the slaves of some defunct economist," as Keynes reminds us! Just think of the impact of neo-liberal growth theory, feeding through structural adjustment and market liberalization into sub-Saharan Africa.

Most NGO personnel lack the skills for such generalization, so collaboration with those who do have them (in universities, other research institutions, and among consultants) is important. One of the lessons SCF has learned from five years of policy-related research is that forging alliances with others is a better way of moving forward than creating a large research department inside an NGO (which begets the suspicions among field workers and other tensions highlighted in Section 3). Of course, the two are not mutually exclusive: NGOs need some independent research capacity of their own, but they need to use it to facilitate research by others in the organization (especially in the field), advise on methodology, promote networking, and so on, rather than to do the research themselves.

Creating collaborative partnerships among NGOs, research institutions, and funders of research is therefore an excellent way of achieving complementarity and promoting synergy among groups with different skills and strengths. In my experience it results in benefits for all parties: a better understanding of field-level realities, more informed practice, better generalization and theory-building, stronger feedback loops, and the promotion of a real learning culture in both NGOs and universities. Indeed, this is an area in which NGOs probably have more of a role than they have realized: David Brown (1994) has made a convincing case that NGOs are "bridging organizations" par excellence. Because of their position as intermediaries between grassroots communities and other institutions (government, universities, donors, and so on) and because of their traditional value base which favours communication and dialogue, NGOs are ideally placed to foster the co-operative relationships among diverse groups that are essential for sustained progress. Taking this point still further, Edwards and Hulme (1995) and Riddell (1997) paint a future for NGOs (especially those based in the North) as actors in multi-layered alliances and coalitions made up not just of "conventional" development organizations but of all sorts of different groups working synergistically towards broad but common goals. If this is true, then the skills of the bridging organization (as of the learning organization) become paramount.

However, fostering collaboration with research institutions and donors is not easy, and it carries risks as well as opportunities. Collaboration takes a great deal of time – to foster relationships of trust, overcome preconceived suspicions and hostilities, allow joint working to evolve organically, and preserve space for independent action when appropriate. Because of their different traditions, NGOs and academics are rarely natural partners. My own experience (Edwards 1996a, 1996b) suggests that close and continuous contact over an extended period of time is required to cement collaborative relationships, with long-term "partnership frameworks" paying dividends in allowing mutual trust and confidence to develop within a constantly shifting pattern of tasks and responsibilities. One way to do this is for researchers to "accompany" particular NGO programmes or areas of work; also useful are staff exchanges (secondments and sabbaticals, internships, reciprocal representation on boards) and incentives from research funders to joint NGO-academic research efforts. NGOs need to move beyond using researchers as short-term consultants. Although obviously useful in certain circumstances, this practice does little to foster longer term collaboration. The links between like-minded individuals in both NGO and research institution are likely to prove crucial, and clearly stated goals and outputs are essential. Roles, responsibilities, and obligations must be agreed in advance, and there must be clear guidelines on the ownership and use of any information generated.

Co-operation must be seen to engender results useful for both sides: more academic publications for researchers and more accessible and action-oriented outputs for the NGO. Partnerships must therefore be extremely flexible.

Another reason for NGOs to collaborate with the formal research community in policy and advocacy work arises from the credibility of different kinds of learning (or information from different sources). Section 3 underlined the importance of decentralizing learning activities in NGOs to give priority to learning in the field, so that learning becomes a natural part of everyone's role (rather than something which is restricted to particular units at headquarters). However, the results of NGO learning are rarely considered by the targets of policy and advocacy work (such as bilateral and multilateral agencies) to have sufficient rigour or credibility to stand on their own. Often, a degree of "academic respectability" is needed to persuade others to take conclusions seriously. A respected NGO and a respected academic may both say the same thing, but because they are respected for different reasons it is often the opinion of the latter that counts, at least in high-level policy dialogue.

This state of affairs will continue to prevail until NGOs become much more adept and professional in their learning role and are able to convince the sceptics that their conclusions are arrived at rigorously and are not simply the reflection of predetermined agendas. By allying themselves with research institutions, NGOs can combine the power of grassroots testimony and clearly articulated normative positions (which are their strengths) with detailed narratives and rigorous enquiry. This is a very powerful combination, though one whose potential for influencing change is largely untapped at present – in part because it is a very difficult combination to achieve. Donald Schon captures perfectly what needs to be done: "the dilemma of rigour and relevance may be dissolved if we can develop an epistemology of practice which places technical problem-solving within a broader context of reflective enquiry, shows how reflection-in-action may be rigorous in its own right, and links the art of practice in its uncertainty and uniqueness to the scientist's art of research" (1983: 69).

But how is this to be achieved? This paper has attempted to map out some preliminary answers – in Section 1 when discussing general principles of NGO learning and in Section 3 when exploring different ways to link grassroots experience with policy and advocacy work. Section 5 tries to take this debate a little bit further. But there is no doubt that this remains a very challenging area.

Collaboration with government donor agencies (either to strengthen channels for policy influence or to gain funding for policy-related research) presents another danger for NGOs: co-option. This is not to say that donors always or consciously attempt to impose agendas and interests onto research that they fund. However, there is a consensus (certainly among the development community in the United Kingdom) that it has become significantly more difficult over the last ten years to undertake research on aspects of development which may be considered controversial. This difficulty arises partly because funding for development research is declining anyway and partly because the funding that remains is heavily dominated by short-term consultancies and research programmes defined by donors and then contracted out to research institutions. There is less space for "foundational research" – the research which explores the most fundamental issues and pushes out the boundaries of what is known.

There are ways of dealing with these problems, of course, centring around protecting the necessary space for independent critical work within broader programmes of research which also offer funders what they want. NGOs have a responsibility here to make some of their own resources available for such work and to be conscious of the dangers of co-option when they undertake their own research. Having seen Save the Children-UK's research budget decline from nearly £500,000 a year to almost nothing as a result of funding cuts imposed during the last two years, I do not underestimate the task of making more NGO resources available for learning and research. But there is great value in NGOs supporting independent work both within their own programmes of research and learning and as part of the linkages with research institutions that this section of the paper has been arguing for. Otherwise, research, which should be a process of searching for the truth, may simply be used to validate what we already think we know.

5 LEARNING, POLICY DIALOGUE, AND PUBLIC ENGAGEMENT

The premise underlying the discussions in this volume is that "NGOs can counter compassion fatigue by demonstrating effectiveness and systematically documenting, evaluating and disseminating their development successes through reasoned policy dialogue and strategic public engagement" (AKF Canada 1995). To do this effectively requires NGOs to become learning organizations. This paper has explored what a "learning organization" might mean in the context of development NGOs today.

However, the link between learning and the wider goal of promoting public support for development assistance is not (or is not necessarily) a strong or convincing one, and for a number of reasons. First, as

Section 1 made clear, learning is as much about failure as about success, or at least about different definitions and interpretations of success where impact is difficult to measure and attribute – the norm in most NGO work (Edwards & Hulme 1995). Thus far, NGOs have disguised their failures through fear that public support will fall away if supporters know the truth about the messy, complicated, and uncertain nature of development work. But this approach is both unsustainable and unhelpful: an inability to be honest inhibits both NGO learning and the development of a strong and stable support base, which requires that supporters not only understand the real nature of development and NGO roles but are also prepared to support them as they evolve over time. Moreover, as Roger Riddell has stressed (1997:42): if the role of development assistance is changing by being placed in the wider context of actions designed to "address more all-embracing aspects of society in the donor country, especially its value systems," then what the public needs to learn concerns less what works in other countries and more what the implications of development are in their own lives. Conventional NGO learning from experience will be of comparatively little help here. It is not that such learning is irrelevant to public support (clearly it can be important, especially in the short term), but that the issue of public support, especially in the longer term, goes much wider than demonstrating that aid is effective.

If the world were a giant machine in which pulling a lever at one level led automatically to the turn of a wheel at another, then one could posit a clear linear relationship between learning, policy, and public support. Policy and public support would be based on, and remain faithful to, what we learn. But we know that the world does not operate in this way. What is intellectually rigorous may not be politically feasible or popular, while what motivates people to support an NGO or undertake some other relevant action may not be related to anything systematic or rational at all. A failure to convince people that development matters to them in their daily lives here and now has been characteristic of NGO campaigning and education work over the last twenty years, and it is one reason why development NGOs have not been able to forge a movement for change along the lines of the environment or women's lobbies. In reality, policy-makers do not wait for what researchers have to tell them and rarely select their options on the basis of research results, unless such results confirm what "gatekeepers" want to hear (Tizard 1990). Policy-making is a much more diffuse and less rational process, subject to a myriad of influences and pressures (of which NGOs are only one small component), and its aim is to reconcile divergent views rather than to select the one which is most convincing intellectually.

In addition, one faces the thorny problem of generalization from diverse and contingent experience that has surfaced regularly throughout this paper. As Barbara Tizard has observed, "on the whole good researchers make poor advocates, because of their awareness of the inevitable limitations of their findings" (1990: 436). Yet generalization is the essence of policy. How are NGOs to confront this dilemma? Section 2 suggested some ways this might be done – by sampling the "edges of experience," "learning by deviation," and identifying common elements rather than generalizing through aggregation. Another avenue is simply to recognize that different stakeholders are going to have divergent interpretations of the same situation, so that some form of negotiated settlement or "combined social judgement" (Fowler 1995) is required before policy can be formed. This addresses the question of "whose reality counts" which was also raised in Section 2: policy-making can be a democratic process or an autocratic one (and is usually the latter, as those with more power and influence impose their interpretation over others). NGOs need to consider where they stand on this issue and adapt themselves accordingly. Equally, if it is true that grassroots experience cannot be aggregated, then why not use it for what it is? In other words, use it as a "reality check" on the impact of policy and as a way of challenging and deepening accepted "truths" rather than trying to generalize it and risk distorting its real power and value.

All this suggests that NGOs need to consider whether they might have more impact in disseminating their learning through diffuse processes rather than narrowly targeted lobbying or public engagement to achieve predetermined goals. Learning can influence policy and public attitudes by challenging existing assumptions, percolating through systems (the media, politics, schools, and so on), and creating an "agenda for concern" (Tizard 1990). In this way, NGOs might help to create committed citizenries that through more diffuse political processes can demand more, and more effective, action for development. Such an approach would simultaneously address the radically new agenda for development action outlined by Roger Riddell (1997) and help NGOs to avoid some of the adverse consequences of over-systematizing their learning and distorting diverse experience by forcing it into narrow policy lobbying channels or selecting lessons learned to convince a sceptical public that aid works. If NGOs get their learning right and release it properly into the right systems and structures (with all this entails), then over time it will form a solid part of the underlying fabric for change on which a sustainable world depends. But this is a very different understanding of learning and its place in NGO strategy, and something which most NGOs in the North have only just begun to think about.

CONCLUSION

How far does this paper take us on our quest for the Holy Grail? Not much farther, you might think, but perhaps this is not so important after all. If it is the journey that matters – the process of learning – then the fact that the destination is unclear, or that there may be many different destinations, or that the destination is constantly shifting, is of no great consequence. What matters is that NGOs do learn, that they try to learn more effectively, and that they don't stop learning even when they think they have found the answers. There will always be tensions between participatory learning and respect for diversity, and the discipline imposed by the need to link learning with policy, advocacy, campaigning, and public engagement. Undoubtedly, NGOs need to develop their ability to manage these tensions more effectively. In this task, what is most important is that NGO personnel continue their quest in the right spirit: a spirit of openness, humility, service, enquiry, sharing, and solidarity. These are the qualities that underlie genuine learning in any organization. They are also the qualities that we used to think made NGOs "special." And they are definitely the qualities which marked out those who embarked on the search for the Holy Grail.

NOTES

1 A full discussion of these developments would require a separate paper, but for those who are interested the following references are particularly useful: Maxwell (1984), Schon (1983, 1987), Lincoln & Guba (1985, 1993), Edwards (1989b, 1994a, 1996a), Uphoff (1992), Booth (1994).
2 As well as SCF (1995), readers who are interested in pursuing this approach might read the special issues of *PLA Notes* (February 1996) and the *Journal of International Development* (September 1996) which provide case-studies of new approaches to children and development.
3 These and many other ideas are contained in a report of a recent workshop, "Bridging the Micro-Macro Interface," organized by the Structural Adjustment Forum and the Development Studies Association at Nottingham University in April 1996. This report is summarized in the July 1996 issue of *Structural Adjustment Forum*.

REFERENCES

AKF (Aga Khan Foundation) Canada. 1995. "Systematic Learning: Promoting Public Support for Canadian International Cooperation." Ottawa: AKF Canada.

Angelides, C., & G. Caiden. 1994. "Adjusting Policy-Thinking to Global Pragmatics and Future Problematics." *Public Administration and Development* 14(3): 223–41.
Argyris, C., & D. Schon. 1978. *Organizational Learning: A Theory of Action Perspective.* Menlo Park: Addison-Wesley.
Booth, D., ed. 1994. *Rethinking Social Development: Theory, Research and Practice.* London/New York: Longman.
Brown, L.D. 1994. *Creating Social Capital: Nongovernmental Development Organizations and Intersectoral Problem-Solving.* Boston MA: Institute for Development Research.
Buchanan-Smith, M., S. Davies, & C. Petty. 1994. "Food Security: Let Them Eat Information." *IDS Bulletin* 25(2): 69–80.
Chambers, R. 1993. "All Power Deceives." *IDS Bulletin* 25(2): 14–26.
Davies, R. 1995. *The Management of Diversity in NGO Development Programmes.* Swansea: Centre for Development Studies.
Drucker, P. 1990. *Managing the Non-Profit Organization.* New York: HarperCollins.
Dudley, E. 1993. *The Critical Villager: Beyond Community Participation.* London: Routledge.
– 1996. "Educating Fieldworkers." In *Educating for Real: The Training of Professionals for Development Practice,* edited by N. Hamdi. London: International Technology Publications.
Edwards, M. 1989a. *Learning from Experience in Africa.* Oxford: Oxfam.
– 1989b. "The Irrelevance of Development Studies." *Third World Quarterly* 11(1): 116–35.
– 1994a. "New Directions in Social Development Research: The Search for Relevance." In Booth (1994).
– 1994b. "NGOs in the Age of Information." *IDS Bulletin* 25(2): 117–24.
– 1996a. "The Getting of Wisdom: Educating the Reflective Practitioner." In *Educating for Real: The Training of Professionals for Development Practice,* edited by N. Hamdi. London: International Technology Publications.
– 1996b. "Development Practice and Development Studies: Working Together." *Development in Practice* 6(1): 67–9.
– 1996c. *NGOs in South Asia: What Breeds Success?* Save the Children Fund, Overseas Department Working Paper 14/South Asia Regional Office Working Paper 5. Oxford: Oxfam (UK and Ireland).
– 1996d. *International Development NGOs: Legitimacy, Accountability, Regulation and Roles.* London: Commission on the Future of the Voluntary Sector.
Edwards, M., & D. Hulme, eds. 1992. *Making a Difference: NGOs and Development in a Changing World.* London: Earthscan.
– 1995. *Beyond the Magic Bullet: NGO Performance and Accountability in the Post-Cold War World.* London: Earthscan/West Hartford CT: Kumarian Press.
Fowler, A. 1995. "Measuring NGO Performance: Difficulties, Dilemmas and a Way Ahead." In Edwards & Hulme (1995).

Gleick, J. 1987. *Chaos: An Emerging Science.* London: Pan.
Hills, G. 1994. "The Knowledge Disease." *Resurgence* 164: 48.
Hulme, D., & M. Edwards, eds. 1996. *Too Close for Comfort? NGOs, States and Donors.* London: Macmillan/New York: St Martin's Press.
Kelleher, D., & K. McLaren. 1996. *Grabbing the Tiger by the Tail: NGOs Learning for Organizational Change.* Ottawa: Canadian Council for International Co-operation.
Lincoln, Y., & E. Guba. 1985. *Naturalistic Enquiry.* London: Sage.
– 1993. *The Paradigm Dialogue.* London: Sage.
Maxwell, N. 1984. *From Knowledge to Wisdom.* Oxford: Basil Blackwell.
Riddell, R. 1997. "Trends in International Co-operation." In *Strategies of Public Engagement: Shaping a Canadian Agenda for International Co-operation,* edited by D. Gillies. Montreal & Kingston: McGill-Queen's University Press.
Roche, C. 1994. "Operationality in Turbulence: The Need for Change." *Development in Practice* 4(3): 160–71.
– 1995. *Institutional Learning in Oxfam: Some Thoughts.* Oxford: Oxfam.
Roy, A., N. Dey, & S. Singh. 1994. *Living with Dignity and Social Justice: Rural Workers' Rights to Creative Development.* Tilonia: Social Work Research Centre.
SCF (Save the Children Fund). 1995. *Towards a Children's Agenda: New Challenges for Social Development.* London: SCF.
Schon, D. 1983. *The Reflective Practitioner.* London: Temple Smith.
– 1987. *Educating the Reflective Practitioner: Toward a New Design for Teaching and Learning in the Professions.* San Francisco CA: Jossey-Bass.
Senge, P. 1990. *The Fifth Discipline: The Art and Practice of the Learning Organization.* London/New York: Random House.
Slim, H. 1993. *Institutional Learning Review and Future Priorities.* London: SCF.
Smillie, I. 1995. "Painting Canadian Roses Red." In Edwards & Hulme (1995).
Tizard, B. 1990. "Research and Policy: Is There a Link?" *The Psychologist* (October): 435–40.
Uphoff, N. 1992. *Learning from Gal Oya: Possibilities for Participatory Development and Post-Newtonian Social Science.* Ithaca NY: Cornell University Press.
– 1995. "Why NGOs Are Not a Third Sector: A Sectoral Analysis with Some Thoughts on Evaluation and Sustainability." In Edwards & Hulme (1995).
Wierdsma, A., & J. Swieringha. 1992. *Becoming a Learning Organization.* London: Addison-Wesley.

3 Effective Policy Dialogue in the North: A View from Canada

TIM DRAIMIN & GERALD J. SCHMITZ

Public policy debates on the future of international development assistance are being played out in the knowledge that there is growing unease about public understanding of and support for development co-operation activities within donor countries. Canada is not immune from these broad trends. Moreover, their influence in the country coincides with acute fiscal problems which offer the government a ready rationale for large and continuing cuts in the budget for official development assistance (ODA). How, therefore, can civil society actors in Canada, specifically those involved in the field of international development, mobilize to turn around a situation that threatens to lead to further decline in support for international development co-operation? How can learning modes and capacities be strengthened and deployed to engage both publics and policy-makers in positive dialogue on and initiatives for development policy?

These are large questions, and we do not claim to offer any definitive answers. We seek only to point to some crucial factors in building a more effective and democratic policy process as the development debate proceeds in Canada – and elsewhere. In the environment which confronts non-governmental organizations (NGOs) and policy-makers today, we are surely long past a time when the elaboration of "enlightened" international goals could be left to a narrow segment of the Canadian state with the passive acquiescence of Canadian society. In their recent book, Ivan Head and Pierre Trudeau offered a retrospective lament about their failure during the Trudeau governments "to raise the consciousness level of the public with respect to the vital importance to Canadian interests of North-South issues" (1995: 161–2). Looking ahead, however, we are convinced that vibrant institutions of parliamentary government and a mobilized non-governmental sector that interacts constructively with policy-makers will both be needed to bring about a better process for the creation of development policy. In the first and fourth parts of this paper, therefore, Gerald Schmitz examines the complex (and sometimes convoluted!) evolution of a parliamentary perspective on dialogue about international development policy. In the middle sections, Tim Draimin reviews this terrain from the specific perspective of NGO efforts to be more effective advocates in the policy dialogue over ODA. We conclude with some suggestions for both policy-makers and NGOs to consider in these challenging times.[1]

1 Policy Dialogue through the Parliamentary Looking Glass: Towards a Canadian Learning Curve

It is not just societies that are under strain and citizens who are anxiously confronted by the pressures from accelerated transition processes (technological, market-driven, demographic, ecological, and, since 1989, geopolitical); stress is also felt by governments, parliaments, and in a particular way by the elected representatives who are among the primary mediating links between the local and the wider worlds of policy action and response. Enabling parliamentarians, who sometimes feel put upon and undervalued, to gain a better appreciation of global development co-operation issues, and thereby to contribute to better policy-making, raises some truly daunting problems. These concerns probably cannot be resolved in a piecemeal or ad hoc manner, or through short-term techniques and increments (an occasional meeting, a few more resources here or there). As NGOs approach political representatives to enlist their informed support for international development goals, they must accordingly consider carefully the constraints and challenges which face those they are trying to influence. Ideally, public spaces and mechanisms can be created which will allow for more mutually satisfying and productive joint deliberation around shared concerns and in which the learning of NGOs could be brought to the table more often and utilized to better effect. That goal remains at some distance; meanwhile, any efforts in this direction will surely strengthen the public policy process in Canada and Canada's role in international development.

THE DOMESTICATION-GLOBALIZATION-DEMOCRATIZATION POLICY NEXUS

Domestication, globalization, and democratization are now commonly assumed to be the operating parameters for policy dialogue in the North (though their meanings are variously interpreted and their desirability sometimes disputed). Each poses distinct challenges for the different stakeholders and political actors in the policy process.

Domestication

Domestication of the policy agenda, a staple theme in studies of Canadian foreign policy for several decades, is showing renewed vigour. Domestication embraces both substantive and process aspects and tends to expand the range of issues put before makers of foreign policy – perhaps even to widen the scope of international affairs to encompass virtually the entire spectrum of public policy. As Canada's minister of foreign affairs observed in 1996: "the term 'foreign affairs' is increasingly an anachronism. More and more developments outside Canada have an impact inside Canada ... We are dealing with the international dimension of national issues. More than ever, Canadians have a direct stake in developments outside our boundaries" (Axworthy 1996: 1). Mr Axworthy went on to recognize the explosion in the numbers of transnational intergovernmental organizations, NGOs, and networking opportunities. A similar paradigm shift had been invoked in one of the more far-sighted NGO briefs submitted to the 1994 parliamentary foreign policy review. It argued that, since most issues of human security could no longer be dealt with by states acting alone (environment being a prime example), a "foreign policy" approach should give way to the development of a "global policy capability" in which civil society actors would be accorded a prominent role (INGO Forum 1994).

Such a progression would go considerably beyond what political scientists have previously defined as the domestic sources of and societal forces shaping a still relatively contained foreign policy agenda – a development about whose value and influence several Realist Canadian scholars continue to be sceptical. Some studies have emphasized the growing government interest in managing domestic public opinion and relations between the state and civil society with respect to international policy objectives (Stairs 1970–1; Keating 1985). Some have looked at increased public involvement through parliamentary processes (Taras 1985; Schmitz 1987). Some have documented a deepening of interest-group participation (Riddell-Dixon 1985), or the efforts of a particular community such as the churches (Greene 1990) to influence foreign policy decisions. Not surprisingly, their findings have been mixed, just as the policy communities examined are often very heterogeneous. Yet it is apparent that opening up the domestic processes for making international policy does not ensure equal advantages for all groups of citizens who might wish to participate. Organizational resources still matter, as do connections to economically powerful interests within the dominant business ethos. The image of interest-group lobbies with rapid "insider" access to top decision-makers fits only a select few, however. In contrast, what Cranford Pratt refers to as the "counter-consensus" of development and human rights NGOs, popular groups, and social movements may look to public education as a long-term strategy to create an environment more conducive to the policy changes they seek. And as the resources of state agencies allocated to public participation in policy development continue to shrink, they may increasingly have to find ways to do so which do not depend support from the public sector.

Domestication is clearly a reality of the times. As Leslie Pal puts it, in a study on the role of Canadian NGOs in international human rights policies, while foreign policy is "still a distinct arena of Canadian policy making ... its boundaries are increasingly permeable to domestic issues" (1994: 214). International development is also a candidate for this sort of domestication and thus for making a potent claim on the everyday consciousness as well as the consciences of Canadians. Yet there are real risks in pursuing this course. A conflation of domestic and international concerns could overload the foreign affairs agenda – and parliamentary attention to it – making it more difficult in practice to establish priorities. Policy-makers, who need a manageable framework and often lack the resources to assess the relevance and credibility of ever expanding information inflows, might simply be overwhelmed by the claims from a proliferation of organizational actors. Demands for more policy dialogue moving back and forth from the domestic to the international might foster an overreaching rhetoric of what global cooperation and governance can achieve. Or, in contrast, the current of domestication might be turned inwards as people either seek insulation from the outside world's troubles or cast international activities largely in terms of domestic objectives and benefits. Indeed, some critics have interpreted the economic priorities set out in the Canadian government's 1995 foreign policy statement, *Canada in the World*, as a retreat from a more generous humane internationalist orientation (Pratt 1994; Cohen 1995).

Globalization

These conflicted processes of domestication coincide with the equally unsettling processes of globalization which suggest, if their more fervent proponents are to be believed, that most existing forms of political interaction and policy dialogue are being overruled or bypassed by major "borderless" forces which are shaping the human prospect and are beyond control by any government or governments. Canadian parliamentarians have recognized the phenomenon. In a 1995 report on international financial institutions, the House of Commons Standing Committee on Foreign Affairs and International Trade (SCFAIT) cited Stanley Hoffmann's diagnosis of a "crisis of liberal internationalism" in which the march of privatized economic globalization is having unforeseen destabilizing effects: "One is the creation of a huge zone of irresponsibility: The global economy is literally out of control, not subject to the rules of accountability and principles of legitimacy that apply to relations between individuals and states ... The other effect has been the frequent domestic backlash against the constraints imposed by interdependence in general, a reaction to the sense that the fate of individuals even in liberal polities is no longer under their control or that of their representatives" (SCFAIT 1995: 55).

An insidious – and worrisome – aspect of this state of disorientation and flux is how easily it could undermine faith in the efficacy of democratic civic action to achieve public goods through the intervention of institutions of responsible government. While there are optimistic Canadian scenarios which seek to reassure, such as the concept of a spreading global "democratic" culture propounded by Gwynne Dyer in his radio series, *Millennium*, contending contrarian views of what is happening to societies and polities under the impact of corporatist power and untrammelled consumer capitalism (Saul 1995; Kingwell 1996) deserve serious attention.

What then can be done by those who want both to "think globally and act locally"? Richard Simeon – working from a Canadian perspective – argues that because globalization's fallout in the domestic arena has indeed broken down the old "social contract," it is more important than ever to construct new deliberative and governance structures which, on both democratic and effectiveness grounds, afford "very strong avenues for participation by interest groups and by individual citizens":

The key point about this process is that it be visible and open, so that the groups themselves can be held accountable and required to confront and debate each other. Here, I believe the key institution is Parliament and legislatures. One of their primary functions should be to provide a forum for consultation and the expression by as wide a range of groups as possible. Legislatures should be able to exploit new technologies to facilitate this process, through interactive hearings and through such devices as the [constitutional] citizen conferences ... a long-term solution ... must be built from a process of genuine and deep public deliberation; it must restore to citizens some sense of control over both governments and the seemingly ineluctable economic forces that rule their lives. It involves, therefore, a greater sense of mutual responsibility, a civic sense. (Simeon 1994: 60–3)

Democratization

It is in the intersection of the global and the local, subjected to forces which are weakening the bonds of both state and society, that the challenges of a democratization project such as Simeon suggests will especially test the ingenuity and good will of both politicians and NGOs and citizens engaged in political action. The American theorist Robert Dahl suggests that raising the general level of "civic competence" enough to be able to address these problems will require not only experimentation with new institutions and techniques but also the promotion of "a widespread capacity for empathetic understanding among citizens" (1992: 54–7). This view suggests that to sustain a democratic civic life that in turn supports a functioning democratic government, civil society cannot be taken for granted as a source of votes (or donations) but must be worked at diligently, perhaps even retrieved in the sense of being able to perform that democratic vocation.

The debate over how to proceed has been preoccupying many liberal democrats, especially in the United States, as shown by the malaise indicated in such titles as Galbraith's *Culture of Contentment* (1992), Lapham's *The Wish for Kings: Democracy at Bay* (1993), Elshtain's *Democracy on Trial* (1995), and Sandel's *Democracy's Discontent* (1996b). What Peter Drucker (1994) has celebrated as the rise of a voluntary "third sector" risks becoming the re-privatization of the (post–World War II welfare) state rather than a democratization of state institutions guided by a public philosophy of the common good. NGOs can be allies of, but ought not to be viewed as substitutes for, democratic government and politics. At a time when more involvement seems warranted, Robert Putnam (1995, 1996) has observed pronounced parallel declines in the United States in both trust in government and membership in civic associations. The nation is producing a "generation of loners." Robert Bly's new book speaks of a "sibling society" afraid to accept adult responsibilities. (Is it a coincidence that the biting political consciousness of the 1970s hit sitcom *All in the Family* has given way to the vapid apoliticism of the 1990s hit sitcom *Friends?*)

In E.J Dionne's view: "At the end of the century, the central problem confronting the democracies is not excessive government or a lack of economic and technical inventiveness, but a decay in the sort of social and political organization that gave power to ordinary citizens, shaped the economy into an engine of mass prosperity, and strengthened democracy." Accordingly, only a "new engagement with democratic reform" will do. "Politics has everything to do with building a more just, more civil, more open society" (1996: 32). At the same time, Michael Sandel points out that: "Self-government today ... requires a politics that plays itself out in a multiplicity of settings, from neighborhoods to nations to the world as a whole. Such a politics requires citizens who can abide the ambiguity associated with divided sovereignty, who can think and act as multiply situated selves." And he adds that people must first learn to become citizens at home before they can think of acting efficaciously as citizens abroad: "The global media and markets that shape our lives beckon us to a world beyond boundaries and belonging. But the civic resources we need to master these forces, or at least to contend with them, are still to be found in the places and stories, memories and meanings, incidents and identities, that situate us in the world and give our lives their moral particularity. The task for politics now is to cultivate these resources, to repair the civic life on which democracy depends" (1996a: 74).

It is noteworthy that the challenge of participatory democracy is being deeply felt even within the world's most developed capitalist democracies, though its application is much wider (Gillies & Schmitz 1992). Writing about contemporary transitions to democracy in developing countries in which there is ideological consensus on the broad parameters of a market economy and political pluralism, Haggard and Kaufman observe that continuing debate "about both policy and modes of representation ... is [nevertheless] an essential component of democratic development." Their conclusion ventures that: "democratic debate and contestation are themselves a form of *collective learning* in which citizens acquire the capacity to reject what fails and to attempt something new. The capacity to learn means that the unexpected is possible, that neither politics nor policy is simply a game of repeating what has come before. It is on this fundamental characteristic of democracy that we pin our hopes" (1995: 379, emphasis added).

To bring these reflections directly to the question of this essay: How can NGOs and politicians in Canada learn – by acting jointly as allies – to make that democratizing process work, and then put it to work on addressing the aims of globally sustainable human development in the twenty-first century? Doing so may mean leaving behind familiar stereotypes and conventional "games" and trying to focus instead on what is in the evolving public interest. And it may require some civic confidence-building measures on both sides because of the widespread perceptions that politicians cannot be trusted (or are only after votes) and that NGOs are only one segment of a proliferation of special-interest groups which often engage in single-issue politics (or are more interested in donations than public education). Clearly there is work to do on the parliamentary side in Canada, for a recent public opinion poll by Ekos Research Associates showed only 15 per cent of respondents had a significant degree of trust in politicians, ranking them just above lobbyists and car salesmen (Toronto *Globe and Mail*, 6 May 1996). NGOs for their part must struggle to mobilize public constituencies and make the case for a greater role in policy development in a time of diminishing government financial support.

In the search for ways whereby legislators and NGO advocates might help each other to strengthen the democratic process and achieve policy dialogue, whether through parliamentary means or various extra-parliamentary techniques, it is as well to begin by evaluating the lessons of past experience with such interactions, which have a considerable if chequered history in Canada. The next two sections offer assessments of some recent NGO efforts, most prominently during the foreign and defence policy reviews of 1994–5, to engage the institutions of Canadian government on issues of international development assistance and thereby to exert the kind of influence on Northern policies that Southern partners see as the priority in bringing about more just and equitable relationships between developed and developing countries.

NGOS ON THE PARLIAMENTARY ROAD: FROM ACCESS TO POLICY INFLUENCE?

The movement in Canada towards a growing number of NGOs speaking out in public forums and an increasing openness of parliamentary processes to policy input from NGOs has so far produced inconclusive results. There are a variety of ways in which NGOs concerned with international development can seek to influence policy-makers – approaches to individual members of parliament and to party caucuses, representations to ministers, consultations with departments and agencies. But the broadest test of their effective political influence has been their response to the periodic public reviews of international affairs policies which have incorporated extensive parliamentary hearings.

As exercises in parliamentary and policy reform, these reviews have elicited increased participation from and raised expectations among Canadian NGOs but have left behind as many sceptics as believers (see Schmitz 1987, 1995; Stairs 1995). The reviews undertaken by the Trudeau government some thirty years ago introduced the promise of participatory democracy to foreign policy making but in reality they were quite circumscribed, as this comment from Denis Stairs makes clear: "That the foreign-policy-making community has not yet found these developments unduly burdensome merely reflects the failure, to date, of the domestic publics to organize successfully in ways designed for applying *significant* pressure on the decision-making process" (1970–1: 234). Thomas Hockin made a similarly troubling observation in describing the 1969 reassessment of Canada's role in the North Atlantic Treaty Organization: "The long work of the committee led to no fundamental reevaluation among the members or the parties of their own biases, prejudices, assumptions and points of view" (1969: 128). The review of international relations conducted by the Mulroney government in 1985–6 ushered in more promises of parliamentary reform and public participation but that process also seemed to lose steam. The means of public policy review was indeed opened up. More NGOs were heard. However, the opportunity for the presentation of views did not lead to a genuine dialogue and shared learning, or to the creation of channels for sustained rather than episodic interaction. (Recommendations to establish regular policy advisory mechanisms were turned aside by successive governments.)

Nor was it clear whether input to these reviews, whatever its quantity or quality, could in the end be effective in bringing about policy changes. Don Page, who had been the senior official in the Department of External Affairs charged with overseeing the official response to the 1986 parliamentary report, later set out the issue in this way: "Effectiveness will depend on Parliament's ability and willingness to hold the government responsible for implementing policy recommendations that arise from outside the bureaucracy. Ultimately, even limited democratization of foreign policy making cannot be effective without the strong leadership of the minister of foreign affairs who is responsible for making it happen. The continued willingness of the public to participate in this exercise in populism will depend as much on the bureaucratic initiative in taking these suggestions seriously in its policy making as on the actual process used to obtain the input. That is the lesson that needs to be learned from the 1985–86 review" (1994: 597).

A similar lesson could be drawn from the fate of the major parliamentary inquiry into Canada's ODA policies and programmes undertaken the next year by the House of Commons Standing Committee on External Affairs and International Trade (SCEAIT). As well as being independently initiated by Parliament (rather than mandated by government terms of reference) and therefore having a clear focus on fundamental reform, this inquiry benefited from inspired chairmanship, careful staff work, and on-site observation of aid projects in Africa. Its report, *For Whose Benefit?* (1987) (commonly called the Winegard report after the committee chair), was also actively embraced by the many NGOs who had participated in the process, and much of its thrust seemed to carry forward into the government's ODA strategy, *Sharing Our Future* (1987/8). Yet, by the early 1990s, this enthusiasm had been replaced by disappointment, even a sense of betrayal, as the bureaucratic élites moved away from that (largely unachieved) strategy and pressure began to build for another public review. It was apparent that sympathetic parliamentary recommendations were insufficient unless some means to follow them through was in place (Pratt 1993–4).

2 The Foreign Policy Review from an NGO Perspective

THE CONTEXT

Before reviewing the role of the development NGOs in the 1994–5 foreign policy review, some background on ODA policy, the evolution of the public policy process, and the policy capacity of the NGO community may be useful to set the context.

ODA Policy

The process that produced the parliamentary report of 1987 on ODA policy (*For Whose Benefit?*) and the government response (*Sharing Our Future*) began very successfully. First, NGOs were prominently involved in the parliamentary process (sparked in great part by the role of the churches' coalition, Ten Days for World Development) and were accepted as credible participants. Secondly, the parliamentarians involved were interested in leading the policy change process and committing time and resources, and they enjoyed ministerial support. However, after the appearance of the new policy framework, *Sharing Our Future*, neither members of parliament nor NGOs paid sufficient attention to the quality of implementation and to governmental accountability. The consequence of this oversight became patently clear as the myriad of problems afflicting the Canadian International Development Agency (CIDA) were made public, first in a consultant's report, *Strategic Management Review Report* (Groupe SECOR 1991), and subsequently in the Auditor General's report of 1993.[2]

The 1988 policy framework coincided with the last years of growth in the ODA budget. That peaked in FY 1991/2, and in FY 1992/3 a series of cuts began which are currently projected to continue until FY 1998/9. The ODA budget has plummeted from $3.183 billion in FY 1991/2 to $2.04 billion in FY 1998/9, a decline of 45 per cent in real terms. The ratio of ODA to gross national product (GNP) has dropped from a high of 0.49 per cent in FY 1991/2 to what will be a thirty-year low of 0.27 per cent in FY 1998/9.[3] Despite the observations of many independent observers that cuts of this magnitude would necessitate significant re-thinking of what CIDA is doing and how it is doing it, the agency has so far attempted to accommodate the cuts through selective downsizing.

Public Policy Process Reform

The increasing scepticism of recent years about traditional political institutions has been reflected most vividly in Canada in the rise of western populism (and the Reform Party) and the growth of separatism in Quebec. The last two federal governments have both attempted to address this by innovations aimed at democratizing the policy process. Discussion about reform and democratization of the public policy process has focused on greater transparency, consultations to create new vehicles for citizen participation, and ways to ensure that the government would treat consultations seriously (Public Policy Forum 1993: v). At the time of the United Nations Conference on Environment and Development in 1992, the Mulroney government summarized its views on public participation in this way: "Decision-making must be transparent. The accountability for solutions must be clear and evident. The process must include all sectors of society" (Charest 1992: 2; see also CIDA 1993). The Liberal Party's platform for the 1993 election reiterated these themes with respect to international policy. This attitude has created many new opportunities for public policy dialogue on international issues. To date, however, the government appears to view policy dialogue more as a form of public *outreach* than a means of policy *development* (see Cameron & Molot 1996; Draimin & Plewes 1996).

NGO Policy Capacity

For many years after World War II, there was in Canada a broad consensus on most foreign affairs issues – often referred to as Pearsonian internationalism. During this time activism on matters of policy was the exception rather than the rule for the majority of Canada's international development NGOs. The exceptions included the ecumenical church coalitions (for example, GATT-Fly [now the Ecumenical Coalition for Economic Justice], Ten Days for World Development, and the Inter-Church Committee on Human Rights in Latin America) and other region- or issue-specific initiatives (for example, Canadian University Service Overseas and Oxfam Canada on South Africa, and those and other organizations on Central America and biodiversity). During the 1980s, however, cracks began to appear in that postwar consensus and the policy activism of NGOs increased. This change sparked different reactions from different government actors.

This rise in policy activism on the part of NGOs was a response to a variety of influences:

- a recognition of the weakness of their past impact in an often hostile macro-policy environment;
- their experiences in preparing for and participating in such international events as United Nations conferences and special sessions;
- their support for various parliamentary committees such as those on ODA policies and programmes, on the Central American peace process, on human rights and international development, and on international financial institutions;
- the encouragement of their Southern partners to take on "Northern-driven" policy issues;
- the evolution of development education towards adoption of a policy approach;
- a recognition that development was a political process;
- the impact of the experiences of the environmental and women's movements which had engaged in policy activism.

For the development community the need to develop and articulate a clear policy agenda became starkly evident in 1989 when Marcel Massé returned to CIDA as president after a term as an executive director at the International Monetary Fund (IMF). Massé "quickly determined that the major responsibility of the bilateral program should be the encouragement and underwriting of the structural adjustment of Third World economies in close cooperation with the IMF and the World Bank." This view of development exposed the growing tensions in CIDA-NGO relations and "created an important gap between the development ideology newly dominant in CIDA and the values and development thinking widely prevalent in the NGO community" (Brodhead & Pratt 1994: 4–5).[4] It became clear that senior CIDA staff (such as Massé and his senior vice-president, Doug Lindores) considered the

NGOs to be executing agencies rather than development and policy partners, even though the secretary of state for external affairs, Joe Clark, remained open to engaging the community on issues of mutual concern (Page 1993: 101).

CIDA's dismissal of NGO policy interests changed in response to a searing attack by the churches on the agency's divergence from the goals of *Sharing Our Future*. Regardless of what CIDA's leaders thought about the merits of the 1991 report of the Canadian Council of Churches, *Diminishing Our Future: CIDA: Four Years after Winegard* (and they contested the way it was released to the press as well as its contents), they recognized the need to manage the NGO-CIDA dialogue in ways which would not publicly embarrass the agency. As Denis Stairs once noted, "one way of disarming a critic is to consult him" (1970–1: 242). The adoption of this approach was reinforced by the Groupe SECOR report in which one of three key recommendations was that "CIDA should increase its ability to dialogue with and influence all of its stakeholders" (1991: 4).

Even before the shift in CIDA's approach to development, the Canadian Council for International Co-operation (CCIC) had reorganized itself in 1987 and created a policy unit to support a more pro-active policy role for the NGO development community. The organizational review led to other changes designed to enhance the CCIC's policy role, including moving to a stronger board model of "policy governance," changing the title of its head to president/chief executive officer to reflect that individual's higher public profile, and strengthening the policy roles of the geographic working groups. These innovations were more a product of the strategy of the council's new head, Tim Brodhead, than any demonstration of the community's clarity on its policy role. Nevertheless, NGOs gradually became more active with respect to both ODA and international policy generally as well as more self-critical in examining their internal policies.[5] Not surprisingly, this evolution brought to the surface the division in the NGO community between those which were "political" (policy active) and those which had chosen an "a-political" (non-active) approach. Over time, however, the legitimacy of policy work gained greater acceptance and these ideological conflicts diminished. Being policy active was no longer confused with being partisan in a political party sense.

In line with its strengthened policy focus (and in anticipation of cuts to ODA), the CCIC held its first annual parliamentary lobbying event in 1989 and initiated a community-wide public mobilization strategy, the One World Campaign, in 1991. Although it has been criticized for goals and objectives which were "too broad and ambitious" (Lagarde 1995: vi), the campaign did prove the desirability and viability of a shared community-wide approach and stimulated the development of important skills for engaging the public and projecting policy goals. Despite these activities the CCIC saw its role as a facilitator of a division of labour on policy rather than as a policy shop for NGOs. It also sought to facilitate policy collaboration between the community, on the one hand, and academics and research institutes, on the other.

Over time, changes at the CCIC were paralleled by changes in individual NGOs: policy projects became more numerous; board members, volunteers, and Southern partners were more actively drawn into policy work; job descriptions changed to include policy work and in some instances new policy positions were created; close collaboration with sympathetic academics increased; contacts with parliamentarians and government officials were more frequent; new policy forums emerged (such as the Middle East Working Group, the Horn of Africa Working Group, and the Central America Monitoring Group) which complemented the work of both the CCIC and the policy-active region-specific funding coalitions (Partnership Africa Canada, Cooperation Canada Mozambique, for example).

An important test for the policy and public mobilization skills of the increasingly policy-focused development community came in the late autumn of 1992 when the Department of External Affairs prepared to seek cabinet approval for its "International Assistance Policy Update." According to critics of the "Update," it "strongly advocated both a major reorientation of aid to tie it more closely to commercial and foreign policy objectives, and a controlling role for External Affairs in the development of policies required by the these objectives" (Brodhead & Pratt 1994: 20). Specific recommendations in the document included: reducing Canada's contributions to the regional development banks and the United Nations, increasing the share of development assistance directed towards eastern and central Europe, cutting the development information programme, cutting NGO "responsive funding"[6] by 50 per cent, and separating "development assistance" ($284 million) and "development cooperation funding" ($427 million) and using the latter to "position [Canada's] private sector for long term penetration" of developing-country markets (External Affairs 1992; Filewod 1993).

Although the document had been prepared secretly for cabinet, it was leaked to the CCIC. Recognizing the sweeping policy implications of its recommendations, the council immediately sought to mobilize the development community against it. The strategy was twofold: oppose the policy changes as undermining the integrity of the ODA mandate and decry the secretive and undemocratic method of making such wholesale changes to policy. NGOs actively lobbied members of parliament, wrote letters to the press, and encouraged the public – successfully – to take up the cause. In the dying moments of an unpopular government, the key issue in the public's (and politicians') eye was the surreptitious nature of the policy play.[7] Barbara McDougall, the secretary of state for external affairs, was forced to back down and the document was withdrawn from cabinet consideration. Although withdrawn, the "Update" obviously represented an important segment of opinion within the bureaucracy on the role and utility of ODA, an opinion that continues to influence the internal debate.

THE FOREIGN POLICY REVIEW

The contretemps over the "Update" document together with the increasing irrelevance of the policy framework for ODA set out in *Sharing Our Future*, the perceived vulnerability of CIDA in view of the criticisms of the *Strategic Management Review Report*, the beginning of cuts to the ODA budget, and the dramatic international changes following the demise of the Cold War combined to reinforce the CCIC's opinion that another review of official development assistance was overdue. In light of the cross-cutting nature of all international policy – a fact ever more evident in the wake of the United Nations Conference on Environment and Development – and in view of the growing debt crisis, regional conflicts, and global trade negotiations, the council believed that any ODA review should take place in the context of an overall review of foreign policy. In addition, it was hoped that a high-profile foreign policy review would provide an opportunity to re-position development in the eyes of a public whose interest and support for ODA had declined.

On 16 February 1993 the CCIC appeared before the Commons Committee on External Affairs and International Trade to propose that the committee prepare the groundwork for a post-election review of aid and "other aspects of Canadian foreign policy including international finance and trade, environmental agreements, defence including peacekeeping etc., immigration policies, and so on." Canada, it argued, "needs an integrated foreign policy framework which promotes the co-ordination of various foreign policy instruments." The CCIC warned that: "a major policy change should not be driven by fiscal restraint to focus on the country's short term economic interests [but develop] a new long term vision of Canada's relations with the Third World within a co-operative internationalist framework ... Any policy review should reassess the meaning of global 'security' in the 21st century to emphasize the threat of environmental degradation and poverty; it should also include an analysis of the current global context, orienting Canada and the world from a North/South rather than an East/West perspective. Our long term security depends on our ability to work co-operatively with other countries to slow down and reverse the rapid escalation of global poverty."

Speaking before a committee which included future ministers of the next government (such as Lloyd Axworthy and Christine Stewart), the CCIC set out a series of recommendations for enhancing the review process which included: promoting a non-partisan approach; seeking the active involvement of all public sectors; expanding the parliamentary committee with outside "eminent persons"; expediting a post-election review by commissioning research during the current parliament; the preparation, once the review was under way, of an interim report which would propose foreign policy objectives, identify major issues to be addressed, and outline the steps to be taken prior to the final report; encouraging Southern voices to be heard; encouraging a parallel "informal" process involving many stakeholders (NGOs and the labour, business, defence, and immigrant communities) which could also build public support for and participation in the formal review.

At the time of the "Update" imbroglio, an internal CCIC document (1993b: 1) had proposed five short-term goals for its policy activities:

- halt the policy update;
- monitor the budget process (and have a contingency plan should development NGOs be subject to the funding cuts for "interest groups" announced in the 2 December 1992 economic statement);
- reinforce the NGO community's legitimate role in the foreign policy process;
- gain support for a post-election policy review;
- prepare to make foreign aid an election issue.

As the country headed towards an election in the autumn, the NGO community appeared to be making headway towards achieving these goals. The "Update" was dropped. The budget was monitored, but the cuts did not materialize. The press coverage garnered and the high-level contacts maintained with ministers' offices, the Privy Council Office, CIDA, and members of parliament showed that the NGO community was accepted as a legitimate policy player. The opposition Liberals responded sympathetically to the call for a foreign policy review, although the party's election platform (set out in *Creating Opportunity* – quickly dubbed the Red Book – and the annexed "Foreign Policy Handbook") did not explicitly commit it to a review if elected.[8]

Having advanced the likelihood of a review, the development community needed to prepare a full-fledged foreign policy platform. The "Update" episode had shown the capacity and ability of public constituencies to stop a policy change, but promoting policy change was a very different activity. To do that would require accelerating the capacity-building activities of members of the development community and thinking about preparing both a process for and the building blocks of a policy framework. To this end, the CCIC organized two training workshops in 1993, one on NGO policy formulation and one on government relations, and focused its May 1993 annual meeting on coalescing community support for its active participation in any foreign policy review and on providing the council with an appropriate mandate to give direction to this role.

The council began to prepare both a framework for the foreign policy review for which it could advocate, and specific recommendations about how the review might be conducted. It organized a major membership policy forum which was to hammer out proposals for the approval of the CCIC board and subsequent presentation to Parliament. In the end, it was decided not to pursue any organized attempt to inject foreign aid into the October 1993 federal election campaign. The timing of the election call (end of summer) coupled with the commitment of resources to other elements of the foreign policy review strategy prevented the preparation of an "election priorities campaign" similar to one the community had organized for the 1988 election. Unfortunately, with the exception of free trade with the United States, foreign policy issues were conspicuously absent from the campaign – thus weakening the momentum for foreign policy change.

Immediately after the election, the CCIC renewed its call for a comprehensive public review of foreign policy. In a letter to the new prime minister, Jean Chrétien, on 3 November, the council urged the government to carry out a review and laid out five challenges to be addressed:

- the growing gap between rich and poor;
- the unsustainable pattern of world economic growth, creating unprecedented and dangerous environmental degradation;
- the need for arms control to reverse the global spread of arms;
- the diminishing influence of national governments over global economic trends;
- the need to find new and significant ways to involve civil society in local, national, and international decision-making.

The letter recognized recent positive changes in the public policy process but noted that "while NGOs have enjoyed more access [to consultations], the quality of policy dialogue has remained relatively limited." However, it continued, "this evolving public policy context suggests the thoughtful exploration of new models of policy dialogue which strike new balances between government and non-governmental actors, between experts and the public at large, between policy formulation and policy implementation, between a vision of what can be and practical evaluation of the tools at our disposal."

This letter was followed up by a sixteen-page report (CCIC 1993c) which expanded on the rationale for a comprehensive review and offered specific proposals for its organization such as integrating the reviews of foreign and defence policy and fulfilling the Red Book commitment on the democratization of foreign policy by piloting innovative ways to promote a "deliberative democracy" looking at facilitating "public judgment" on complex issues.[9] The report also outlined a number of specific recommendations about the conduct of the review.[10]

Following the election the government quickly became embroiled in numerous reviews of domestic policy. It was with some reluctance, therefore, that it agreed to a review of foreign policy. In December 1993 it was announced that there would be two reviews – one for foreign policy and one for defence policy. Each would be conducted by a joint committee of the House of Commons and the Senate. Jean-Robert Gauthier, the Commons co-chair for the foreign policy review, was a veteran member of parliament but he lacked strong foreign policy experience. The Senate co-chair was Allan MacEachen – an ironic choice to lead a public review. Although twice secretary of state for external affairs and highly knowledgeable, he had discouraged his department's officials from public dialogue and engagement during his first term in that office and even forbade it for a time during his second term (Page 1993: 100). The committees were announced in February 1994 and began work as the government held its first National Forum on Canada's International Relations, an annual consultation on foreign policy between concerned Canadians and various ministers.

The choice of separate reviews by joint committees had several effects on the overall process. First of all, it diluted the influence of the new opposition parties (the Bloc Québécois and the Reform Party) and strengthened the already dominant hand of the government. Secondly, it ensured that a majority of the members of the Defence Committee would be sympathetic to the Department of National Defence.[11] Thirdly, it brought the Conservatives who had lost official party status in the Commons into the process (through the party's members in the Senate). Fourthly, it undermined the chance of creating a comprehensive framework for Canada's international affairs. An additional concern for constituencies promoting reform agendas was the dramatic shift in the political centre of gravity that arose from the presence of a vocal right (Reform) and a virtually invisible left. (The New Democratic Party also lacked official party status and was not represented on either committee; the Bloc, while social democratic in orientation, had no sustained interest in foreign policy.) In consequence, the government's attention was focused on managing pressures from the right and it was able to ignore, to a large extent, those from the left.

The CCIC already had its policy development process under way with broad membership involvement. Papers had been commissioned on three main topics: sustainable human development and ODA, human rights, and economic justice. In February 1994 a policy conference was held involving members and overseas partners at which policy positions were refined. These were subsequently reviewed, adjusted, and endorsed by the CCIC's board. The resulting 55-page document, *Building and Sustaining Global Justice: Towards a New Canadian Foreign Policy*, appeared in May and became the council's brief to both committees. The construction of a common policy agenda was a remarkable watershed for the NGO community which in the past was known more for its divisions than its cohesion.

Besides the general CCIC brief, approximately half of the council's 100-plus members made presentations to the committees, either directly or as members of consortia or working groups. A CCIC-commissioned survey of these and selected allied briefs noted "a very high degree of consistency and similarity among the various briefs" and suggested that "part of this homogenization of opinion may be the product of the CCIC/member collaborative approach to the construction of the policy alternatives" (Rowe 1994: 8). The intent of the CCIC was that its brief would provide a general framework while the briefs of individual members would provide detailed programme and country illustrations and examples of policy points. In practice, however, only a small proportion of individual NGO briefs were region- or country-specific.

Unfortunately, the failure to carry through on this plan left many committee members (particularly those on the Defence Committee) with the impression "that they were being bombarded over and over again by orchestrated repetitions of the same superficial and poorly substantiated message from a closely interconnected coterie of the likeminded." In addition, some committee members believed the groups "were ultimately motivated by self-serving interests" (Stairs 1995: 98). If Stairs's analysis is indeed an accurate reflection of the views of many committee members, then the attempt of the development community to anticipate the needs of the committees (and those of a participatory public policy process) were certainly misconstrued.

The CCIC policy presentation strategy (a consensus overview brief plus individual NGO presentations) was constructed with the objectives both of strengthening community policy capacity and providing the committees with a strong broadly based agenda which could not be dismissed as unrepresentative of the sector. In addition, the pre-developed NGO position was designed to aid the committees if they chose to create multi-stakeholder forums to facilitate consensus-building between sectors (they didn't) or when the time came to balance the contributions from so many presenters. (For example, the Foreign Policy Committee received 561 briefs, including 277 from NGOs, 155 from individuals, 70 from education and culture groups, 49 from business, 6 from labour, 4 from international organizations, 2 from military associations, and 1 from a lower level of government [SJCRCFP 1994a: 85].) The CCIC brief did not make a narrow, sectoral appeal for self-interested proposals. In fact, by taking on the broader issues of Canada's international policy framework, it could be perceived as having strayed too far from its core areas of competence. Of course, by choosing sustainable human development as a framework for ODA, programme areas where NGOs are strong would presumably be beneficiaries of reform. According to CIDA's own research on basic human needs programming, it is areas of NGO activity which have the highest impact in the provision of basic human needs (Van Rooy 1995).

It may be that NGOs would have been criticized regardless of the approach they employed. The recent vilification of voluntary sector organizations as "special interest groups" placed NGOs in a negative context even before they reached the floor of a committee hearing room – a striking change in attitude from the 1987 hearings of the Winegard Committee. One brief – from the IDEA Group (1994), an informal association of senior NGO executives – inadvertently fuelled this negative view with its criticism of CIDA ("increasingly shrouded in mystery and silence or indecision and doubletalk") and its staff and by statements such as "no other institutions or organizations in this country do this work as effectively as NGOs."

3 Outcomes – An NGO Insider Viewpoint

SPECIAL JOINT COMMITTEE REVIEWING CANADIAN FOREIGN POLICY

Overall, the report of the Foreign Policy Committee – *Canada's Foreign Policy: Principles and Priorities for the Future* – held few surprises, changes, or innovations. In fact, it was disappointingly general (presenting few challenges to the government as it prepared its reply) and offered no cogent and comprehensive framework for Canada's role in the world. The report stayed within Canadian traditions, rocked few boats, and began the slow turn towards a less dynamic internationalism in Canada's foreign policy. For example, Canada was advised to practise "directed multilateralism," a euphemism for opting out of some international organizations. Overall, there was little sense of urgency about the pressing needs of the global community. On the specific issues of the CCIC's brief, the report's responses were mixed.

Once the committee's report was released, attention switched to the minister of foreign affairs and his officials, especially those responsible for drafting the government's reply. Less than three months after the committee reported, the government released its response: *Canada in the World* provided a general statement and a companion document, *Government Response to the Recommendations of the Special Joint Parliamentary Committee*, addressed each recommendation in turn (Canada 1995a, 1995b).

The CCIC had kept in touch with policy staff in the Department of Foreign Affairs and International Trade (DFAIT) throughout the review process to ensure the NGO community's concerns were known. In December 1994, after seeing the committee's report, the council had written to the minister to highlight four of its priorities: an integrated framework for international policy; reform of international financial institutions; a legislated mandate for the ODA programme, retaining Africa as a priority and promoting reciprocal North-South relationships utilizing models such as "development pacts"; and democratization of policy including creation (at arms length) of the Centre for Foreign Policy Development (promised in the Red Book).

How did the NGO proposals fare? On the four specific issues cited above, results were uneven. In *Canada in the World* the government recognized the need for coherence and consistency across international policy (and with all foreign policy instruments). "Security" was given a new comprehensive definition (multi-generational, embracing environmental degradation, social inequality, lack of economic opportunity, overpopulation, disease, mass involuntary migration, etc). Values were given prominence throughout the response. However, the three overriding foreign policy objectives chosen by the government (promotion of prosperity and employment, protection of security within a stable global framework, and projection of Canadian values and culture) were inward-looking rather than internationalist in outlook. The only response to the desire for reform of international financial institutions was to offer a somewhat anodyne "review." The government did, however, agree to push for a strengthening of poverty reduction as an objective of soft loans from the International Development Association. ODA was not to have a legislated mandate, but Africa would remain a priority. No change was proposed in the framework of Canada's North-South relationships. And the government agreed only to a "mechanism" for foreign policy consultation and outreach to be lodged within DFAIT.

On a more general level, there were some substantive gains. ODA had a clearer (though still weak) mandate but was recognized as "just one part of a larger effort – one that involves the resources of developing countries themselves and other factors, such as international trade and investment" (Canada 1995a: 41). Environmental sustainability had a higher profile. And there was frequent recognition of the roles of actors other than government (such as NGOs and civil society) in international policy. Specifically on ODA, the government did accept the committee's recommendations for its programme priorities, except that the sixth priority ("public participation") was replaced with "infrastructure services." (This was a precursor to budget cuts which entirely eliminated funding for development education except for that of overseas programming NGOs.[12])

But overall the dominant impression was that the new policy was a business-oriented one with, as the CCIC put it, "the promotion of Canada's economic interests as both a cornerstone and a yardstick of Canadian foreign policy." During the whole of the review process, the development community was in fact fighting a rearguard action against a rising and narrow economic agenda. In DFAIT the tension between the views of the development community and business was seen as one between values and interests. Some in the department saw its report as "driving up the middle." Perhaps confirming that, one review insider has observed that the values-based approach of NGOs found a natural resonance among parliamentarians but had its most important impact influencing people at DFAIT. The department, of course, was feeling the pressure from the minister for international trade, Roy MacLaren, who was fond of joking that "trade policy *was* foreign policy." During the Cold War security concerns eclipsed economic ones; perhaps it was not surprising that the post–Cold War era would see such a definitive rise of economic interests. Indeed, had it not been for the activism of Canadian NGOs, the erosion of Canada's traditional policy might have been much greater.

SPECIAL JOINT COMMITTEE ON CANADA'S DEFENCE POLICY

The review of defence policy was a revisiting of the status quo. The committee reported in early November 1994 and the government's white paper appeared on 1 December (more than two months before the government's foreign policy statement). While one of the committee's "major findings" was that the concept of security had broadened to "reflect political, economic, social, environmental and even cultural factors" (SJCCDP 1994: 5), Robert Lawson notes that the white paper "ignores entirely the issue of an expanded notion of security" (1996: 110). Suggestions from the NGO community that Canada shift its stated defence requirements from general capability armed forces to forces focused on peacekeeping (and thus render up a "peace dividend") were also ignored. Thus, "while the 1994 defence review began as an attempt to democratize the process of defence policy formulation, it quickly became an exercise in the construction of a new policy consensus supporting the status quo" (Lawson 1996: 113).

WHITHER PARLIAMENTARY REVIEWS?

The limited impact of external constituencies on the outcomes of the 1994–5 reviews of foreign and defence policy can be partly explained by several special circumstances emerging from the 1993 election: the dominance of the House of Commons by the Liberal Party (177 of 295 seats), the lack of a nationally representative official opposition, and the fact that two-thirds of those elected were neophytes. As a result, the government has had almost complete control of the national agenda, leading some observers to see the Liberal caucus, rather than Parliament, as the venue of real political debate.

In addition, the continuing crisis over national unity has meant that the goals of all federal programmes are examined to ensure they support the government's objectives on this matter. CIDA, as a major "discretionary" spender within the federal budget, was therefore under pressure to direct significant amounts of its domestic spending to Quebec. This pressure was reinforced by the fact that André Ouellet, the minister of foreign affairs who was the minister responsible for ODA in the Chrétien government, was also the political minister responsible for Quebec. Finally, while much public attention was focused on the public reviews, the real action in shaping government priorities seemed to be taking place in private deliberations by cabinet as it carried out its budget-cutting review of all programmes.

The obvious question therefore is whether optimal conditions existed for an effective parliamentary review process in the latter part of 1994. Analysts who have studied the public policy process and Parliament's role in it have noted the following criteria for success:

- Parliament's influence depends on "the idiosyncratic variables; the right issue, the right minister, the right timing" (Taras 1985: 16).

- "An energetic and non-partisan chairman, a minister ... willing to support and encourage the inquiry, a small but knowledgeable staff, objective and serious committee members, and the capacity to sustain an inquiry over the several years that might be necessary to complete it" (Canadian Study of Parliament Group 1984: 12).
- "Policy change is fundamentally a political process that requires political leadership, an agenda that steers, the mobilization of analytic resources ... and the crafting of political coalitions" (Stein 1994–5: 20).

The committees established in 1994 to review foreign and defence policy lacked the time to focus, opportunities for research and travel, and the ministerial mandate and support to question fundamental assumptions. Without political leadership (in cabinet and in committee), the opportunity for public policy discourse was circumscribed. Undoubtedly, stronger and better-constructed ideas contributed by NGOs and the creation of non-traditional coalitions on policy positions could have expanded the space for dialogue.

Overall, what was the impact of the NGO development community on the policy agenda, policy process, and outcomes?

Policy Agenda

The NGOs did significantly influence the policy agenda, ensuring that important ODA and international policy issues were on the public agenda in an increasingly hostile environment.

Policy Process

Development NGOs along with other organizations and constituencies did ensure a public parliamentary review. Given the lack of resources and leadership available to the committees, it was a blessing in disguise that the reviews of foreign and defence policy were separate.

The NGO community had made numerous suggestions for the review process (most of which were ignored) but a major omission, assuming resources were available, was a failure to mobilize the public to bring pressure to bear on the government and Parliament during the reviews. The NGO organizations were mobilized (hence the large number of briefs and presentations) but the public was not. Ideally, formal reviews should be complemented by extra-parliamentary activities to enhance the impact of policy initiatives suggested by NGOs. Significantly, NGOs are now accepted as a central constituency to be reckoned with in the foreign policy arena.

Policy Outcomes

Here results are less clear. While many of the forward-looking aspects of the NGO agenda were not picked up, it can be argued that the wholesale retreat from many ODA principles (as envisioned in the 1992 "Update" paper) was stymied. And the importance of international policy integration and coherence (supported by others besides the development NGOs) became an accepted principle (although its implementation remains to be confirmed).

In very modest fashion, the government tinkered around the edges of ODA policy. Despite the vastly changed environment for international co-operation following the end of the Cold War, the foreign policy review ignored compelling arguments and important opportunities to re-think and re-configure ODA as an important fulcrum facilitating the shift from a Third World development framework to a global development framework (Plewes, Sreenivasan & Draimin 1996).

LESSONS LEARNED

Did the development NGOs push their reform agenda strongly enough? In an era of declining public support for ODA, reform proponents find themselves in a Catch-22. Critiques of ODA are seized upon by its opponents to attack its legitimacy. The press, without a conscious hostile agenda, indirectly supports this attack by focusing the public's attention on a "drip of horror stories." How can one promote needed structural reform of ODA without inadvertently undermining its already fragile basis, making ODA bureaucrats more defensive, and abusing public support? How do we change the bath water without throwing out the baby?

Rather than submitting to and suffering from self-censorship, perhaps the "reform" of ODA has to be tackled head on: reformers may best counter growing public disenchantment by acknowledging the need for reform and promoting an agenda for significant change reflecting a world in flux. This Catch-22, where critique and reform meet public opinion, highlights the need to reconcile the tension between the role of NGOs in policy activism and their role in seeking public support for ODA. In any case, it is probably dangerous for those of us in the ODA "business" to confuse existing public support for ODA with support for the status quo on ODA policy.

Looking over the long term, the foreign policy review was an important learning opportunity for an NGO community engaged in a rapid capacity-building process for policy activism. While some critiques of the impact of NGOs focus on their limited policy experience, in fact the review process strengthened the NGO policy agenda (giving the CCIC its first comprehensive policy mandate) and built skills throughout the community. Nevertheless, future effectiveness in shaping policy will require NGOs to extend and deepen their professional capacities.

Does the dependence of NGOs on CIDA funding have a negative effect on their role in shaping policy (or just on the perception of them by others)? According to one study, "in 1991 16 of the 18 largest agencies reported that more than two-thirds of their total resources were from government sources" (cited in Brodhead and Pratt 1994: 3). Yet the sharpest NGO critique of CIDA during the foreign policy review came from the brief of the IDEA Group which is composed of the heads of many of those large CIDA-dependent agencies. The correlation isn't immediately clear.

Certainly NGOs would benefit from greater recognition by government of their important and legitimate concern with policy development and government accountability. At one point CIDA actually approached the NGO community about creating a "policy fund" to strengthen NGO capacity by jointly funding policy development initiatives. The offer was subsequently withdrawn. Two years of dialogue between NGOs and CIDA on the draft of the recently issued CIDA document, *Canadian Voluntary Organizations and CIDA: Framework for a Renewed Relationship* (1996), created an opportunity for serious policy engagement which needs to be evaluated. Three early observations would be: that NGOs can marshal useful and detailed policy input; that policy change at CIDA is not easy; and that the consultative process and mechanisms for shared learning can be improved.

4 Outcomes – A Parliamentary Insider View

THE 1994 PARLIAMENTARY REVIEWS

NGOs in the development community had reason to hope that a new public review could deliver both substantial policy reform and a better process for continuing policy dialogue. In opposition the Liberal Party had sought out NGO views and its "Foreign Policy Handbook" emphasized NGO and parliamentary roles in the "democratization of foreign policy" and contained ambitious proposals on how this would be done. Yet the review processes set up by the incoming Chrétien government in 1994 left a number of these hopes and ambitions on the drawing board. The balance sheet in terms of parliamentary and civil society/ NGO actors has been surveyed by the authors elsewhere (Schmitz 1995; Draimin & Plewes 1996). Here, we want to look at possible explanations for why expectations of a breakthrough in policy renewal and process were frustrated.

Many NGOs put a great deal of time and effort into their presentations to the committees. The CCIC in particular strove to put forward a coherent vision of how the development community's priorities of global justice and sustainable human development affected the whole spectrum of foreign and defence policies. To some extent this did happen, and several groups – for example, the Interchurch Fund for International Development – were able to bring in Southern partners to describe concrete experiences and thus reinforce messages about reciprocal policy dialogues (SJCRCFP 1994a: issue 20). Unfortunately these presentations were often made to very few parliamentarians. The Foreign Policy Committee split into three separate panels to deal with the volume of requests to appear. Even so, this *oral* testimony (which was key since few committee members would have time to read the hundreds of briefs received, no matter how diligently prepared) was typically squeezed into long days covering a multitude of issues.

The one organized round table dealing with the role of civil society actors in the formulation and delivery of foreign policy was held in the middle of the summer recess and therefore suffered from lack of attention and poor attendance. That session began with a leading question being put by the committee co-chair, Jean-Robert Gauthier, to the effect that, with so many NGOs receiving government funding for delivering programmes, should this work perhaps be more co-ordinated by government and the "multiplicity" of organizations restricted (SJCRCFP 1994b: issue 48: 6)? The round table left NGOs with the impression that, while big business can take care of itself and has other more effective channels of influence than public reviews, NGOs along with other less well-represented groups in society are more problematic communities to involve in the making of policy. Alison Van Rooy has observed, however, that although NGOs will inherently resist co-ordination from above or outside (their autonomy being a virtue), they should be regarded positively as receptive to inclusive forms of co-operation in policy development. Moreover, such government-society channels have the benefit of breaking down the insularity of the established bureaucracies. She put forward the North-South Institute's proposal for an overseas development council that would "institutionalize and regularize a system of interaction and consultation with NGOs, so new policy actors can become involved, and it must be with agencies other than CIDA alone" (SJCRCFP 1994b: issue 48: 9).

It is ironic that the "democratization" proposals and ideas set out in the "Foreign Policy Handbook" were not subjected to a systematic examination during the reviews. (Indeed, at the round table they were barely mentioned.) Also ironic, in view of Gauthier's remark about an unco-ordinated multiplicity of foreign policy actors, is that NGO efforts to mobilize among themselves to deliver a more coherent and reinforced message were perceived very differently by some observers – as confirming instead a stereotypical image which worked against that message's intended impact. As Denis Stairs observed: "The result was that the representations of the NGOs in the minds of their political targets were lumped into a single, stereotyped category ... In this perceptions-editing process, much of the texture was lost, and with it an opportunity to buttress a powerful moral case with vivid displays of emotionally appealing evidence" (1995: 98).

It is possible to overstate this effect, but certainly one of the flaws of the review process was that some of the most sophisticated briefs got rather short shrift. NGO proposals for global education and the development of public awareness provide an example. The Kawartha World Issues Centre of Peterborough, which submitted a very professional and forward-looking brief in early April, was given a few minutes to present in late July, the day after the round table. What developed was a rather testy exchange with the co-chair and a minimal engagement on the important issues raised in the written submission. These issues also got sidetracked by an individual presentation, slotted into the same time period, which lumped NGOs in with a dubious and huge "assistance industry" (SJCRCFP 1994b: issue 49: 96).

There does not appear to have been any attempt to compensate for the lacunae in the oral testimony on development partnership and education during the summarizing and editing process leading to the final report. It probably did not help that the position paper on foreign aid by economist André Martens, commissioned at the behest of the committee's co-chairs, found Canadian NGOs to be a problematic bunch despite their "generally impressive achievements." In Martens's view, these problems included potential deficiencies in cost-efficiency and political accountability. He also suggested that some NGOs had developed an unfortunate "aversion" to developmentally necessary market-economy and governance institutions (1994: 78–9). While it is difficult to ascertain how much influence any of these "second thoughts" had, the report offered a rather ambiguous set of messages related to ODA partnerships under the heading "improve results." The committee's sole recommendation linked maintaining or increasing support for NGO programmes to "where partners have a clearly demonstrated record of effectiveness and efficiency" as well as to "the strength and depth of the Canadian support base as measured by such things as the commitment of volunteers to the organization and the ability to generate matching contributions" (SJCRCFP 1994a: 56–7).

POST-REVIEW PROSPECTS

Although the government's response to the committee report affirmed the principle of NGO roles in policy development and delivery, it was less than reassuring on specifics: "any decision as to the relative share of ODA allocations to NGO partners must take into account the severe fiscal situation that the Government and CIDA itself face. Preference will be given to those partners who demonstrate the most effectiveness and efficiency, and who provide programming that is complementary to the objectives of the Government in promoting sustainable development. In addition, special attention will be paid to supporting partners who can contribute their own financial resources and the time of volunteers, or who allow young people to serve abroad" (Canada 1995b: 70).

In his budget, tabled a few weeks later, the finance minister sharply cut ODA funds; subsequently, CIDA funding was eliminated to some NGOs whose focus was development education and consciousness-raising in Canada. NGOs as a whole are still struggling to cope with the overall impact of these cutbacks. But they are also moving on to elaborate new strategies for public engagement and policy dialogue.[13] A year into the aftermath, largely in response to concerns raised by the CCIC, these challenges received televised parliamentary exposure through presentations to an all-day special forum on the subject of promoting greater public understanding of international development issues which was held by the House of Commons Committee on Foreign Affairs (SCFAIT 1996).

This may have been a first step, albeit limited and delayed, towards what the Foreign Policy Committee had in mind when it closed the chapter of its report on "reforming international assistance" with the assertion of a "need for greater understanding and dialogue on the aid program" and a consequent recommendation for "the establishment of broader-based consultations on development co-operation, including the participation of Parliamentarians" (SJCRCFP 1994a: 58–9). However, this section of the report, like the final musings on democratizing foreign policy making, remained underdeveloped – almost an afterthought. The government's response was accepting but vague, acknowledging a commitment to "information sharing and ongoing consultation" and promising to "work to strengthen its consultative process on development co-operation" and invoking in this regard "future meetings of the National Forum on Canada's International Relations" (Canada 1995b: 73). The formal government statement, *Canada in the World*, released at the same time, addressed somewhat more directly additional ways to strengthen partnerships with NGOs, enlarge parliamentary roles, expand consultative processes, and, not least, establish a new departmental "mechanism ... for foreign policy consultation, research and outreach that will bring together government practitioners, parliamentarians, experts and citizens" (Canada 1995a: 48ff).

Despite this apparent attention, the foreign policy review exercise did not deliver any significant new resources to enable the broadening and deepening of a more deliberative dialogue with Canadians over foreign policy. As the co-chair of the first National Forum, Janice Stein, has observed, it evaded the issues of concrete support "for the organization of the analytic capabilities of the policy community in Canada and for parliamentary monitoring of policy implementation" (1994–5: 56). The second National Forum, held in September 1995, and in which one of the authors participated as a working group chair, returned to the theme of promoting the participation of civil society in developing Canada's international relations and, specifically, encouraging the increasing transnational presence and potential policy contributions of NGOs. Significantly, the other co-chair of the 1994 forum, Pierre Pettigrew, has since become minister for international cooperation and briefly addressed the Commons Committee's April 1996 forum on public understanding of development.

Political leadership from the executive level of government and from parliament is important because some crucial post-review issues remain outstanding. To enlarge participation in productive civil society-parliamentary-government policy dialogues, in which learning can go both ways, will entail a clear and material commitment from the state to such participation, including the creation of appropriate spaces, supported by adequate resources, for deliberative "public judgment" to take place. That the realization of such a project will not be easy is suggested by the conclusion of the co-editors of the 1995 *Canada among Nations* volume: "The foreign policy review was in fact designed to manage stakeholders, not to encourage mass participation. For government officials, an excessively high level of participation would politicize the foreign policy process, alienate business, and hinder the management of the affairs of state" (Cameron & Molot 1996: 21). The hazards of superimposing ambiguous concepts of democratization on a foreign policy establishment (which, moreover, considers itself already overburdened in facing ever more issues with less time and a diminishing budget) are further explored in a recent provocative essay by the editor of *Canadian Foreign Policy*. While Evan Potter agrees that "there is a greater, not lesser, need for closer consultation between Canada's foreign policy practitioners and non-governmental actors," he deflates any illusions about its likely impact:

125 Policy Dialogue in the North: Canada

Many groups outside government seem to be under the misapprehension that there is a direct causal relationship between consultation and influence on policy outcomes. When a policy emerges that does not conform with their recommendations, letters of regret are swiftly remitted to ministers' offices; NGO press releases inform that Ottawa is not meeting its foreign policy targets, a favourite complaint being that Canada's total Official Development Assistance is not anywhere near 0.7 per cent of its G[ross] N[ational] P[roduct]. With the frontlines thus drawn, contacts between non-governmental organizations and policy makers have in the past resembled dialogues of the deaf and paralysed constructive consultations between officials and citizens, which in turn has militated against giving Canadians a larger stake in the decision-making process. This lack of mutual trust ensures that societal pressures make little headway in changing the conduct and directions of Canadian foreign policy. (1996: 15)

It is apparent that the present international policy environment affords no group the benefit of comfortable assumptions and may challenge NGOs to rethink their own approaches (as the CCIC attempted to do.) There is at least a suggestion in Roger Riddell's paper for this volume that NGOs come across more strongly to policy-makers as well-intentioned (but often naïve) moralizing advocates, or as alternative service providers, than as reliable agents of learning and effective problem-solving. Indeed, in regard to the latter, he concludes by quoting a rather humbling admission from an Oxfam-UK paper: "The most striking thing about development practice over the last 30 years is how wrong people have been when they were convinced they were right, and how systems of mis-information become self-sustaining" (Roche 1995: 4). There is no reason to believe the Canadian experience will be an easier one. This is obviously a problem when governments hardly need further reasons to slash spending on "discretionary" expenditures such as international aid. While NGOs may not be responsible for what Ian Smillie refers to as aid administration fatigue, along with government and other sectors they must learn to do a better job of addressing with candour and imagination growing public and political doubts about the effectiveness of much Northern development assistance in achieving aims such as poverty reduction (Boone 1995; Schmitz 1996). They need to communicate to legislators as clearly as possible how what they have learned – from mistakes as well as successes – makes them key participants in policy solutions.

NGOs must also learn to overcome arguments such as that put forward by Kim Richard Nossal to the effect that corporatist "stakeholder politics" tends not to be very democratic at all (Nossal 1996). This too will not be easy because many Canadian NGOs are clients as well as critics of government. Nossal is among those who see Parliament, the country's supreme public interest forum, as the most appropriate venue for a deliberative dialogue on foreign policy to take place. In that regard, Lloyd Axworthy told the SCFAIT, in an early appearance as the new minister of foreign affairs to defend the government's spending estimates (which again reduced foreign aid): "We want your committee to become engaged in helping define our new agenda, and through you, NGOs and interested Canadians ... It would be my wish to make this an annual process, reinforcing the role of Parliament in opening up foreign policy and bringing more Canadians into a dialogue about our role in these changing times ... You must be the main vehicle, the 'clearing house' for exchanges between Canadians, Parliament and Government" (Axworthy 1996: 4).

Yet there is some evident exasperation in the wake of resource cutbacks, which have also affected parliamentary committees, that previous reviews seem not to have done very much to sort out the policy muddles, while the powers that be have also shied from deep structural changes. Policy evolution still seems to be incremental at the margins at a time when bolder actions and choices are called for. For example, following the 1996 budget, a *Toronto Star* editorial of 24 March 1996 urged the government "to fund more research and encourage a free-wheeling debate about the over-all shape of Canada's defence and aid programs ... Parliament can decide, after hearing the arguments. The current approach – trying to do the same things with one-fifth less money in defence and one-third less in foreign aid – looks increasingly like a recipe for not doing very much very well."

Under such circumstances, parliamentary institutions and civil society actors are being invited to a policy dialogue table which may test their patience as well as overwhelm their capacities, especially when these are not being bolstered relative to the tasks at hand. That needs to be stated plainly. And the responsibility for providing the infrastructure to allow democratic policy development to take place cannot simply be devolved by government to parliamentarians and NGOs. It would take another round table to tackle the dimensions of this subject, however, and such considerations should not detract from exploring ways in which existing capabilities for interaction might be utilized most effectively. That may mean learning to accept that there is room for qualitative improvements in parliamentary processes and in NGO approaches which could benefit from, but do not depend on, adding on more resources, and which avoid adding more elements to the policy dialogue process than can be properly attended to.

5 By Way of Conclusions

DEMOCRATIZATION AND THE CHANGING PUBLIC POLICY ENVIRONMENT

This paper has focused primarily on the public policy environment surrounding Parliament and an infrequent policy review process. The lessons learned, however, may be applicable to the much broader daily context of policy development.

Any evaluation of the non-governmental community's role in public policy has to come to grips with the rapidly evolving character of this amplified public environment described above. All signs point to more democratic policy-making, although the pace of change might appear slow to those measuring it in months. In an era of declining resources more democratic and participatory policy-making can make effective use of informed resources outside government to develop better policy, help revitalize political institutions, build greater social consensus, further engage citizens, and build up citizenship and civic space. Governmental and non-governmental policy resources not only need to complement one another but to build new models of horizontal linkages reflecting the fact that both are foreign policy actors.

Discussion of the democratization of policy merits more attention so that all the players, governmental and non-governmental alike, can be clearer in making explicit decisions to strengthen the process and improve its outcomes. This could include ensuring that shared learning takes place. Some of the questions faced are straightforward. How do NGOs improve their policy contributions? How does government facilitate the creation of greater "space" for policy dialogue and a better enabling environment for non-governmental participants? How can greater trust be developed between government and non-government participants? What "confidence-building measures" can be employed? How can all the different strands of international policy development activity be more mutually supportive? How is the public policy process moved from one of managing stakeholders to managing policy development? How can the rules of the game be clarified so that each policy activity has clear objectives and realistic expectations among all participants? How does public policy activity overlap with and relate to citizen engagement and public mobilization? What are the respective governmental and non-governmental responsibilities in each case?

Past experience has shown that intermediate parastatal organizations, such as the Canadian Institute for International Peace and Security, the International Development Research Centre, and the

International Centre for Human Rights and Democratic Development, can use their "good offices" to create new space for developing new ways of working on policy. In light of current financial constraints (and the demise of the Canadian Institute for International Peace and Security), careful thought could be given to promoting "virtual" hybrids, or joint ventures, able to nurture opportunities (including confidence-building measures) for enhanced public policy dialogue. Developing and promoting new institutional arrangements which could expand policy "space" might be an important role for the new Centre for Foreign Policy Development.

In looking specifically at Parliament's role in policy development, one has to ask if the growing expectations of that role (as suggested by the growing complexity of the policy issue "nexus" and government's view that it become the "clearing house") will be matched by the resources dedicated to its committees. The impact of Parliament's policy role depends on its accountability functions as well as its policy development functions.

In international policy, apart from parliamentary forums, there are a large number of consultative activities currently under way. By some accounts, the most effective appear to be the International Trade Advisory Committees and Sector Advisory Groups on International Trade. These business-dominated forums have regular meetings, staff support, and financial resources. What are the lessons here for other policy areas? Recently both DFAIT and CIDA carried out reviews of their range of consultative initiatives. Those reports (unavailable at the time of writing in summer 1996) should form part of the basis for thinking through new and better means to strengthen policy development.

One key preoccupation for those interested in the quality of democratic policy development must be the continuing series of government funding cutbacks. These could significantly reduce the capacity of smaller independent organizations to participate, leaving only larger institutions and a reduced spectrum of experiences and viewpoints. Should the most institutionalized policy development processes be dominated by business or a handful of large NGOs? Or should policy endowment funds be created? Or a policy "lottery" fund-raiser conducted?

RECOMMENDATIONS

- Convening government-parliament-multi-stakeholder initiatives to help clarify the evolving public policy context and current and potential roles for the different participants; in the case of international policy, a joint DFAIT-CIDA-stakeholder task force could review

the performance of existing policy forums, examine international parallel initiatives, and make recommendations; the new policy mechanism in the department and the John Holmes Fund could co-ordinate this activity.
- The CCIC could co-ordinate a review of NGO policy dialogue effectiveness in order to focus recommendations it could make to its membership and government on next steps; perhaps a "learning circle" model, involving other policy active sectors, could be employed.
- Strengthening NGO policy capacity through:
  - strengthening the ability to build and scale up policy knowledge from micro development experience;
  - facilitating a continuing division of labour (to build on the strengths of a diverse community);
  - enhancing learning capacity;
  - encouraging greater collaboration and alliances between NGOs and academics;
  - increasing financial and human resources committed to policy;
  - ensuring capacity to "stay the course" in monitoring ODA policy implementation to ensure accountability;
  - expanding the capacity to relate to other government departments besides CIDA to build and maintain a perspective of the breadth of international policy and to avoid been seen as a "client" of any one department.
- Expanding training modules for civil servants involved in international policy to include multi-stakeholder policy development and consultation; consider joint training sessions involving governmental and non-governmental participants.
- Acknowledging that government has a role "to help improve the performance of Third Sector organizations in their dealings with policy-makers," as highlighted in a report recently commissioned by the Department of Canadian Heritage. Recommended innovations from that report include: establishing model government-third sector policy development relationships; setting up communications with key stakeholders which move beyond annual exchanges; making more broadly available a wider range of information relevant to the policy development process on key issues – "as a means of improving the transparency of the policy-making and decision-making process, government departments should provide stakeholders with an up-to-date account of those officials in various departments and agencies involved with a particular issue" (Voluntary Action Directorate 1995: 26, 27).
- Supporting an enabling regulatory environment for enhanced policy work by revising antiquated rules governing charities. For

example, the Income Tax Act prohibits registered charities from spending more than 10 per cent of their total resources to support political activity, policy included, and many groups primarily involved in advocacy or public education are deemed ineligible for tax status as a charity (Phillips 1995: 17). As government funding declines, a regulatory change is also needed which encourages contributions to NGOs from smaller donors by increasing the size of their tax credit.

From the parliamentary side, we might add a few modest practical suggestions for strengthening NGO policy effectiveness with Parliament:

- Do your homework. If NGOs wish to be taken seriously by policy-makers, they also need to take the political process seriously and to inform themselves as fully as possible about the institutions of parliamentary government that they are trying to influence. If they are appearing before a parliamentary committee, for example, they should make preparatory contacts to ensure they understand the setting in which their presentations will be received. NGOs should also verify that any information they supply is accurate and can be backed up if necessary.
- Establish credibility. NGOs should be able to provide straightforward information about themselves: vital statistics, who they are speaking for, what their aims are, relevant accomplishments, and so on. This is a general rule, but it is especially important for those with a lower public profile. NGOs should not assume that they are "on the side of the angels" or that this should be enough to translate into effective influence. While NGOs should be confident about their distinctive contribution to the policy debate, they should avoid making exaggerated claims or indulging in rhetoric that suggests that they are more representative of the public interest or society at large than are elected members of parliament.
- Know what you want to say and focus your message. In most policy processes, time is limited and information overload a major problem. The parliamentarians NGOs will most want to influence often will have the most crowded schedules. In committee reviews, groups may have only one brief chance to make an impact. They should make it count. Experienced observers of the process know that effective presentations are clear, succinct, and to the point. They avoid jargon and include observations based on direct knowledge of issues which appeals to the concerns of legislators. Longer, particularly more technical, submissions should always include an executive sum-

mary which highlights a limited number of key points and recommendations. Policy prescriptions should follow logically from the analysis offered, not be encoded in abstract philosophizing, or merely asserted as argumentative polemic.
- Be concrete and realistic. It is one thing to be idealistic and visionary, but policy recommendations should be specific and emphasize the achievable. Asking for what cannot possibly be delivered is a recipe for frustration on both sides. NGOs should bear in mind that the Canadian Parliament is not the United States Congress, and that Canada must usually work with many other countries if it is to accomplish its international objectives. No one said that genuine policy dialogue and reciprocity would be easy!

Finally, we want to return to the need for some concrete confidence-building measures to persuade aspiring policy actors to invest significantly in an uncertain exercise of policy deliberation. In a climate of tight, often shrinking, resources, and open scepticism about existing political processes, we need not only expressions of good faith and intentions but working examples of demonstrable benefits from policy dialogue and shared learning in action. With perseverance and political courage, we can build those experiences and new norms.

A sagacious observer once stated that "in an era of ODA resource growth one talks programmes and in a time of cutbacks one talks policy." Welcome to the age of policy!

NOTES

1 The authors would like to thank those who have shared their ideas including Tim Brodhead, Peter Padbury, and staff at the Canadian Council for International Co-operation particularly Gauri Sreenivasan, Rieky Stuart, and Brian Tomlinson, as well as those in government. The authors, of course, remain responsible for the content. This document is the product of a "virtual" Internet-based collaboration.
2 In 1987 *For Whose Benefit?* began by saying that Canada's ODA "is beset with confusion of purpose" (SCEAIT 1987: 7). Six years later the auditor general concluded that CIDA was losing ground in meeting development needs and that "it is difficult for CIDA to concentrate on putting poverty first ... while ... it has commercial and political objectives that do not always lend themselves to dealing with poverty in a direct way" (Canada, Office of the Auditor General, 1993: 31).
3 The 1998/9 figure should be lower because it includes about $200 million for "refugee support," an item that only began to be calculated as part of

ODA in 1993/4. If it is excluded, the ODA/GNP ratio drops to 0.24 per cent in 1998/9.
4 This section shares much of the analysis of the Brodhead and Pratt paper (1994).
5 For example, the CCIC-commissioned study by Ian Smillie (1991) provided a critical framework for looking at Canadian NGO performance.
6 Responsive funding is a block grant mechanism allowing NGOs substantial autonomy in decisions concerning the use of ODA funds.
7 See, for example, the editorial in the *Ottawa Citizen* of 26 January 1993 and a press communiqué issued by opposition party critics on 20 January 1993: "[Lloyd] Axworthy and [Christine] Stewart Object to CIDA's Major Restructuring without Public Input."
8 The CCIC and its members actively participated in Liberal caucus round tables and discussions with caucus members and their legislative and research staff as foreign policy positions were being developed.
9 The CCIC's proposals were significantly influenced by the ideas of Daniel Yankelovich. See, for example, Yankelovich 1991.
10 These recommendations included: ensuring the foreign policy committee enjoys high-level leadership by a secretary of state or knowledgeable backbencher; opening the committee to non-parliamentarians with specialized experience; constructing a committee strategy for citizen involvement; building an expanded and co-ordinated research support based on seconded departmental staff and non-governmental input; creating multistakeholder working groups and other forums to facilitate consensus building on key issues; reaching out and involving provincial and municipal politicians; international committee travel, presentations by international partners of Canadian organizations, and establishment of an international advisory group for Southern contributions and feedback; a media strategy for public outreach and creation of special funding mechanisms for public discussions; mandating the review to include the establishment of objectives for monitoring and accountability mechanisms for follow-up; employing the vestiges of the Canadian Institute for International Peace and Security, then re-profiled as the Cooperative Security Competition Program, for facilitating public contributions to the review (CCIC 1993c).
11 According to Denis Stairs: "The Committee itself could hardly be described as unfriendly [to the Department of National Defence], and from that point of view a collision over fundamental matters of principle was unlikely. The majority of its members had seen military services themselves, some in very senior ranks. Others had important constituency stakes in the defence establishment" (1995: 105). See also Lawson (1996: 102–3).
12 The February 1995 budget made dramatic (and unbalanced) three-year cuts to Canada's international policy programmes. In the first year (1995/6) Foreign Affairs was cut 7.5 per cent, National Defence 4.9 per cent, and

ODA 15 per cent. Over the coming three years the cuts were: Foreign Affairs 17.3 per cent, National Defence 14.2 per cent, and ODA 20.5 per cent (divided 15–0–6.5). In 1995/6 the voluntary sector was cut by a disproportionate 18.5 per cent. The preceding autumn the CCIC had argued in front of the Commons Finance Committee (charged with pre-budget consultations) that the Department of National Defence should be cut dramatically with most of the savings going to deficit reduction and ODA and a lesser amount to Foreign Affairs. The March 1996 budget added a further 7-percent ($150 million) cut to ODA for FY 1998/9.

13 In 1995 the CCIC established a special task force to examine the development community's public mobilization strategies, and its May 1996 annual meeting was organized around the task force's proposals for re-tooling the community's public engagement tactics and strategies (CCIC 1996).

REFERENCES

Axworthy, L. 1996. "Foreign Policy at a Crossroad." Address by the Minister of Foreign Affairs to the Standing Committee on Foreign Affairs and International Trade. Ottawa: DFAIT, statement 96/12. 16 April.

Boone, P. 1995. "Politics and the Effectiveness of Foreign Aid." Working Paper 5308. Cambridge MA: National Bureau of Economic Research, October.

Brodhead, T., & C. Pratt. 1994. "Chance for a Fresh Start: CIDA, the NGOs and the 1994 Foreign Policy Review." Mimeo.

Cameron, M., & M.A. Molot, eds. 1996. *Canada among Nations 1995: Democracy and Foreign Policy.* Ottawa: Carleton University Press.

Canada. 1987/8. *Sharing Our Future: Canadian International Development Assistance.* Ottawa: Supply and Services Canada. Although dated 1987, this report was not released until 1988.

– 1994. *1994 Defence White Paper.* Ottawa: Supply and Services Canada.

– 1995a. *Canada in the World: Government Statement.* Ottawa: Canada Communication Group.

– 1995b. *Government Response to the Recommendations of the Special Joint Parliamentary Committee Reviewing Canadian Foreign Policy.* Ottawa: Canada Communication Group.

– External Affairs and International Trade. 1992. "International Assistance Policy Update." Mimeo. Ottawa. This document was not officially released but leaked to the CCIC.

– Office of the Auditor General. 1993. *Report of the Auditor General of Canada to the House of Commons 1993.* Ottawa: Supply and Services.

Canadian Council of Churches. 1991. *Diminishing Our Future: CIDA: Four Years after Winegard.* Toronto: Interchurch Fund for International Development/Committee on International Affairs, Canadian Council of Churches.

Canadian Study of Parliament Group. 1984. *Parliament and Foreign Affairs.* Ottawa: The Group.

CCIC (Canadian Council for International Co-operation). 1993a. "Preparing for the Twenty-First Century: Canadian International Policy from a North/South Perspective." Mimeo. Ottawa: CCIC, 16 February.

— 1993b. "Notes towards Next Steps." Mimeo. CCIC internal document. February.

— 1993c. *Putting People First: Towards a Canadian Foreign Policy for the 21st Century.* Ottawa: CCIC.

— 1994a. *Building and Sustaining Global Justice: Towards a New Canadian Foreign Policy.* Ottawa: CCIC.

— 1994b. *A Review and Analysis of the [Special Joint Committee] Report's Recommendations.* Ottawa: CCIC.

— 1995a. *"Canada in the World": A Review and Analysis of the Government's Foreign Policy Statements.* Ottawa: CCIC.

— 1995b. *Canada's Voluntary Sector in International Development.* Ottawa: CCIC.

— 1996. *From Donors to Global Citizens.* Ottawa: CCIC.

Charest, J. 1992. "National Statement of Canada to UNCED," Rio de Janeiro, 11 June.

CIDA (Canadian International Development Agency). 1993. *CIDA's Policy on Consultations with Canadian (Civil Society) Stakeholders.* Ottawa: CIDA, 22 September.

— 1996. "CIDA and Canadian Voluntary Organizations: Framework for a Renewed Relationship." Draft. Ottawa: CIDA.

Cohen, A. 1995. "Canada in the World: The Return of the National Interest." *Behind the Headlines* 52 (summer).

Dahl, R. 1992. "The Problem of Civic Competence." *Journal of Democracy* 3 (October): 45–59.

Dionne, E.J., Jr. 1996. "Why the Right is Wrong." *Utne Reader* (May-June): 27–32.

Draimin, T., & B. Plewes. 1996. "Civil Society and the Democratization of Foreign." In Cameron & Molot (1996).

Drucker, P. 1994. "The Age of Social Transformation." *Atlantic Monthly* 277 (November): 53–80.

Elshtain, J.B. 1995. *Democracy on Trial.* New York: Basic Books.

Filewod, I. 1993. CCIC Review of the Department of Foreign Affairs International Assistance Policy Update. Ottawa: CCIC.

Galbraith, J.K. 1992. *The Culture of Contentment.* Boston: Houghton Mifflin.

Gillies, D., & G. Schmitz. 1992. *The Challenge of Democratic Development: Sustaining Democratization in Developing Societies.* Ottawa: North-South Institute.

Greene, B., ed. 1990. *Canadian Churches and Foreign Policy.* Toronto: James Lorimer.

Groupe SECOR. 1991. *Strategic Management Review Report.* Montreal: Groupe SECOR.

Haggard, S., & R. Kaufman. 1995. *The Political Economy of Democratic Transitions.* Princeton NJ: Princeton University Press.
Head, I.L., & P.E. Trudeau. 1995. *The Canadian Way: Shaping Canada's Foreign Policy, 1968–1984.* Toronto: McClelland and Stewart.
Hockin, T.A. 1969. "Innovation and the Decision Makers." In *Alliances & Illusions: Canada and the NATO-NORAD Question,* by L. Hertzman, J. Warnock, & T.A. Hockin, 119–29. Edmonton: Hurtig.
IDEA (International Development Executives Association). 1994. "The NGO Imperative in Canada's Foreign Policy." Mimeo. Ottawa: IDEA, May.
INGO Forum. 1994. "Towards a Canadian Global Policy." Submission to the Special Joint Parliamentary Committee Reviewing Canadian Foreign Policy on behalf of International Non-Governmental Organizations with Secretariats in Canada, Montreal, 17 May.
Keating, T. 1985. "The State, the Public and the Making of Canadian Foreign Policy." In *Contemporary Canadian Politics,* edited by R. Jackson et al. Scarborough ON: Prentice-Hall Canada.
Kingwell, M. 1996. *Dreams of Millennium.* Toronto: Viking.
Lagarde, F. 1995. *Evaluation of the CCIC One World Campaign Public Awareness/Education Component, Final Report,* 31 January 1995. Ottawa: CCIC.
Lapham, L. 1993. *The Wish for Kings: Democracy at Bay.* New York: Grove Press.
Lawson, R.J. 1996. "Construction of Consensus: The 1994 Canadian Defence Review." In Cameron & Molot (1996).
Liberal Party of Canada. 1993. *Creating Opportunity: The Liberal Plan for Canada.* Ottawa: The Party.
Martens, A. 1994. "Foreign Aid & Development Revisited: Reflections with Special Reference to Canadian Aid." In Canadian Foreign Policy: The Position Papers. Ottawa: Special Joint Committee Reviewing Canadian Foreign Policy.
Nossal, K.R. 1989 and 1997. *The Politics of Canadian Foreign Policy.* Scarborough ON: Prentice-Hall Canada.
– 1996. "The Democratization of Canadian Foreign Policy: The Elusive Ideal." In Cameron & Molot (1996).
Page, D. 1993. "The Foreign Service and the Canadian Public." In *The Canadian Foreign Service in Transition,* edited by D.C. Story. Toronto: Canadian Scholars Press.
– 1994. "Populism in Canadian Foreign Policy: The 1986 Review Revisited." *Canadian Public Administration* 37 (winter): 573–97.
Pal, L. 1994. "A World of Difference? Human Rights in Canadian Foreign Policy." In *The Real Worlds of Canadian Politics,* by R. Campbell & L. Pal. Toronto: Broadview Press.
Phillips, S.D. 1995. "Redefining Government Relationships with the Voluntary Sector: On *Great Expectations* and *Sense and Sensibility.*" Ottawa: Roundtable on the Voluntary Sector, November.
Plewes, B., G. Sreenivasan, & T. Draimin. 1996. "Sustainable Human Development as a Global Framework." *International Journal* 51 (spring): 211–34.

Potter, E. 1996. "Widening the Foreign Policy Circle: Democratization or Co-optation?" *bout de papier* 13 (spring): 14–16.
Pratt, Cranford. 1993–4. "Canada's Development Assistance: Some Lessons from the Last Review." *International Journal* 49 (winter): 93–125.
– 1994. "Development Assistance and Canadian Foreign Policy: Where We Now Are." *Canadian Foreign Policy* 2 (winter): 77–85.
Public Policy Forum. 1993. *Making Government Work.* Ottawa: Public Policy Forum.
Putnam, R. 1995. "Bowling Alone: America's Declining Social Capital." *Journal of Democracy* 6 (January).
– 1996. "A Generation of Loners?" In *The World in 1996.* London: Economist Publications.
Riddell, R.C. 1997. "Trends in International Co-operation." In *Strategies of Public Engagement: Shaping a Canadian Agenda for International Co-operation,* edited by D. Gillies. Montreal & Kingston: McGill-Queen's University Press.
Riddell-Dixon, E. 1985. *The Domestic Mosaic: Domestic Groups and Canadian Foreign Policy.* Toronto: Canadian Institute of International Affairs.
Roche, C. 1995. "Institutional Learning in Oxfam: Some Thoughts." Oxford: Oxfam, Programme Development Team, Policy Department.
Rowe, B. 1994. "A Review of Selected CCIC Member and Non-Member Briefs to the Special Parliamentary Committee Reviewing Canada's Foreign Policy – Summer 1994." Mimeo. Ottawa: CCIC.
Sandel, M. 1996a. "America's Search for a New Public Philosophy." *Atlantic Monthly* (March): 57–74.
– 1996b. *Democracy's Discontent: America in Search of a Public Philosophy.* Cambridge MA: Harvard University Press.
Saul, J.R. 1995. *The Unconscious Civilization.* Concord ON: Anansi.
SCEAIT (House of Commons Standing Committee on External Affairs and International Trade, Canada). 1987. *For Whose Benefit? Report ... on Canada's Official Development Assistance Policies and Programs.* Ottawa: Supply and Services Canada.
SCFAIT (House of Commons Standing Committee on Foreign Affairs and International Trade, Canada). 1995. *From Bretton Woods to Halifax and Beyond: Towards a 21st Summit for the 21st Century Challenge.* Ottawa: SCFAIT.
– 1996. "Forum on Promoting Greater Public Understanding of International Development Issues." *Minutes of Proceedings and Evidence,* Issue 9 (18 April).
Schmitz, G. 1987. "Parliamentary Reform and the Review of Canadian Foreign Policy: Where to Now?" Paper presented to the annual meeting of the Canadian Political Science Association, Hamilton, June.
– 1995. "The State, the Public, and the Decennial Refashioning of Canadian Foreign Policy: Democratizing Diminished Expectations or Demanding a New Departure?" Notes for a presentation to the annual meeting of the Canadian Political Science Association, Montreal, June.

- 1996. "The Verdict on Aid Effectiveness: Why the Jury Stays Out." *International Journal* 52 (spring): 287–313.
Simeon, R. 1994. *In Search of a Social Contract: Can We Make Hard Decisions as if Democracy Matters?* Toronto: C.D. Howe Institute.
SJCCDP (Special Joint Committee on Canada's Defence Policy, Canada). 1994. *Security in a Changing World.* Ottawa: Canada Communication Group.
SJCRCFP (Special Joint Committee Reviewing Canadian Foreign Policy, Canada). 1994a. *Canada's Foreign Policy: Principles and Priorities for the Future.* Ottawa: Canada Communication Group.
- 1994b. *Minutes of Proceedings and Evidence.* Issues 22 (2 June), 48 (26 July), and 49 (27 July).
Smillie, I. 1991. *A Time to Build Up: New Forms of Cooperation between NGOs and CIDA.* Ottawa: CCIC.
Stairs, D. 1970–1. "Publics and Policy-Makers: The Domestic Environment of Canada's Foreign Policy Community." *International Journal* 26 (winter): 221–48.
- 1995. "The Public Politics of the Canadian Defence and Foreign Policy Reviews." *Canadian Foreign Policy* 3 (spring): 91–116.
Stein, J. 1994–5. "Ideas, Even Good Ideas, Are Not Enough: Changing Canada's Foreign and Defence Policies." *International Journal* 50 (winter): 40–70.
Taras, D. 1985. *Parliament and Canadian Foreign Policy.* Toronto: Canadian Institute of International Affairs.
Van Rooy, A. 1995. *A Partial Promise? Canadian Support to Social Development in the South.* Ottawa: North-South Institute.
Voluntary Action Directorate. 1995. *Reconsidering the Federal Government's Relationship with the Third Sector.* Ottawa: Department of Canadian Heritage.
Yankelovich, D. 1991. *Coming to Public Judgment: Making Democracy Work in a Complex World.* Syracuse NY: Syracuse University Press.

4 Effective Policy Dialogue in the South: Pakistan's National Conservation Strategy

ABAN MARKER KABRAJI

This paper offers a practitioner's view of lessons learned in the business of environment and development in the countries of the South, most specifically in Pakistan. Many of the views of non-governmental organizations (NGOs) on policy dialogue and development aid are derived from personal experience and a knowledge of what works and what doesn't in the complex and byzantine world of Pakistan's body politic.

There are sound objective reviews of the role the World Conservation Union (IUCN) has played in the changing environmental landscape in Pakistan, and there are a plethora of reports and studies on Pakistan's National Conservation Strategy (NCS). While they are listed at the end of this paper (see, for example, Runnalls 1995) and I refer tangentially to their findings, I have tried to break new ground by filling in some gaps and drawing out some particular threads of the canvas to highlight the more subtle and less obvious features of an extraordinarily complex picture.

What makes for success in a policy formulated between a government and an NGO? Many things of course, but perhaps the most important of all is integrity – of purpose, of goal, of intellect, and of accountability. It is such amorphous nuances that this paper attempts to track and document using as a case-study the policy dialogue in Pakistan on the development and implementation of the National Conservation Strategy.

Pakistan's NCS is viewed as a success story: of policy impact within the developing world, of Canadian aid, and of the genre of strategies variously called national conservation strategies, national environmental action plans, green plans, or sustainable development strategies, depending on the year, the country, and the donor. But this explosion of plans is fairly new and when work began on the NCS in 1985, the IUCN had only the vaguest inkling of what it was about to achieve, and very little real appreciation of the potential of the process that the NCS would generate. At that time – pre-Brundtland, pre-Agenda 21, pre-Rio – the only lead came from a slim document called the World Conservation Strategy which had been prepared jointly by the United Nations Environment Programme (UNEP), the World Wildlife Fund (WWF), and the IUCN. This document introduced the concept of *sustainable development* and stressed that its objectives should be pursued and implemented through the framework of a national strategy.

In 1985, a number of circumstances combined to launch the process of developing a national conservation strategy in Pakistan, but perhaps the most critical was the genuine need for one that was perceived by the inspector-general of forests, a civil servant who was a visionary but who also knew how to work with a resistant, even unyielding, system of government. Although it is an unfashionable concept to espouse in developmental terms, the value and impact of individuals in societies like Pakistan where there is a major breakdown of the mechanisms of governance and a historical residue of mismanagement must not be underestimated. In a nation in a state of dysfunction, there is room for individuals and institutions to carve out niches and establish relationships that would be difficult if not impossible to achieve in more settled, institutionally robust societies. Chaotic systems create space for individuals and institutions to work in ways that ordered well-run systems do not.

To work within those spaces successfully, however, the individual or institution must have a thorough understanding of the role and impact of power and its manifestations within the political landscape of the developing world. Only then can a successful policy dialogue be achieved. Without it, there is a grave danger that any initiatives that intend to challenge and alter the status quo in any fundamental way will be unsuccessful, and in this context, "unsuccessful" may not be manifested just as a matter of failure to succeed but in the elimination of the person or institution who dared to challenge the status quo. Thus, survival and growth in themselves become indicators of success and political savvy, a prerequisite for successful policy dialogue, drawing the critical dividing line between incremental change which earns respect and grudging admiration or a backlash that earns the proponent scorn and contempt and will bury good ideas until memory dims.

THE NATIONAL CONSERVATION STRATEGY OF PAKISTAN

On 1 March 1992, the cabinet of Pakistan approved the National Conservation Strategy (GOP/IUCN 1992a). This 406-page document had been prepared by a team of experts over a three-year period under the supervision of the deputy chairman of the Planning Commission, one of Pakistan's most powerful bureaucrats. It had involved more than three thousand people through workshops, comments on drafts, and other consultations. The document begins by describing the stark reality of the country's deteriorating resource base and the consequent implications for an economy that is still largely based on natural resources. It then sets forth the beginnings of a plan to integrate environmental concerns into virtually every aspect of Pakistani economic life.

The NCS has three overriding objectives: conservation of natural resources, sustainable development, and improved efficiency in the use and management of resources. Reaching these goals depends in turn on three operating principles: first, achieving greater public partnership in development and management; second, merging environment and economics in decision-making; and, third, focusing on durable improvements in the quality of life of Pakistanis.

Part I of the report surveys the state of Pakistan's environment in the broadest sense by examining the quality of its land, water, and air, its energy use, the health of its people, and the institutions and policies that deal with these concerns.

The report points out that less than 20 per cent of the country's 88 million hectares has the potential for intensive agricultural use – an amount which nearly matches the current area under cultivation. In addition, among today's states, Pakistan has one of the smallest percentages of land surface covered by forest in the world (4 per cent). There is ample scope for increased agricultural production through multiple cropping and higher yields per hectare. However, to achieve this level of intensity, serious problems of water and wind erosion, salinity and sodicity, waterlogging, flooding, and loss of organic matter from the soil must be tackled. Deforestation must be arrested and reversed.

Pakistan relies on irrigation for more than 90 per cent of its agricultural production. Although the amount of water available per acre has increased by more than a third over the last thirty years, the efficiency with which it has been used has not. Even when measured by the standards of the rest of Asia, the efficiency of Pakistan's irrigation system is low. Only about 30 per cent of the water diverted from the river systems actually reaches the crops. The rest is lost in poorly maintained, largely unlined, often weed-infested canals and watercourses and through poor farming practices.

The arid and semi-arid rangelands which cover much of the country are in poor condition because of chronic overgrazing and poor maintenance practices which are responsible for productivity losses of up to 40 per cent. In a dry country like Pakistan, such misuse is often a prelude to desertification.

Pakistan's considerable marine resources are under threat. Untreated urban sewage, mangrove cutting, siltation, and unplanned urban development affect the coastal areas, particularly those around Karachi. Fresh water resources are becoming increasingly polluted.

As the report points out, Pakistan is both energy poor and energy profligate. Rural dwellers have little access to commercial energy sources and are often forced to rely upon the nation's dwindling forest resources and other biomass for fuel for cooking and heating. Yet the "modern" sector uses the commercial energy that is available very inefficiently. Pakistan's energy use per unit of the gross national product is as high as that of the United States, one of the world's most wasteful energy consumers.

Pakistan suffers from high levels of pollution. Only half the urban excreta is disposed of in sewers, and virtually none of that is treated before it flows into the rivers and the sea. While 44 per cent of the population has access to piped water, surveys of most urban locations suggest that none of that water is safe for human consumption. Gastrointestinal diseases account for more than a quarter of all hospital cases, and approximately 60 per cent of infant deaths are due to infectious and parasitic diseases, most of them waterborne. The national report of Pakistan to the United Nations Conference on Environment and Development estimated that 80 per cent of illnesses and 40 per cent of urban deaths were caused by unhygienic water (GOP/IUCN 1992b).

Untreated sewage has contaminated many of the country's rivers and streams. The NCS cites the example of the Ravi River downstream from Lahore where pollution has cut fish production by 5000 tons a year. Solid waste is also a problem. Only about half of the country's solid waste is collected by the municipal authorities. In Karachi, a city of 11 million people, only 55 per cent of households have garbage collection. Most of these wastes are disposed of in poorly sited and badly maintained dumps. The balance of the city's household wastes is simply left on the street or dumped on vacant land. Nor are domestic wastes the only pollution problem. A 1985 survey of 100 hazardous chemical industries by the Pakistan Council for Scientific and Industrial Research showed that only three plants treated their wastes to commonly accepted standards.

As if current problems were not sufficiently serious, the report points out that Pakistan's population growth rate of 3 per cent a year is one of the highest in the world. And even the most optimistic forecasts do not see that figure dipping below 2 per cent for at least twenty years. With at least 122 million people, Pakistan was the world's tenth most populous and fourth most densely populated country in 1992. At the current rate of growth, it is estimated that Pakistan will double its population in twenty-three years. Therefore, without major changes in Pakistan's current development pattern, efforts to provide these quarter-billion people with a decent standard of living will result in environmental and poverty problems which would dwarf the current crisis.

But the NCS is not a document of gloom and doom. Most of the report deals with solutions to these problems. Part II contains detailed recommendations for various sectors of the economy. It makes a strong statement about the urgency of merging economics and the environment in decision-making and the use of economic instruments rather than regulation to control pollution. It also identifies a series of cross-cutting intersectoral programmes for population, education, communications, research, and the role of women.

Part III contains sixty-eight different programmes which would boost the government's spending on projects broadly related to natural resource management and the efficiency with which resources are used from about 4 per cent of national investment to 8 per cent by 2000. Perhaps most important, it sets out a wide-ranging set of recommendations to reform the way in which economic decisions are made. Fourteen core areas are listed as priorities:

- maintaining soils in croplands;
- increasing irrigation efficiency;
- protecting watersheds;
- supporting forestry and plantations;
- restoring rangelands and improving livestock;
- protecting water bodies and sustaining fisheries;
- conserving biodiversity;
- increasing energy efficiency;
- developing and deploying renewables;
- preventing and abating pollution;
- managing urban wastes;
- supporting institutions for common resources;
- integrating population and environment programmes;
- preserving the cultural heritage.

Since the adoption of the NCS by cabinet and its subsequent publication, some steps have been taken to ensure its implementation.

WHY PAKISTAN?

At first glance, Pakistan would seem to be an unlikely candidate to produce the best plan for environmental improvement and sustainable development among the 50 or more countries which have prepared conservation strategies, national environmental action plans, and the like. Throughout much of its history the country has been ruled by repressive or unstable regimes. Indeed, since the time the NCS was first conceived in 1985, there have been some dozen changes of government.

Pakistan has experienced a rapid rate of economic growth by South Asian standards. Real gross domestic product has grown at roughly 6 per cent per annum since the 1960s and per capita income has more than doubled since 1972. Yet, "in 1990, 80% of the population still had no sanitary facilities and close to one third of the population were classified as living below the poverty line. Between 1970 and 1990, adult literacy increased by only 15% cent, to just 35% of the population. For women, the situation is much worse: 79% of Pakistani women have received no formal education ... As a percent of total government expenditures, the Pakistani government's budgets for health and education are among the lowest in the South Asian region – about half the level of neighbouring countries like Sri Lanka and Bangladesh" (IUCN 1993b: 9).

Caloric intake in Pakistan is below the mean for other low-income countries, and life expectancy and infant mortality rates compare unfavourably with those of poorer Asian countries. And the human rights records of some of its governments have been the subject of much comment by international organizations such as Amnesty International.

Why then has the NCS taken root so firmly in Pakistan? The answer lies partly in the international environmental debate which has been unfolding since 1972, partly in the strategy's approach to sustainable development, and partly in the "made-in-Pakistan" nature of the plan. Its success rests on a combination of factors, often dimly understood, some serendipitous and some planned, which made for a successful policy dialogue among the three key partners, the government of Pakistan, the Canadian International Development Agency (CIDA), and the IUCN.

THE KEY PARTNERS

A number of recent studies analyse the way the government of Pakistan functions (much as any post-British colonial civil service) and offer suggestions about how it should be restructured to serve the needs of a modern state more successfully, but it is generally accepted that the key lies with strong, enlightened, political leadership: leaders who are willing to put aside the ties that bind to land, feudal structures, the military oligarchy, and the addiction to absolute power in favour of the principles and demands of genuine democracy. It may well be true that in the developing world more than anywhere else (with the sterling exception of Nelson Mandela) "the natural resource in scarcest supply of all is good political leadership" (Ramphal 1993).

Thus those who must wrestle with the task of exerting policy influence upon the government of Pakistan must also contend with the need to understand the severe limitations within which it functions. Not only is the structure systemically flawed, and responsive to political whim rather than to reason and plans, but there is little hope within the present political environment of the sort of leadership emerging that will direct or allow for the dismantling of the status quo in the short or medium term.

How do donors and organizations like the IUCN operate in this environment? If one assumes that the primary purpose of development aid is to improve the quality of life of the people of the country in question (whether because of the old-fashioned ideals of altruism or the new globalized vested self-interest), then it is inevitable that even though the framework for official development assistance remains government to government, in circumstances in which the state is ineffective, the preferred mechanism for delivery of that aid lies with the voluntary and private sectors.

This situation, in turn, unleashes tensions and forces among these players as they negotiate positions of ownership, influence, and accountability. The institutions that achieve their goals will be those which demonstrate the ability to comprehend that the playing field is not level, and was never intended to be, but that "leading from behind" can get the players where they want to go.

Not all NGOs are capable of playing such strategic roles, nor, frankly, do they need to be. Policy dialogue and influence can work at various levels, and the origin, composition, and raison d'être of the average NGO (Northern or Southern) defines its role in policy influence. Arguably, it is only a particular kind of hybrid institution which combines aspects of both government and NGO that is allowed to play so strategic a role. Building on Korten's (1989) definition of the three institutional sectors – commercial, government, voluntary/NGO – it is clear that a new sector is emerging. This is the world of the government-organized NGO (or GONGO), a hybrid entity combining features of both government and NGO. This fourth sector institution increasingly appears to be the shape of things to come as state and market change form and function. The IUCN is one such organization.

Founded in 1948, the World Conservation Union brings together states, government agencies, and diverse non-governmental organizations in a unique world partnership. It is one of the very few international organizations that both governments and non-governmental bodies can join. The IUCN's present membership is 865: 72 states, 100 government agencies, 603 national NGOs, 56 international NGOs, 34 non-voting affiliates. This membership is drawn from 133 countries. The stated objectives of the IUCN are:

- To ensure the conservation of nature, and especially of biological diversity, as an essential foundation for the future.
- To ensure that when the earth's natural resources are used this is done in a wise, equitable, and sustainable way.
- To guide the development of human communities towards ways of life that are both of good quality and in enduring harmony with other components of the biosphere.

Taking advantage of its unusual structure, the emphasis in the IUCN's work is on partnership. The union provides a neutral forum where organizations from different sectors can meet, exchange views, and plan joint action. It builds partnerships between governments and environmental organizations – whether to develop a conservation strategy, to test a new idea through a field project, or to build local and regional capacity. The union has helped many countries to prepare national conservation strategies, and it demonstrates the application of its knowledge through the field projects it supervises and supports. Its operations are increasingly decentralized and are carried forward by an expanding network of regional and country offices located principally in developing countries.

The IUCN's work is driven by the needs of its members. It works to strengthen them and to help them accomplish their individual missions. To do this, the IUCN provides information and technical knowledge based on the latest science. It promotes a common approach to the world's environmental problems, ensuring that lessons learned in one place or context are available in others. And as a global advocate for the environment, it represents the views of its members on the world stage.

As an employee of the IUCN, I am acutely aware that one could be accused of bias in supporting the argument that it is only hybrid institutions like the IUCN – which, chameleon-like, can identify with and be owned by both government and NGO – which can forge the sort of relationship that was demonstrated when CIDA, the government of Pakistan, and key NGO and private sector players in Pakistan created the policy dialogue which makes the NCS work. But it is important to grasp the essence of the argument, namely, that only those institutions that can demonstrate the ability to function in this hybrid role (and their origins and own internal structure of governance usually determine this) will become players of real influence in effecting macro-policy change. Most NGOs and advocacy groups are good at having an impact at the local or micro-policy level where relationships are usually adversarial and change comes from winning and losing. More sophisticated and complex macro-policy change is the work of institutions which can have an impact on government mainly because they are accepted as trusted collaborators and allies – almost as extensions of the government machinery itself.

THE PROCESS

When Pakistan's inspector general of forests approached the IUCN in 1983, it was as a member-state of the IUCN requesting technical assistance from the organization. The IUCN did two things: organize an assessment, and look for a donor. At that time most strategies were requested by and developed by ministries and consultants from the traditional IUCN heartland sectors of forests, wildlife, and parks. This was consistent with the original impetus of Pakistan's NCS. It was the choice of assessors that probably set the NCS onto a different and broader track. The initial survey was done by an economist from the London-based International Institute for Environment and Development who was on the cutting edge of sustainable development thinking and by a historian who was aware of the importance of central planning. They insisted to the government of Pakistan, and their local representative, that to respond adequately to the request for assistance would mean developing the NCS within the Planning Division because the essence of the strategy was to create a multi-sectoral plan which cut across the traditional sectoral structures of government. This recommendation was resisted by both the requesting ministry and by Planning; the former for reasons of turf, and the latter because it thought the project of little importance. A compromise placed development of the strategy in a newly created environment division within the Ministry of Urban Affairs but, at the IUCN's insistence, under a committee headed by the deputy chairman of the Planning Commission, a former civil servant who had once tried forest management as a district commissioner and who took a personal interest in environmental issues. Once such a prominent person had agreed to head the NCS steering committee, it became much easier to convince both donors and the institutions of government to take the process more seriously.

The proposal went out to donors and CIDA agreed to fund the original prospectus, provided a Canadian was employed to do it. Tied aid can be a millstone or an opportunity depending on how it is handled. Viewed as an opportunity, one can respond by insisting to the donor that the very best from their country be used and, with a little effort, the recipient country can be in a position to name the person and products they want. Most bureaucracies are too diffident or too lazy to pursue this course on their own, but in partnership with a non-governmental institution which is willing to share the risk and which makes good quality a prerequisite of its projects, it becomes possible.

Thus, the NCS benefited from a Canadian who brought with him not only a good knowledge of the issues but also a remarkable ability to make friends and lead from behind (projecting the bureaucrat as always in the lead). He also was experienced in using the round table process and the "search conference" format and in the practice of consensus building through participatory planning. It cannot be stressed enough how radical this concept of consultation and participation was and still is in the Pakistani governmental context. Its use in the creation of the NCS accounts for much of the strategy's subsequent success, and a decade later it is still the approach used for most environmental initiatives that stem from within the NCS family of policies.

Government anywhere is wary and mistrustful of public consultation in the formulation of policy, but most particularly in countries with a history of failed democratic processes. To some extent, environmental issues were a fortuitous choice to try out these techniques in Pakistan because in the mid-1980s these issues were viewed as marginal to political processes and therefore safe areas in which to experiment. There is, however, another reason for their success: the more complex but important interrelationship between the institution outside government (the NGO) and its perceived character and credibility. The IUCN offered the advantage of being both "international" with quasi-United Nations status (since Pakistan belonged to it as a state, as did other government agencies) and also national in character (headed and staffed mostly by Pakistanis). Thus while the Canadian consultants might work on the substance of the strategy, they did so under the partnership umbrella of the government of Pakistan and the IUCN which was perceived to be national in character. This arrangement created legitimacy and trust. It was seen as Pakistani-to-Pakistani and so it was far easier to challenge the bureaucrats we worked with in the context of "our needs," "our agenda." In fact, there was many an occasion when introducing the objectives of the NCS that an attempt was also made to introduce the IUCN which was barely known inside the country, and the bureaucrat's response was "that's okay, but the basis upon which we work with you is that we know you, we know where your people are coming from, and thus we trust you."

As the years passed, this response has been internalized and evolved into trust in the institution, but that was earned on the basis of initial trust in the individuals who represented it. This is an advantage which many a national NGO also has but is only gradually learning to use, namely, to establish credibility with government by being up front with "who you are" and "where you are coming from."

It is also worthwhile for the NGO to assume a core nationalism in most civil servants, and to appeal to it. When we speak to government, we speak of an agenda which is important to all Pakistanis, stressing that "we are in this together." In twenty years of work in the development business, I have never met a bureaucrat who is unresponsive to this appeal and who, when approached in this manner, does not listen. A productive and successful NGO-government partnership must be based on mutual respect for each other's role in society, and an appreciation of the power balance. In the mid-1980s (under the military regime of Zia-ul-Haq) this was seen to lie entirely with the government. But as the forces of globalization, free trade, and democracy increasingly affect Pakistan, spaces open for those who wish to push consultative and participatory agendas. In these circumstances, the visionary within the bureaucrat emerges to work the system in a way that opens up room for policy dialogue – between government and other sectors. The recent public consultation (government, private sector, NGO) on the formulation of the new Environmental Protection Act is one such example.

All these avenues were explored and traversed as the NCS was formulated. Once the search conference built the consensus required to identify the main environmental issues of concern, and the NCS prospectus emerged, CIDA agreed to fund the next step, the writing of the strategy itself. A small IUCN-managed team of Canadian advisers and Pakistani project personnel was placed in the Planning Division, to consult, commission, and workshop their way through issues, sectors, and policy impact. Using the increasingly popular participatory approach for the process, public hearings (borrowed from the Brundtland Commission's methods and the Canadian experience) and village meetings were held. Government, NGOs, and the private sector all participated, and the critical reaching out to stakeholders – and the sense of ownership of the NCS that resulted – was thus begun even as the document was being formulated. This approach allowed for policy dialogue between government and stakeholder, using the partnership with the IUCN as the "implementing agency for the project."

THE PARTNERSHIP

The partnership between the government, the donor, and the IUCN has been in place for eleven years, and under the present arrangement for full NCS implementation is to continue until the end of the decade. Over the years, all three partners have adjusted their positions based on perceived needs, the reality and fashions of aid, international trends, and the personalities of the decision-makers. The styles have changed as CIDA has changed over the last decade, as the government of Pakistan has had to respond to the many different administrations in power since work on the NCS began, and as the IUCN (Pakistan) has grown from a one-person outfit to a 120-person programme. With the completion of the NCS document, the government partners became both the Environment Ministry and the environment section in the Planning Division. It is significant that during the formulation of the NCS, the area of government concerned with environment grew from the status of a division to a full ministry, and as with the IUCN, it was the design and subsequent implementation of the policies of the NCS which powered that growth.

On completion, the NCS was adopted as Pakistan's environmental plan by the federal cabinet in 1992 and subsequently by all donors who designed their environmental aid programmes within its framework (including, under duress, the World Bank, which grudgingly accepted its equivalence to a national environmental action plan, thus making Pakistan eligible for funding from the Bank's soft-loan window).

The relationship with CIDA has perhaps been the most pivotal in the success of this policy exercise, and it is doubtful that, apart from the individuals who were directly involved, there is full comprehension within the agency of the true impact of the $20 million which will have been spent over two decades when the project draws to a close. Two major environmental institutions been created and strengthened (the Sustainable Development Policy Institute – SDPI – and the IUCN in Pakistan), one (SDPI) specifically to advise government on policy formulation and to do the attendant independent research which makes the findings credible. The process itself has spawned awareness and become a driving force for change, for democratization, for NGO mobilization, for private sector dialogue with government, and for the translation of the implementation of the national strategy into the provinces through provincial conservation strategies.

CIDA initially approached the process very much in the conventional mode of bilateral aid, government to government, viewing the IUCN's role as that of a quasi-consultant or technical agency. There was an early presumption that once the work of the document was completed, the role of the IUCN would be fulfilled, and the serious business of implementation could then be left to the government. Fortunately, there were enough people in the agency, both in Ottawa and Islamabad, who realized that this was not a conventional infrastructure project with the IUCN offering its usual technical advice. A review was commissioned by CIDA to chart the way forward (Ramsay et al. 1992). The CIDA-sponsored team concluded that it was crucial that the IUCN remain a partner with the government in order to maintain institutional continuity and commitment to the process. CIDA came to perceive the IUCN not as a mere executing agency (although that may still be the technical terminology) but as a full institutional partner which was as important to the project's success as the government of Pakistan itself. This was, for a bilateral development agency, a major shift in perception of an NGO's role, and its very useful spin-off was the greater legitimacy and credibility given to the IUCN in the eyes of the government. A tripartite partnership composed of special relationships among NGO, government, and donor thus emerged. It was extended to the institutions created by the NCS (such as the SDPI) and to the style and design of the provincial strategies. These strategies were developed in the heart of the provincial planning process (placed in planning and development departments, reporting to the additional chief secretary who chaired a multi-sectoral steering committee) and forged the same tripartite relationship between donors, government, and the IUCN.

During this process CIDA had also to deal with the issue of contracting a relatively large project through its bilateral aid programme using a non-Canadian organization. It was able to do so partly by arguing that Canada is also a member of the IUCN, partly by emphasizing the unique institutional development nature of the project, and partly by allocating a major chunk of funding for Canadian linkages through a Canadian partner organization (which, significantly, reports to the Pakistani implementing partners). By doing this, CIDA also acknowledged the importance of institutions that do not function in the consultancy mode.

The procedures of most aid agencies make it mandatory for bids to be presented for major projects. While these methods may have the virtue of competition and accountability, they are skewed against the involvement of NGOs or other institutions which are not structured to bid for projects. In Pakistan, consulting companies are viewed by most government agencies as primarily concerned with profit, with little interest in or commitment to quality and accountability, and with their primary loyalty to their paymaster, the donor. They are therefore subject to manipulation, graft, and bullying, and generally not taken very seriously except as deliverers of reports. Most significantly, their products are treated in a cavalier "take it or leave it" fashion, since their style and modalities of work seldom allow for real ownership or involvement in the development of the product by the government counterpart. A consultant who works outside the continuum of an institutional framework risks being seen as transitory and unaccountable and, as a consequence, his or her product is viewed as peripheral to central concerns, unless it is politically expedient to do otherwise. Had the NCS been formulated in the usual bilateral style, by a Canadian consultancy reporting to the government of Pakistan, it is highly likely that the report would today be languishing on a dusty shelf in a government department like so many other worthy policy documents.

The partnership between government, NGO, and donor agency created in the case of the NCS is now mirrored increasingly in the environment/development world of Pakistan. The consequences of the partnership, and its considerable demands on all partners, as well as the attendant conflict resolution, productive work patterns, and shifting turf and power bases are a matter of analysis and discussion elsewhere. The lessons are still being learned and documented but perhaps the primary achievement is the realization that such a model can emerge, can work, and could form a new paradigm for NGOs and governments to explore elsewhere with donors involved in development aid.

THE LEARNING

A great deal of knowledge has emerged from the NCS process: some learning has occurred by osmosis within the NGO world, the rest through a multiplicity of workshops, papers, newsletters, and academic studies. These are some of those lessons:

- The worlds and reality of NGO, government, and donor are different. This may seem platitudinous, but it is important to remember when one is trying to work together. The reality from which each operates is so dramatically different and the power bases of the three so enormously uneven that unless the imperatives that drive the different institutions are factored into the dialogue, there is usually a breakdown fairly early on. This is particularly true in the case of the NGO which attempts to work with a Southern government (their own) and a Northern government (donor).
- While the basis for dialogue and joint project planning might ostensibly be a development goal, it is political expediency that drives and frequently hijacks the process. Thus the NGO often has to play a

flexible and nimble role as an honest broker simultaneously juggling donor priorities, project goals, and government imperatives while ensuring the process stays on track. The more successfully an intermediary NGO institution does this, the more likely it will gain the respect of the other partners.

- To present one's institution as credible to government, there must be a clear agenda and legitimacy of origin and purpose. Integrity and honesty of agenda, an ability to prove one can deliver what one says one will, and a sense of alliance and commitment to national goals are essential attributes of successful government-NGO partnerships and dialogues.
- Institutions outside government that appear viable and secure and offer a challenging work environment attract the brightest and the best of local talent and manage to retain them. Donors have yet to appreciate the enormous positive impact on development such institutional capacity-building provides. Only too often institutions they have helped set up are left struggling for survival after arbitrary project cycles come to an end because time and resources were never provided for the Holy Grail of "financial sustainability" to be achieved. In the absence of endowments or any secure revenue from government for NGOs in most Southern countries, donor reluctance to make long-term commitments to institutions rather than to projects leaves most NGOs to lurch from project to project with little time to devote to the work of policy design and influence. Until donors and development aid seriously address the issue of the financial viability of Southern NGOs, it is unlikely they will find many institutions that will be able to play a serious role in macro-policy dialogue.
- To work successfully with both the government of one's own country and that of the donor, it is essential for the NGO to study and be responsive to the imperatives of both. In the case of the NCS, a constant flow of information through the Canadians with whom the IUCN worked helped both in interpreting and advising responses at an official level and in assisting the more informal behind-the-scenes dialogue. One was prepared, for example, to gear up to "results-based management" by having forewarning of the changing mood at CIDA.
- The greater the flexibility and capacity of the NGO to change style and modality in the dialogue, the greater the chances of success. Some sensitive issues are best addressed behind the scenes, others are best approached through public dialogue. Some issues yield to consensus building and negotiation; others are non-negotiable and require a combination of strong advocacy and, sometimes, confrontation to be retained. Much of the work of the NCS followed a simul-

taneous route of public and private dialogue, with elements of advocacy, consensus building, and negotiation running through both. It is however important to remember that transparency and accountability are in the non-negotiable category. Any compromise on either and one risks the questioning of one's integrity and objectives, which in turn leads to a loss of credibility with one's constituency and a negative backlash on the partnership's integrity.

- With the exception of institutions such as the SDPI, the Aga Khan Development Network, and the IUCN, there are few institutions in Pakistan today that can engage in effective policy dialogue. This is not to say that a number of smaller NGOs are ineffective. There has been much effective change at the micro-policy level, particularly in the new models of rural support programmes that have emerged, but the impact is limited to their geographical spread and has not in most cases worked back into macro-policy. This is a gap that the NGO sector has not bridged. Many of the reasons for this failure derive from the origins of the NGO sector in Pakistan. Suffice it to say that the potential to engage with government on macro-policy issues exists, but save for the few institutions mentioned above, such dialogue is not evident except at the micro-level or on issues with a direct impact on the NGOs. (One example is the recent bill which represents an attempt by government to regulate and control the NGO sector). The capacity to engage in international or regional dialogue is similarly constrained, although this is beginning to change within the circle of NGOs which form the IUCN's membership in Pakistan because by being members of the IUCN they effectively become part of a global network, linked with Northern NGOs and advocacy groups.
- An important emergent area of effective policy dialogue which has been largely ignored so far is that between the NGO and the private (business) sector. As trade, the Internet, and the World Trade Organization affect the environment in which government, NGO, and private sector operate, a dialogue on issues of national interest becomes more and more important. A recent illustration of this was the hard bargaining to build a consensus among business, government, and NGOs for the implementation of the National Environmental Quality Standards in Pakistan.

In conclusion, it is probably fair to say that we are still a long way from learning all the lessons from the work done on Pakistan's NCS. This paper offered an initial and tentative attempt at drawing out the most important features from the perspective of a practitioner. Its aim is to spur debate and discussion among those who share the goal of developing the new partnership paradigm.

REFERENCES

Brown, D.L., and D.C. Korten. 1989. *Understanding Voluntary Organizations: Guidelines for Donors.* Washington: World Bank.

Burki, S.J. 1996. "If We Do Not Wake Up in Time." *Dawn* (Karachi), 2 June.

GOP (Government of Pakistan), Environment and Urban Affairs, and IUCN. 1992a. *Pakistan National Conservation Strategy: Where We Are, Where We Should Be, and How To Get There.* Karachi: GOP & IUCN.

– 1992b. *Pakistan National Report to UNCED.* Karachi: GOP & IUCN.

IUCN (World Conservation Union). 1993a. "Flash in the Population Pan." *NCS Bulletin* 5 (March): 8–9.

– 1993b. *The Way Ahead: IUCN's Programme in Pakistan.* Karachi: IUCN.

– 1996. *Mission, Objectives and Activities.* Brochure, Gland.

IUCN, UNEP, and WWF. 1980. *World Conservation Strategy: Living Resource Conservation for Sustainable Development.* Gland: IUCN.

Morgan, P., W. Backler, H. Baser, R. Malpas, Z. Qureshi, and N. Sipra. 1996. *Capacity Building for the Environment: A Background Study for the Pakistan Environment Programme.* Karachi: IUCN.

Morgan, P., Z. Qureshi, J. Holmberg, and N. Sipra. 1993. *Capacity Building for the Environment: A Review of IUCN – The World Conservation Union in Pakistan.* Karachi: IUCN.

Qureshi, S.A. 1995. *Background Paper on Governance Issues and Pakistan 2010 Report.* Islamabad: World Bank.

Ramphal, S. 1993. SDPI-IUCN Distinguished Lecture on Sustainable Development.

Ramsay, J., D. Beckett, F. Bregha, and T. Gangopadhyay. 1992. *Building on Success: Directions for Canadian Support for Implementation of the National Conservation Strategy in Pakistan.* Ottawa: CIDA.

Runnalls, D. 1995. *The Story of Pakistan NCS: An Analysis of its Evolution.* Karachi: IUCN.

Schwass, R. 1992. *Implementation Design for the NCS for Pakistan.* Karachi: GOP & IUCN.

Smillie, I. 1995. *The Alms Bazaar: Altruism under Fire – Non-Profit Organizations and International Development.* London: Intermediate Technology Publications.

United Nations Development Programme. 1992. *Balanced Development: An Approach to Social Action in Pakistan.* Islamabad: UNDP.

World Bank. 1991. *Managing Development: The Governance Dimension.* Washington: World Bank.

World Commission on Environment and Development (Brundtland Commission). 1987. *Our Common Future.* New Delhi: Oxford University Press.

5 Strategies of Public Engagement

ERIC YOUNG

No doubt most of the development community would agree that development is still the most urgent challenge facing the human race. The problem lies with the lack of broad acceptance of this view in the North. Does this arise from the fundamental failure of past attempts at development communication? Is it a failure of development itself to deliver on its promise – in marketing terms, there's an old adage: "nothing kills a bad product faster than good advertising." Or is it a failure of public will in the face of problems whose scale and complexity seem so daunting? I believe that there is some truth in all three of these suggestions.

Clearly, twenty-five years or so of development communication have failed to produce a critical mass of public understanding in the North about the issues, urgency, and realities of development, and the presumed support that would come from such an understanding. At the same time, however, is it not possible that the public's understanding, though intuitive rather than grounded in knowledge, is not far off the mark: that foreign aid has been largely ineffective, that "three decades of foreign development assistance in the Third World have failed to lift the poorest of the poor in Africa and Asia much beyond where they have always been" (French 1996)? Finally, is it perhaps simply asking too much of people who are wrapped up in the confusions and anxieties about the direction of their own lives to factor into their consciousness a meaningful concern for places and people that they will never know, for those whose plight, though profound, is faraway?

WHAT DO PEOPLE THINK?

The pollster's dipstick has been dropped into the Canadian psyche fairly regularly to measure attitudes to and support for development. What does it reveal?

Well, the picture isn't entirely clear.

On complex issues, opinion is a shallow measure of what people really think. Development is a complex issue; and these are complicated times. Government spending has been a fairly easy target for public opinion in recent years. But on today's fiscal battleground, it is becoming increasingly evident to the public that government spending is not simply a spectator sport. Canadians face crucial and painful decisions which call into question their shared values and principles, which challenge their heritage of institutions and social capital, and which directly affect the way they live together as a people and the way as a people they live together with the rest of the world. Pollsters ask for their opinions on all kinds of issues. They reply with relative ease (anonymously and without accountability) by selecting from codeable multiple-choice responses, but they are rarely given an opportunity to say: "I'm confused as hell and can't take it any longer."

There are those who seek to understand the public mind and plot the direction of public purpose by poring over survey results as though they were tea leaves. (Professional pollsters are more cautious in their interpretations.) But tea leaves are inert. The human mind is not. Ideas are not fixed. Perceptions and choices are shaped by context. Indeed, context is critical in seeking to make any useful sense of public views on international development co-operation. Reading papers – drawn from a variety of sources – on the state of public support for development assistance, the term "compassion fatigue" crops up fairly regularly. As well, there are a considerable number of references to the resilience of humanitarian compassion in public sentiment. Neither of these assessments should be discounted lightly.

Some of the apparent instability of public opinion can certainly be attributed to differences in survey techniques and approaches. But, more significantly, it indicates the weak grip the development issue has on the public mind. The rise and fall of measured support for development does not reflect the shifting attitudes of an *engaged* public. Quite the opposite. Development is poorly understood, rarely considered, and not a major preoccupation of most people.

Most people in Canada appear to feel that we have some obligation, as a rich country, to provide assistance to those in need in the rest of the world. This opinion seems to have tracked at a fairly consistent level (about 70 per cent in agreement) over the last twenty years. Most

Canadians felt a sense of compassion and moral responsibility in 1977. And most feel it now. But how deeply? While there are strong pockets of *support for* and *opposition to* development assistance at the ends of the spectrum, researchers classify at least 60 per cent of the population as essentially neutral in their views.

Spending on foreign aid is another matter. Here research reveals a marked erosion in public support. Over the last ten years, the number of Canadians who believe that the country spends too much on aid has risen steadily from about 15 per cent to just under 50 per cent of the population. Only one in ten Canadians now believes that not enough is spent on aid (down from one in four in 1985).

Yet another way to gauge the strength of public support for aid is to see how it stands up in competition with other potential areas of government spending. Here it fares very badly. In a 1994 study which asked Canadians to rank nineteen areas of public spending, aid came dead last. Development assistance is a weak competitor in a field of pressing concerns. This status is particularly significant in an era of deficit-driven decisions and aggressive social restructuring. Compassion is not dead – but it is not sufficiently vital or focused to translate into meaningful resistance. Development may be the most urgent challenge facing the human race, but it does not have much political valence in Canada. There is no public outcry when budgets are slashed. And, at election time, the issue is hardly on the agenda; international co-operation has no part in shaping voter behaviour. At best, Canadians are fair-weather fans of foreign aid.

Support for development faces intense competition not only from other priority issues but also from people's perceptions. Indeed, it is interesting that opposition to development assistance is not stronger in light of the serious misgivings about it which have been brewing for some time.

For the most part, people see a wall of problems, not solutions. They have little sense – and even less understanding – of development. Rather, they view the Third World as a place of intractable misery. A sense of crisis – not a vision of progress – shapes their perceptions. The widespread sense of hopelessness, which is reinforced constantly by media reports and fundraising campaigns, understandably fuels responses that range from apathy to antipathy. While clinging to the belief that "we must do something," the conviction that "nothing we do can make a difference" has become deeply entrenched. There is, as well, a very widespread sense of mistrust. A large majority of Canadians (80 per cent) believes that Canada's aid never reaches the intended beneficiaries. They are cynical about government involvement in foreign assistance – perceiving waste, inefficiency, and mismanagement at this end and blatant corruption at the other. They are inclined to trust non-governmental organizations (NGOs) over government for the delivery of aid, but they believe there are too many organizations and that this profusion contributes to the problems of waste and inefficiency. And while they are predisposed to assistance that "helps people to help themselves," 60 per cent of Canadians remain concerned that aid promotes rather than relieves dependency.

With little or no substantive understanding of development, people are moved primarily by a sense of moral discomfort and altruism. They are discouraged by a sense of futility. There remains some feeling of obligation but little sense of personal relevance or self-interest. People see international development assistance essentially as a one-way street. Increasingly, they suspect it is a dead end.

This is what Canadians seem to think about international development assistance. When they think about it. But that isn't very often. Most of the time they are thinking about the idiot boss, the ailing parent, the cute thing the baby did, the deteriorating neighbourhood, getting a new car, getting out of debt, getting a job, getting a mate, getting home to watch *Seinfeld* and, maybe, the news. People's lives are here. Their broader concerns are naturally focused on their own well-being and the well-being of those they care about – especially at this time of waning confidence in the future. The economy, jobs, health care, education, crime, and community problems matter in direct and material ways. Sustaining a way of life while reinventing the infrastructure that provides it is the accepted challenge – by some people with reluctance, by others with eagerness.

Nevertheless there are core values at play underneath these immediate challenges. These are not lost in changing times. Indeed, probably more than ever, people now want their values to be addressed and engaged. In a recent major study of Canadian values, the researchers noted that "discussion group findings shed a different light on public values than what might be assumed as a result of shifts in the electoral process ... In offering a 'grey zone' for discussion that avoids the confines of polarized political and ideological debates, the public judgment process elicited opinions that contrast with the results of recent Canadian elections" (Peters 1995). (That discourse yields very different ideas than top-of-mind opinion has important implications for the engagement of the public on development issues – a point to which I will return.) The Peters study goes on to observe that in twenty-five discussion groups in eight cities across Canada, participants were almost united in their adherence to the following values: "self-reliance; compassion leading to collective responsibility; investment, especially in children as the future generation; democracy; freedom; equality; and fiscal responsibility." Another study reports that Canadians desire "a search for real change; higher ethical standards; ... individual participation; a moral community; and people first investment" (Ekos 1994).

These people were not, of course, talking specifically about international development. They were talking about the kind of society they want to live in and want their children to inherit. But within the values they espouse, there are seeds of hope for renewed support for development among Canadians – or, to put it somewhat differently, for engaging their interest in the kind of *world* they want to live in and want their children to inherit.

In some ways, of course, global considerations have begun to shape the public perspective in Canada. The country's political and economic leaders have been hammering home the need to compete effectively in a global arena. Canadians are coming to view the world as an integrated circuit of global markets, global capital, and global communications. Development NGOs were early promoters of the theme of global interdependence. But it is global competition – with its attendant risks and opportunities – rather than global co-operation which is shaping the dominant frame of reference. Still, this opening of a global perspective (made more possible as the psychic dismantling of the Berlin Wall changed our view of international relations) offers some potential for engaging meaningful public interest in global co-operation. However, it must be recognized that while globalization is a dynamic new story, development is an old and tired one.

One final observation on what people think about development. Many commentators have noted the poor quality of public opinion on this issue. People's ideas are rooted in a very shallow base of knowledge or understanding. They have little familiarity with the nature of the problems being addressed, the kind of programmes being delivered, and the longer term perspective. Even the term "development" is almost meaningless. Their sympathies are visceral, their values are charitable, and their expectations are simplistic. It is no wonder that ambivalence – rather than outright support or opposition – characterizes the public response to development.

The gulf between public and expert understanding of the issue seems enormous. And yet, at one fundamental level, both informed and ill-informed opinion appear to be arriving at the same place. How different really is the public's lack of confidence from that of the experts? Within the development community, there is much pessimism, uncertainty, and talk of crisis. This concern is not focused just on the state of financial support. For some, it has led to calls for a re-examination of the basics. So, in acknowledging the pressing need to renew public confidence in official development assistance (ODA), it is important to ask: is the development community attempting to convince the public of something about which the community itself is not convinced?

PUBLIC ENGAGEMENT – IN WHAT?

Dwindling political support for development assistance has made the need to find new and effective strategies for public engagement all the more urgent. But the perceived need to engage the public is not new. In Canada, there has been a generation of development education programmes and multiple communications initiatives by players like the Canadian International Development Agency, the Canadian Council for International Co-operation, Aga Khan Foundation Canada, and other individual NGOs (to say nothing of countless fundraising campaigns). Though in comparison with those of marketers of beer, toothpaste, or banks, budgets have been constrained, over the years tens – perhaps hundreds – of millions of dollars have been spent on development communications (again excluding fundraising campaigns). There have also been serious attempts to develop a fairly comprehensive strategic orientation to the challenge, both in Canada and internationally. These studies provide good and thoughtful analyses of the problem. Yet in surveying the literature, it strikes me that a fundamental question receives little attention: what do we actually want people to do? Past discussions have focused much more on the *techniques* of engagement than on the *outcomes* of engagement. But in the long run, it is impossible to craft techniques and co-ordinate them into a clear strategy for change if there is no clarity about outcomes.

The fundraising strategies of development agencies are, of course, clear about what they want people to do: send money. But is money still the primary motivation of broader development communications efforts? The emotional, simplistic, and often paternalistic approaches of fundraising campaigns are often criticized as counterproductive to the aims of promoting deeper public understanding of the issues. Is the real purpose of development education essentially to get the public to voice its support (directly to government officials and indirectly through opinion polls) for the protection of aid allocations? Or are there other meaningful roles the public can play? Does the development community view the public (collectively) as a necessary third-party endorser of its activities, or does it believe that the thoughts and actions, input and involvement, of ordinary citizens in the North are a critical component of future attempts at global co-operation and development?

Public engagement is a costly undertaking. It costs money, time, energy, and attention; intellectual, creative, and emotional resources;

leadership and management involvement; and a significant level of participation from a network of (inevitably strapped) allies at the grassroots level. So it is important to consider whether the undertaking is worth the effort. Various studies suggest that while "it is widely taken as axiomatic that there is close correlation between expressed public support for aid and government spending on it ... evidence for this is in fact less than clear" (Winter 1996: 4). And Roger Riddell (1997) cites studies by G.R. Olsen and V.W. Ruttan which indicate that public opinion seems to have little bearing on the decisions of governments about development aid policies and allocations and that "the influence of the popular view will be reduced still further in future" (Olsen 1996: 352).

This is not an argument for abandoning public engagement strategies but for clarifying them.

If development is still the most urgent challenge facing the human race, if the escalating polarization of wealth, power, consumption, opportunity, and well-being is dangerous and abhorrent, and if the increasing "ghettoization" of vast numbers of disenfranchised fellow human beings is to be resisted forcefully rather than accepted as inevitable, then it is understandable that those who have been working in and for development should feel that it is imperative to close the "sensibility gap" between themselves and the public. And if today's world is a globally interconnected one, then it is only right that foreign policies should reflect the values of people, not simply the interests of state and market.

But this brings us back to the fundamental question: what do we in the development community want people to do? Are there practical ways for people to become involved, to convert moral discomfort, good intentions, and a desire to make a difference into meaningful action? In other words, before addressing the question of how to engage people, we must work out the ways in which people can be engaged. Otherwise, public interest will be lost in the gap between concern and action.

A sense of efficacy – personal and/or collective – in the minds of target audiences is a highly significant precursor to effective attitude and behaviour change. This is one of the important lessons from social marketing campaigns which have attempted to influence change on issues ranging from fitness, smoking, AIDS, and drinking and driving to healthy environments and community revitalization. Information alone does not produce transformation; messages, by themselves, are relatively weak motivators of change. People must be able to see clear and concrete paths of action, believe their action will make a difference, and feel it is within their means to take action. So, for example, telling junkies to avoid drugs because of the risk of AIDS is not likely to have much impact. A much more effective approach (attuned to the realities of the target audience) is to promote clean needle use and to make that a viable approach by demonstrating needle-cleansing techniques and providing convenient and non-threatening opportunities for needle exchange.

Without a sense of efficacy and opportunities for involvement, there is nowhere for people's anxieties or good intentions to be channelled.

Over the last ten years or so, the environmental movement has been good at making the connection between broad concerns about the environment and specific actions people can take. "Think globally/act locally" makes sense because there are some very direct ways for people to engage. By recycling, choosing environment-friendly products, walking or cycling to reduce automobile use, participating in community clean-ups, and so on, people can participate in the solution. They are encouraged to take action when they see others like them taking action. (This is another important lesson from effective social marketing campaigns – the perception of peer interest, involvement, and momentum is a powerful influencer of attitude and behaviour change in others.) People know that their actions alone, and even the aggregate of actions by their fellow citizens, will not be sufficient to solve the environment crisis. But once they have taken some personal responsibility and action, they also become more demanding in the action and responsibility they expect from governments and corporations.

In the development area, the success of child sponsorship programmes demonstrates the same link. Clearly, these programmes provide a meaningful and sustainable form of engagement for many people. They are widely scorned within the development community as sophisticated money grabs (from mostly unsophisticated people), as misleading, and as trivializing the real issues. But this leads again, then, to the question: where are the more appropriate – but equally engaging – alternatives for people who wish to get connected?

NGOs see popular participation in the South as essential to successful development there. Does the same hold true in the North? Does public involvement by Northern publics genuinely contribute to development? Or do NGOs really view the public as the third point of a triangular relationship, with government and themselves at the other two points – and see public involvement as important only in so far as it is able to influence government to make decisions about policy and dollar allocations congruent with NGO interests?

Perhaps as the development community grapples with the strategy for and structure of development assistance in these challenging times, answers to these questions will become clearer.

In this light, however, it is interesting to reflect on comments made by Chris Rose, the campaign programme director for Greenpeace-UK, in a lecture on the future of environmental campaigning (1996): "There is an increasing move to recognize politics without politicians ... People increasingly want to base actions on values. If the formal political system does not allow them to do this, they will find other ways ... in the future, environmental campaigning will be based much more on new, informal political processes, such as between NGOs and companies and the public as consumers, than on old, formal, malfunctioning political systems. There will be much more direct action, whether it is occupying a tree in the path of a road or the use of your money as a consumer. These actions and the consequent 'environmental agenda' will be based more on arguments about ethics, values and responsibility than on 'science' and policy."

Rose goes on to talk about Greenpeace's relatively recent decision to adopt what he calls "solutions campaigning" strategies: "The point is not whether these are complete solutions. The scandal is that industry could do much which it is not doing. We know from supporters that one of the great turn-offs of environmentalism is its perceived negativity: campaigning *against* things, bringing *bad* news – the doom and gloom brigade. We campaign on solutions because it is an effective way to speed up positive change."

Solutions campaigning also makes sense for development. The point is not simply to tell positive stories about what has worked, but to move aggressively to make it clear that extraordinary progress is possible. In this way a moral and pragmatic imperative for development is established. If the situation is hopeless (and if there is no legitimate role for ordinary citizens), people can be excused for turning their backs; but if solutions are possible, they are simply abrogating their most basic human responsibilities and, at the same time, sacrificing their own future security. The challenge is to demonstrate and facilitate meaningful ways for ordinary people to become involved.

FROM PUBLIC OPINION TO PUBLIC IDEAS:
TOWARDS A COMMON SENSE

People who develop social marketing campaigns (I'm one of them) try to pay a lot of attention to the preconceptions, knowledge, values, priorities, anxieties, desires, social circumstances, and information sources of those we seek to influence. "Think backwards from the target market's place and point of view" is a credo of the discipline. It is in the understanding of the audience that strategic opportunities are identified. Some of my remarks to this point have reflected this orientation. It makes sense to think about people when we are thinking about public engagement. It makes sense to respect their starting positions, the quality of their ambivalence, the strength of their values, the legitimate tensions between their self-interests and more altruistic inclinations, their capacity for judgment, their habits of withdrawal. However, it is important to consider not only the dynamics of human nature but also the dynamic nature of ideas themselves.

Ideas have a life in society. And society has a life around ideas. Not everyone has to be informed or even in agreement for certain ideas to have a shaping force on collective decisions and actions. The environment, gender equality, deficit reduction, global competitiveness, and "Nike is cool" are all recent examples of such interaction. History provides thousands more. In stable societies, shaping ideas rule with little opposition. But in changing societies, the competition of shaping ideas is turbulent and intense. Thus, when we in the development community speak about public engagement in international co-operation, I think what we really mean is that "the most urgent challenge facing the human race" should become one of the shaping ideas in our society and in our time – that it should become a driver, not a victim, of other priorities.

How do certain ideas come to have this force? How do they become the matter of public belief? Noam Chomsky once said: "When you get to cultural patterns, belief systems and the like, the guess of the next guy you meet at the bus stop is about as good as that of the best scientist. Nobody knows anything. People can rant about it if they like, but they basically know almost nothing" (1993: 72).

Here are some guesses from my bus stop. We use the term "public" loosely, as though it refers to something real and identifiable. The public comprises many individuals, as alike and different in attitude, temperament, circumstance, and personality as you are from your neighbour or the next stranger at the bus stop – and as distinct from the general category of "public." There is no public. But there are public ideas. Individuals hold private ideas. But we are held together as a public by shared ideas. The life of a public idea is different from the life of a private idea.

A public idea takes time to form. Its genesis may be rooted in the expertise and/or conviction of a small number of people, but it passes through gateways into the broader social arena where it is shared and shaped by many. The process is not so much one of consensus as of convergence. What wasn't important becomes important; what was marginal becomes mainstream. The collective perspective shifts; collective priorities become realigned. A public idea is a social construct, and it has social consequences. Its influence is normative. Trivial, dumb, dangerous, and progressive ideas can all follow this course. From the clothes we wear to the goods we covet to the enemies we demonize to the common good we define, we can see the pattern at work. The "Red menace" helped etch the dividing lines necessary to sustain the Cold War's energy in the West. In the East, the red tab on Levi jeans helped to erase those lines.

About twenty years ago, the British biologist Richard Dawkins developed a theory of something he called "memes." Essentially he proposed that ideas can be thought of as organisms with their own evolutionary force. Technical and conceptual inventions, cultural artefacts, and moral and organizational systems are all memes. Some survive and replicate with enormous vigour; some die away quickly. Human consciousness is the environment in which memes breed. Attention is the energy they require to evolve successfully.

In his book, *The Evolving Self,* Mihaly Csikszentmihalyi draws upon the concept of memes in arguing that an adaptive response in human consciousness is necessary if we are to achieve a more harmonious and sustainable future. The ideas that fuel social transformation "must be shared to become effective ... Values are so ephemeral that they require the joint psychic input of a group to retain their hold on each person's attention ... To face the third millennium with confidence we must join together in a community of shared belief about the future" (1994: 281). Whether one takes the concept of memes literally or metaphorically, it helps in understanding that the kind of ideas that shape society and shape the future are formed in a process of complex cultural interaction.

Public engagement must thus be viewed as a *public* activity. And it is not just a matter of public learning, but of public discovery. Information and rational argument play a part, but so too does an emerging *common* sense of how things are and might be. In other words, public engagement requires not only an engagement with ideas but also an engagement with others around ideas.

In a very real sense, then, the term "public engagement" really refers to "citizen engagement." Our interest is not simply in the aggregate of everyone's private thoughts about international development at any given time but in the collective view that is shaped, and the directions, priorities, and responsibilities that view entails. The word public means "of or pertaining to the whole, done or made in behalf of the community as a whole." It is a product of interaction, not an arithmetic sum of individuals. As Benjamin Barber says: "common civic activity constitutes what we mean by political judgment. The journey from private opinion to political judgment does not follow a road from prejudice to true knowledge; it proceeds from solitude to sociability ... Political judgment is defined by activity in common rather than by thinking alone ... citizenship suggest[s] individuals transformed by membership in a political association into common seers who produce a common judgment" (1988: 199).

We Canadians have not arrived at common judgment around international development. We have not – as a public – taken a measure of the consequences and our own accountability. This is not to say that we are oblivious to the issue. It has some affinity with our values; but it has no political weight.

Daniel Yankelovich, one of the deans of public opinion research and an extremely thoughtful commentator on the nature of communication in a democratic society, offers an important perspective on public judgment – both the concept of judgment and the practical implications for nurturing it more effectively. In his words, public judgment differs from both expert and public opinion in that it exhibits: "(1) more thoughtfulness, more weighing of alternatives, more genuine engagement with the issue, more taking into account a wide variety of factors than ordinary public opinion as measured in opinion polls, and (2) more emphasis on the normative, valuing, ethical side of questions than on the factual, informational side" (1991: 5).

Public judgment is not a measure of what people know, or simply what they think, but rather what they have resolved after a process of meaningful consideration. The process for arriving at public judgment is both psychological and dialogical: people have to be given the time (and motivation) to "work through" their internal resistances, inconsistencies, and conflicts around an issue. There also has to be a legitimate form of deliberative discourse between experts/leaders and lay citizens and among citizens themselves. I would argue that the process for arriving at public judgment is also observational – people have to see that the issue is being taken seriously in the public arena, that respected opinion leaders and institutions are responsibly engaged.

Yankelovich stresses that "engaging" the public – especially on issues that are morally demanding and where change or sacrifice is required – is an altogether different process from "selling" the public on an issue or policy. The latter takes the form of conventional top-down and one-way communication aimed primarily at informing and persuading. It implicitly assumes that lack of information is the key factor characterizing the gap between public and expert opinion. And it implicitly neglects the complex web of values, convictions, prejudices, anxieties, life experiences, and capacity for judgment people bring to issues of public importance. It does not give people the credit, or time, or framework for true deliberation. Yankelovich suggests that "instead of seeking to inform and persuade as in the top-down model, leaders need to stimulate people to be more thoughtful, to confront their own prejudices and resistances, to embrace long-term goals as opposed to the impulses of the moment, to weigh the pros and cons of policy choices seriously and responsibly" (Yankelovich & Immerwhar 1994: 49).

Yankelovich is absolutely right in advocating this approach. I believe that if this approach were more integrated into Canadian political processes, it would go a long way towards restoring the essential qualities of trust and accountability that have leached out of our practice of democracy. However, it is important to assess whether, in practical terms, an NGO-led public engagement initiative could command the sustained media participation that would be required to see it through on a sufficiently large scale.

Although the frame of reference was somewhat different, it could be argued that past efforts at development education did attempt to engage the public in a more substantive, thoughtful, values-based working through of the issues. Development educators may have been successful at helping those they reached come to a deeper understanding and more supportive judgment of international co-operation. But a generation of development education did not produce a substantial enough result throughout the population. There was little to no diffusion effect and no critical mass was achieved.

To mobilize international co-operation as a public idea, it will almost certainly be necessary to direct some significant effort to "influencing the influencers." The term influencer is used here to denote those people who can command some degree of public attention and who have some effect on public thinking – a relatively small élite comprising political leaders, business leaders, the media (editors and influential journalists), public intellectuals, and social commentators (those the English refer to as the chattering classes). Whether we like it or not (Yankelovich, for one, views it as a dangerous trend), élites increasingly set the terms of the public debate in our society. Whether they like it or not, élites are increasingly forced to deal with an agenda of significant change; that is to say, their focus is not on protecting the status quo (which is different from protecting their interests) but on reinventing social and institutional priorities and practices.

In the United States in particular, think-tanks have played a powerful role in germinating and legitimizing ideas. Think-tanks on the right are the cauldrons in which conservative ideas (and ideals) have been reinvigorated and given new force. Not simply places of research and scholarship, they have become more and more adept at marketing their ideas. Position papers, lectures, books (and promotional tours), op ed pieces, compelling spokespeople, sound bites, and sound arguments are all part of their working arsenal of "influencing tools." As influencing organizations, they have an impact not only on policy-making but on the agenda of issues around which public debate forms. Some of these organizations may work on campaigns aimed directly at the public, but for the most part it seems that much can be accomplished by targeting (and sustaining) communication to influencer audiences. In other words, it is possible to mobilize a public idea not only by being a popularizer of an issue but also by being a crystallizer. Clearly, convincing influencers is a different exercise from attacking them, or pleading for their support. It requires the ability to transmit conviction as well as knowledge.

Probably more than other elements of society, élites understand (some of) the global realities of today's world. If development is still the most urgent issue facing the human race, the lack of understanding and/or attention to this challenge among élites is a serious impediment to progress. The urgency of the challenge must begin to shape their frame of reference and their lexicon. Again, the strategic purpose here is not just to influence their decision-making but to stimulate their capacity to disseminate the idea into the public sphere – to help move it from a marginal to a mainstream priority, to help transform it into a public idea.

But is the development community currently positioned to marshal and market a compelling case for development to influencers? Certainly, the prevalent world-view, values, and aspirations within the community of élites will often be a source of resistance. However, the obstacles to influence may not reside only in the audience. To some degree, the development community exists in an ideological and self-referential bell jar. For those who are not insiders, the language of that community may seem opaque and the reasoning suspect. If the broader society is to rally around a common sense that international development is essential, perhaps more than anything the development community itself will have to find a voice of leadership – a voice that communicates moral clarity, enthusiasm, and a genuine sense of possibility.

LOOKING AHEAD

How then should the development community proceed if it is to persuade people to become engaged in and supportive of international development co-operation?

Engage People in a Vision

Despite the competition of and preoccupation with other pressing social and economic concerns, I believe that the single biggest obstacle to revising the response of people to development is the current overriding perception that the situation in the Third World is hopeless and that interventions by the developed countries are futile. This mind-set is rooted not only in the negative images to which people are exposed with crushing regularity but also in a fundamentally charitable response to the problem. People are moved to act primarily from purely altruistic motives rather than from the hope of achieving a lasting transformation. Therefore, a crucial step in building public support is to smash through feelings of hopelessness and engage people in "a vision of possibility."

I do not minimize the challenge. First, the general temper of these times is neither optimistic nor confident. Secondly, the development community itself seems dispirited and equivocal. Like "the best" in Yeats's apocalyptic poem, they seem "to lack all conviction." Can a dramatic case be made for possibility? If so, it should be founded in a sense of *people's* capacity to make a difference. This is why the current burgeoning of civil society around the globe is so significant. My hunch is that this phenomenon provides a foundation for building an inspiring new vision; but it is for those who are expert in the realities of development to determine whether this is truly a reason for renewed hope.

Assuming that a vision of possibility can be crafted, it cannot be projected in small compartmentalized pieces of information. If one wants people to see the big picture in a different way, that picture must be painted for them. It can be substantiated with details, but it should not require a laborious, educative, and information-driven process before people can grasp the vision.

Creating a vision of possibility does not mean diminishing a sense of urgency or consequence. Development should be positioned as the most urgent challenge facing the human race. It does have a profound bearing on the world we live in and will leave to our children. Rampant poverty and the increasing polarization of wealth and opportunity do destabilize the social ecology as much as pollution and overconsumption destabilize the natural ecology. Our future depends upon our will and ability to redress that balance.

Engage People in Dialogue and Action

While a vision of possibility can probably be projected through one-way communication, it will be important to engage as many people as possible in the kind of deliberative dialogue that Yankelovich talks about.

There are some models for this. In the United States, the Kettering Foundation has developed an extensive network encompassing hundreds of communities across the country which allows ordinary citizens to meet to deliberate and work through large issues of national concern. These forums have dealt with issues like the environment, crime, immigration, the public debt, health care, education, and freedom of speech. As Yankelovich says, "the Kettering Foundation has succeeded in taking the concept of choicework out of the realm of theory and putting it into everyday practice" (1991: 248). While the discussions are very open, they are not unstructured. Kettering has spent considerable time developing an effective model for these forums. It creates a framework that positions and describes the issue in terms that are relevant to the lay public and then provides several viable choices that represent different perspectives (with different implications for action) on the issue. There are no straw dogs in these choices. A good part of the art is to present the options non-judgmentally, giving credibility to each perspective. In other words, the forums have no manipulative intention, save for trying to foster a thoughtful and constructive deliberation. It is in working through the choices with one another that people move from their initial opinions to more considered judgments. Participants arrive at a view (not necessarily consensual) of the direction society should take on an issue. They may also determine specific actions that they can take, either as individuals or as a small group, to get involved.

In Canada, a project based on these principles called The Society We Want has recently been created. (This was done for the Canadian Policy Research Networks and grew out of their research project, Exploring Canadian Values.) A number of national organizations have signed on as partners and are mobilizing community-level discussion groups through their own networks. These kinds of discussion groups hold a lot of promise. However, it is important to stress the obvious: they don't happen automatically. They require a great deal of work at the developmental stage and even more work at the implementation stage to ensure widespread adoption and acceptance.

As a corollary to engaging people in dialogue, I would suggest that to obtain a more sensitive and nuanced understanding of how people think about international co-operation, the development community should rely less on opinion surveys and more on the kind of qualitative research that focus groups yield.

Earlier in this paper, I asked: what does the development community actually want people to do? Engaging people in dialogue is constructive, but I still believe it is essential to give people meaningful opportunities to become actively involved. I am not sure what those opportunities are. However, I am certain that we should not assume a continuum that imagines vast numbers of people moving from ignorance to awareness to political activism. Some people will follow this progression, of course, and, where appropriate, that should be encouraged. But some people will never be activists, and this attitude should not preclude offering them opportunities for other kinds of involvement – as students, consumers, investors, donors, professionals, and members of domestic civil society organizations.

Engage Influencers

I have already noted the importance of influencing the influencers, and there is little more to say except to stress that the time may be opportune. As Peter Drucker says: "Every few hundred years in Western history there occurs a sharp transformation ... Within a few short decades, society rearranges itself – its worldview; its basic values; its social and political structures; its arts; its key institutions ... We are currently living through just such a transformation" (1993: 1).

Within the ranks of today's influencers, a transformational agenda has been embraced and the concept of globalization has taken root. Notwithstanding the general swing to the right and the idolization of the marketplace as the fairest organizer of human interaction, there also seems to be a growing recognition (among some) of social interdependence and the fragility of existing systems. The concept of social capital and the importance of a strong civil society (as a basis for viable democratic and economic systems) is beginning to receive some attention. Marketplace values may be ascendant, but the theme of corporate social responsibility is definitely on the map. The traditional lines of opposition – or even demarcation of public, private, and third sector responsibilities – are becoming blurred.

Of course, ideas like "the good society," "the importance of our children," and "securing a future they can inherit" receive more support in homily than they do in practice. But vectors of thought can become vectors of action. Those with a genuine interest in social, environmental, and global well-being are right to mistrust lip service (and self-service); but it is also important to recognize where the potential for convergence of agendas and momentum for positive change exists.

Ted Newall, in his speech as retiring chairman of Canada's Business Council on National Issues (1995), identified poverty as "*the* national issue where we must focus our energies and resources." Newall, of course, is a firm believer in a competitive private sector but that did not prevent him from saying to his corporate peers: "I suggest to you that one of the most critical measures of success in our society, and one of the most critical measures of whether or not that success can be sustained for the long haul, is the quality of life for those in our society whose income is in the lowest 20%. Our highest priority for using the wealth created by growing economic success should be raising the quality of life for this segment of society."

It should not be an impossible stretch to make global human security a factor in this perspective.

REFERENCES

Barber, B. 1988. *The Conquest of Politics: Liberal Philosophy in Democratic Times.* Princeton NJ: Princeton University Press.

Chomsky, N. 1993. *The Prosperous Few and the Restless Many.* Berkeley CA: Odonian.

Csikszentmihalyi, M. 1994. *The Evolving Self: A Psychology for the Third Millennium.* New York: Harper Perennial.

Drucker, P. 1993. *Post-Capitalist Society.* New York: Harper Business.

Ekos Research Associates. 1994. *Rethinking Government '94: An Overview and Synthesis.* Ottawa: Ekos.

French, H. 1996. "Second Thoughts on Foreign Aid." *New York Times,* 12 April.

Newall, J.E. 1995. "BCNI Past and Future: A Reflection." Speech delivered at Members' Dinner, Toronto, 24 April.

Olsen, G.R. 1996. "Public Opinion, International Civil Society and North-South Policy since the Cold War." In *Foreign Aid towards the Year 2000: Experiences and Challenges,* edited by O. Stokke. London: Frank Cass.

Peters, S. 1995. *Exploring Canadian Values.* Ottawa: Canadian Policy Research Networks.

Riddell, R.C. 1997. "Trends in International Co-operation." In *Strategies of Public Engagement: Shaping a Canadian Agenda for International Co-operation,* edited by D. Gillies. Montreal & Kingston: McGill-Queen's University Press.

Rose, C. 1996. "The Future of Environmental Campaigning." *RSA Journal* (March).

Winter, A. 1996. *Is Anyone Listening? Communicating Development in Donor Countries.* Geneva: United Nations Non-Governmental Liaison Services.

Yankelovich, D. 1991. *Coming to Public Judgment: Making Democracy Work in a Complex World.* Syracuse NY: Syracuse University Press.

Yankelovich, D., & J. Immerwhar. 1994. "The Rules of Public Engagement." In *Beyond the Beltway,* edited by D. Yankelovich and I.M. Destler. New York: Norton.

Future Directions

DAVID GILLIES

The question which binds the essays in this book is whether systematic learning can enhance the capacity of development organizations to influence policy and to strengthen support for their objectives amongst the public. The issues were approached largely from the vantage point of the non-profit sector. More specifically, how are Canadian non-governmental organizations (NGOs) to adjust to increased funding pressures and reorient themselves in an aid system in which Southern NGOs are increasing in importance?

A key message that emerges from the essays is that the "old story" of development has lost some of its appeal and relevance both within the aid community and among the wider public and the political élite. Development organizations need to move beyond their long-time focus on working through specific programmes and projects and integrate their overall objectives with the larger agenda of interconnected global issues. Without abandoning the focus on poverty reduction and capacity-building, these organizations must consider how their work is affected by a range of transnational issues such as migration, environmental degradation, population, civil conflict and complex human emergencies, democracy, human rights and good governance, the arms bazaar and the drug trade, global disease, and North-South economic relations.

TRENDS IN INTERNATIONAL CO-OPERATION

Development organizations have to adjust to several current trends in today's world. These include an accelerating, market-driven globalization of national economies, the reduced role of the state in delivering public goods, the increasing importance and capacity of Southern NGOs and civil societies, growing material inequality both within and between countries, a reduction in real terms in the volume of global aid, and the declining relevance of aid in financial flows to the South and in determining the economic and development prospects of developing countries. While this constellation of influences is prompting reflection among development professionals about the fundamental purposes of aid, about the apparent fall in donor support for development assistance, and about future aid management, the current sense of fatigue is nothing new. The aid regime has faced "crises" before and they have been overcome.

While no direct connection can be drawn between international trends and action to maintain public support for development assistance (in view of the diversity of aid agency missions, resources, and capacities), Roger Riddell argues that campaigns to increase public engagement should not be focused defensively on issues such as the volume of official development assistance (ODA) but should be framed more positively around aid quality and the voiced needs of recipient countries and communities.

This does not mean that the voluntary sector can abandon the issue of aid volume. Messages centred on aid quality will clearly be irrelevant if volume continues to fall and international co-operation is relegated to the backwaters of Canadian public policy. Although meeting the United Nations ODA target of 0.7 per cent of gross national product now looks almost meaningless in a Canadian context, what must be communicated is that small savings in expenditure have a disproportionate opportunity cost in terms of programmes that can no longer be delivered by Canada to the poorest communities in the South.

The implications of international trends for both operations and public engagement are less clear-cut. A more holistic development paradigm may require some organizations to become generalists. Others will need to build issue-driven alliances with an array of national and international NGOs, with the domestic non-profit sector, and with non-traditional stakeholders, such as the private sector.

The challenge of deepening and broadening the development knowledge base raises the issue of capacity and resources. Who pays? Ironically, Canadian NGOs need to demonstrate competence and sophistication on a range of complex global issues at a time of reduced public spending on development education and limited human resources for policy development.

However, not everyone is convinced that NGOs can or should engage a broader range of global policy issues. As Michael Edwards underlines, the comparative advantage of NGOs in contributing to discussion of such issues lies in their field experience. Yet NGO efforts to use the lessons from that micro-experience to influence macro-economic policies have had limited impact: witness attempts to affect the work of international financial institutions, for example. The paucity of credible, NGO-sponsored primary research on the local impacts of macro-economic policy puts them at risk of not being taken seriously.

There is a broad consensus that the purpose of ODA is to improve the quality of life, redress market failures, promote human rights, democracy, and good governance, and enhance capacities for self-reliant development. However, some of these emphases appear to have reduced the salience of direct poverty alleviation as the prime rationale for ODA. Globalization appears to deliver economic growth but widens the gap between rich and poor and does not necessarily alleviate poverty. It may be that the greatest contribution of Northern NGOs to the development debate has been their constancy in focusing on poverty alleviation as the goal. Consequently, there is legitimate concern about further marginalizing the poorest countries and communities by falling back on "socially reactionary" arguments (for example, that development reduces migration by helping people survive in their own countries) to maintain public support for international co-operation.

This range of opinion underscores the sense of anxiety, including a fear of market influences, prevailing in some parts of the Canadian international development community as it adjusts to uncertainty, change, and the reduced importance of foreign aid in public life.

What are the implications of a more holistic development paradigm for aid management? The logic of moving from an aid to a global-issues paradigm is to integrate ODA more closely into national security and trade objectives. The functional absorption or closer co-ordination of aid agencies with foreign policy, security, and commercial departments of government has potential costs as well as benefits. A possible benefit is the opportunity to ensure that development concerns are considered in the broader array of issue-areas and in the policies and operational management of several line departments. The potential cost is the drowning of development issues in the sea of the policy priorities of larger and more powerful departments.

In some Nordic countries, the functional integration of aid agencies with foreign policy ministries is fairly advanced, and Riddell believes that the initial fears of Scandinavian NGOs have not been borne out. In practice, integration appears to have proceeded without a significant erosion of the poverty focus and development priorities of official aid agencies. Nevertheless, the costs and benefits of functional integration for Canada's international relations must be judged in their own context. The debate on an independent development agency versus some form of amalgamation turns on the basic objectives and time horizon of Canadian ODA. If the goal is development and a long-term vision, a separate agency is indispensable; if the agenda is to pursue domestic interests and short-term objectives, such as market penetration, then there are advantages in folding development aid into the Department of Foreign Affairs and International Trade.

These issues first came to the surface in Canada during the mid-1980s, in the context of mixed credits (the blending of concessional aid with commercial loans) and with greater force in the early 1990s in an internal policy brief of the Department of External Affairs which called for a substantial appropriation of ODA to further the market penetration of Canadian firms in the developing world. The issue of integration and co-ordination has resurfaced since the election of the Liberal government in 1993 because a reorganization of responsibilities has meant that currently the foreign minister no longer deals with a junior minister for development but with a cabinet equal, the minister for international cooperation, who has the autonomy to sign all submissions to the Treasury. Meanwhile, the (rechristened) Department of Foreign Affairs and International Trade must deal with a widening agenda of global issues despite diminishing resources. The department's recently created Global Issues Bureau, for example, has no clear counterpart in the Canadian International Development Agency (CIDA); a case of good ideas without targeted funds to manage or programmes to implement.

Some in government recognize that the current system of policy co-ordination on international issues is not optimal. Inter-agency co-ordination works well when it is event-driven, such as for a summit of the G-7 industrialized countries or a United Nations conference, but appears to be less successful on more routine issues. The technical complexity of many of today's foreign policy issues means that formalized inter-agency consultations are useful as stocktaking opportunities but do not function well as decision-making forums.

Six member-countries of the Organization for Economic Co-operation and Development (OECD) have moved towards a more centralized model for managing foreign policy. There have also been lively discussions in the United States and the United Kingdom about the possible integration of their development agencies into the State Department and the Foreign Office, respectively (Gordon et al. 1996). Despite this international trend, there are reasons to beware the silver bullet of a foreign policy super-ministry in Canada. The bottom line is performance, co-ordination, and foreign policy coherence across a welter of agencies and departments, and in a rapidly changing international environment.

In pursuit of this goal, structures may not be decisive. Private sector experience shows that high-performance organizations are marked by good leadership, sound communications, and clarity of role – attributes that transcend the particularities of structure.

The conceptual framework for managing Canada's foreign policy is integration. And the intellectual leap linking the long-term development priorities of CIDA to the peace, security, and commercial preoccupations of Foreign Affairs has been taken. But the optimal organizational form for creating policy coherence and co-ordination remains a conundrum.

Irrespective of the foreign policy structure in Canada, however, an enhanced knowledge base and pragmatic issue-based alliances will become increasingly important to Canadian development NGOs if they are to be significant contributors to the integration of aid policies within an increasingly variegated policy environment.

SYSTEMATIC LEARNING

A consciously induced and managed process of creating, acquiring, and disseminating knowledge is imperative as development organizations adjust to an aid regime in the throes of rapid change. At a time of reduced public spending on aid and increased concern among donors about aid effectiveness, public support can only be maintained by making both a moral and a practical case for international co-operation; one based on enlightened self-interest.

As CIDA has begun to recognize, NGOs whose focus is programme management in the South are well placed to disseminate the lessons of that experience to the Canadian public. And there are signs that some Canadian NGOs have become more interested in accurately documenting and disseminating the lessons learned from their development interventions as one way to demonstrate effectiveness to the sceptics. However, NGOs and the donor agencies that fund them need to be more honest in explaining to themselves and to their publics what aid can and cannot do.

Michael Edwards argues that effective organizational learning means reflecting on the lessons of experience and putting new knowledge into action for enhanced performance, informed policy dialogue, and effective public engagement. One very important litmus test of effective learning is the ability to acknowledge and deal with "discordant information" including field experiences which fail or whose results conflict with an organization's assumptions or beliefs. Development interventions are inherently open-ended, experimental, unstable, contingent, and diverse. A sound learning culture thus requires a spirit of openness, humility, inquiry, and sharing. While more and more NGOs have begun the difficult journey towards becoming a learning organization, for most the Holy Grail is still far in the future.

There are no magic bullets on the path to organizational learning. It is clear that it takes organizations a long time to absorb and act upon the learning that leads to change and renewal. Edwards cautions that there may be no immediate external payback from organizational learning but is convinced that the "inner" organizational journey through the process of learning is at least as important as the destination or concrete policy and public engagement outcomes. He warns as well that the lessons-learned approach of documenting and disseminating field experience is a necessary but not sufficient step on the road to organizational learning. The danger of this "banking concept" is that acquired knowledge stays with a few specialists, remains unused, or has a limited shelf life.

Even when an organization has been transformed into a learning organization, there is no linear or necessarily causal connection between that better learning and more effective policy dialogue and public engagement. If development is as much about contingency, failure, and adaptation as it is about success, then there will be times when "honest" lessons produce "discordant information" at odds with the pressure to package success stories. Edwards suggests the need for learning strategies geared to several levels: grassroots, project-based, policy- and advocacy-based, and research for innovation. NGOs need to strike a balance between these types of learning but recognize that as a community they excel at learning from grassroots and participatory experiences.

From a learning perspective, the NGO sector has generally not exploited its location as an intermediary between grassroots communities and policy-makers and research institutions. As classic "bridging" agencies with a value base which favours dialogue, NGOs have a largely unrealized potential to be catalysts promoting collaborative learning networks among diverse constituencies (researchers, governments, communities) with a stake in the development process.

EFFECTIVE POLICY DIALOGUE

Based on case-studies of policy-influencing strategies in Pakistan and Canada, Kabraji and Draimin and Schmitz addressed the scope for NGOs to set agendas and influence processes and outcomes in unhealthy or constrained policy environments and in societies without a strong tradition of consultation on national policy.

In many "developing" societies, the preponderance of state power, the propensity for abuses of power, and the potentially fatal human and institutional consequences of failure call for different indicators to judge effective policy dialogue. Institutional survival and growth are indices of political savvy and the building blocks for successful policy dialogue. Games of skill and position are decisive in policy environments that are fundamentally unhealthy or dysfunctional.

The genesis of the National Conservation Strategy (NCS) in Pakistan over twelve years and as many governments underscores that substantial agendas for policy reform can sometimes be maintained in the face of political instability and flawed governance. The NCS story may hold clues for effective policy dialogue in other developing countries. One lesson is that only those institutions that have established their credentials as trusted collaborators and allies of government are capable of influencing major policy reform. Another lesson is that large national NGOs, international NGOs, and especially hybrid NGOs which "represent" both the state and civil society have particular advantages in seeking to influence national macro-policy debates.

This country-specific observation appears to contradict the general NGO claim that they are well-placed to use the lessons from their micro-experience to affect larger policy debates. It would be misleading, however, to generalize from a single example. Small NGOs can and do have an impact on policy disproportionate to their size. For example, Gonoshasthaya Kendra, a Bangladeshi NGO, virtually singlehandedly lobbied for the creation of a national drug policy which made medicines cheaper and thus more accessible to the poor in Bangladesh (see Smillie 1995).

The NCS process helped strengthen the institutional capacity of two environmental NGOs and drew on Canadian consultative practices, such as search conferences and other consensus-building mechanisms. It also helped transform CIDA's engagement from one of control and technical transfer to one of partnership and capacity development.

Both essays on policy dialogue evoke considerable interest in the potential of hybrid institutions that are constitutionally or functionally located between state and society to serve as "public spaces" for the articulation and mediation of policy choice. They provide opportunities for NGOs, the government, and non-traditional stakeholders such as the business community to discuss international development issues. In Canada such institutions include the International Centre for Human Rights and Democratic Development (ICHRDD), the International Institute for Sustainable Development, and the International Development Research Centre.

The ICHRDD is an interesting example of the potential of such hybrids. First proposed by a parliamentary committee in 1986 and established by statute in 1988, the centre is funded from the public purse but functions at arms length from government. Its legislated mandate is to "initiate, encourage and support cooperation between Canada and other countries in the promotion, development and strengthening of institutions that give effect to the rights and freedoms enshrined in the International Bill of Rights." The centre has positioned itself as a donor advocate. Because its funds are limited, its real value is to call domestic and international attention to grave or intractable human rights problems. Examples of its public awareness and policy-influencing roles include the 1992 mission of the Nobel peace laureates to Thailand to call for the release of Aung San Suu Kyi, and its advocacy on behalf of "Nada," a Muslim woman whose struggle for refugee status in Canada led to the addition of a gender-based fear of persecution to the criteria for refugee determination in Canada. The potential of the ICHRDD as a hybrid organization is perhaps best illustrated by its convening, in partnership with the Business Council on National Issues, a national dialogue on the relationship between trade and human rights.

In these times of deepening distrust of political institutions, there is little consensus in Canada on the effectiveness of Parliament as a public space for policy deliberation and influence or of the scope for civil society to influence policy through newer modalities, such as the annual National Forum on Canada's International Relations, the Canadian Centre for Foreign Policy Development, or the John Holmes Fund for Policy Research.

The foreign minister, Lloyd Axworthy, is trying to breathe new life into the parliamentary foreign affairs committees which he describes in Bagehotian terms as "the main vehicle, the 'clearing house' for exchanges between Canadians, Parliament and Government" (1996: 4). And he has broadened the annual National Forum to include a series of regional meetings. Nevertheless many interested Canadians doubt that Parliament has much influence on the outcomes of foreign policy processes and believe that the parliamentary committees have been deliberately weakened, that the National Forum is an élite mechanism, and that the policy research groups located within government departments primarily serve state priorities. Others, however, view the decline of government resources, notably for policy research, as an opportunity for productive collaboration between the state, NGOs and universities.

A nation's political culture and the characteristics of its development "community" can influence the way in which the non-profit sector engages policy issues. Canada's NGO sector is very diverse in size, in geographical reach, in mission, and in approaches to policy dialogue. A tradition of strong operational and policy autonomy, coupled with a tendency towards duplication and, increasingly, competitiveness in a constrained financial environment, has complicated the development of a single NGO policy voice on some key issues.

One feature of the Canadian voluntary sector is the general absence of charismatic leadership in support of Canadian international co-operation. By contrast, as Aban Kabraji's essay underlines, charismatic leadership is a defining feature of the NGO sector in many developing areas, such as South Asia. In Pakistan, key individuals located both in government and in the non-profit sector were decisive in the genesis of the National Conservation Strategy. Canadian development NGOs have historically been leadership averse. Where are Canada's global heroes? Where is its Greenpeace of global poverty? Teenager Craig Kielberger's single-minded upstaging of the government on child labour during the government's Asian trade mission in 1996 is a rare example of a public campaign on a development issue that caught the imagination of people.

In Canada, decisions on overall budgetary allocations to international co-operation are the purview of the cabinet and senior mandarins, and decisions on allocations within departments and on modalities largely rest with the bureaucracy, the so-called permanent government. More than 560 briefs were submitted by Canadian civil society organizations and individuals when Parliament last reviewed foreign policy. It would be difficult to point unequivocally to any single government policy outcome that can be traced to the submissions of Canadian NGOs. But while the voluntary sector has had little impact on general aid funding decisions, Canadian NGOs can point to successes on specific policy issues.

The Canadian Council for International Co-operation helped to strengthen the civil society and sustainable development component of CIDA's policy framework for engaging the voluntary sector. Several small NGOs have played a disproportionate role in policy advocacy and in promoting public awareness of international issues. Canada Mines Action helped convince the Canadian government that it should adopt an assertive role in promoting an international land mines agreement. The Steelworkers Humanity Fund is an articulate and credible advocate on child rights and labour standards. The Rural Advancement Foundation International (RAFI), a small international non-governmental organization led by Canadian plant scientist Pat Mooney, works in international forums to oppose patenting of living organisms, and with indigenous and rural communities worldwide to defend and develop intellectual property rights based on their knowledge of local plant and other biological resources. More controversially, the East Timor Alert Network has kept the issue of self-determination in East Timor in the public eye, publicizing alleged inconsistencies between Canada's human rights policies and its growing trade links and investment portfolio in Indonesia.

Canadian experience suggests that even where the prospects for policy influence are limited, NGO engagement in policy dialogue is important as a way of enhancing the capacity of the NGO sector to participate in processes which help preserve trust and accountability in the country's public institutions. Engaging in successive Canadian foreign policy reviews has enabled the Canadian Council for International Co-operation to build its policy capacity and raised its credibility among its membership as a legitimate advocate on behalf of Canadian development NGOs.

EFFECTIVE PUBLIC ENGAGEMENT

Those who seek to educate the public about development face a daunting challenge. First, there is a disconnect between the funds available and the "staggering growth" in communications as a field of expertise. But even with sophisticated messages tailored to segmented audiences, such as youth, women, and political élites, the evolution in communications technology and techniques is relentless, consumers are becoming more discriminating, and the competition for attention grows more intense. Canadians are drowning in media messages.

Secondly, some professionals lament the erosion of funding for development education. But given the well-known diagnoses of the weaknesses of development education, do we need to spend more, or just do development education smarter? In the future, development educators will need to make the most of their modest resources by becoming far more outwardly focused and by turning themselves into managers of external expertise rather than trying to do everything themselves – as is still too often the case. This will require a culture change that will not be easy to achieve. But the alternative is a gradual drift into irrelevance (Winter 1996).

Government must also adjust to reduced communication resources and seek new ways to stretch its development education dollar. A potential model is the Norwegian experience. NORAD, Norway's development aid agency, has attempted to stretch its communications resources through a structured collaboration with some of the country's largest corporations and cultural institutions.

For social marketers like Eric Young, the key attributes of effective public engagement are initiatives which reach large numbers of people, which promote dialogue and the active involvement of citizens, which are sustained processes rather than single-shot actions, and which use accurate development knowledge to help citizens deliberate meaningfully about the value of international co-operation.

The ingredients for successful public engagement include building a vision of achievable outcomes, convincing citizens that they can make a difference, credible leadership, and peer involvement and momentum. Strategies for public engagement need to be developed on several levels: with mass publics, with specialized audiences such as the private sector, the media, or youth, and with the political élites and opinion leaders.

Pollsters confirm that in Canada public support for international co-operation has remained relatively steady; it is political confidence that appears to be more in question. Nevertheless, in contrast to issues such as gender equity and the environment, global development is not a "public idea" near the front and centre of national life. Among the reasons for this state of affairs are a perception that aid does not work, evidence that Canadians are preoccupied with their own anxieties about the future, and the stark reality that development issues rarely affect the daily lives of people. Another reason may be that the development community has lost conviction and purpose; that it has become an isolated élite which connects poorly with the domestic voluntary sector and other professions (the media, law, medicine, educators) and which has limited ability to develop sustained voluntary engagement in support of international co-operation.

But strategies to build durable public support for development co-operation are also bedevilled by the absence of any clear or compelling answers to the hard-nosed question: "What's in it for me?" Short of the ethically dubious tactic of preying on public fears (about immigration and disease, for example), global poverty has little visceral impact on the daily lives of most Canadians. It may also be a tough sell to persuade politicians and the public that development interventions are capacity-building experiments and that failure is as much part-and-parcel of *our* learning and *your* tax dollars as is success. One answer may lie in Riddell's argument that one way to demonstrate development effectiveness is to show that programmes leave local ownership behind. The public engagement implication of this claim is that development assistance should be packaged for its ability to help kick-start independence and self-reliance and not be positioned as a form of welfare that perpetuates dependence. (Recent Environics Research polling data, for example, show that 59 per cent of respondents agreed that foreign assistance makes recipients too dependent – SCFAIT 1996.)

Development education initiatives in Canada have suffered from several disabilities. First, they are still sometimes undertaken primarily as a means to garner funds. This has had the perverse effect of prompting an almost chronic need to package success stories to elicit largely passive support. Secondly, the size and diversity of the country has meant that many genuinely innovative development education activities have focused on local experience; few have been taken to scale. Thirdly, there is a belief, not easily supported by domestic and international opinion polling, that increasing public support will influence the volume or modalities of development spending.

If aid volume and direction are not significantly influenced by levels of public support, then development organizations need to be clear about their objectives and desired outcomes before investing scarce resources in public campaigns. Public engagement should be recognized as a valuable end in itself rather than as a means to more instrumental objectives. In addition to informing Canadians about the reality of and solutions to global poverty and other international issues, a primary purpose of public engagement is to deepen Canadians' sense of global connectedness, promote active citizenship, strengthen national values and unity, and restore trust in public institutions. These objectives suggest a need to distinguish more sharply between public engagement and fundraising which relies on passivity, fear, charity, and pity or which distorts the complex reality of the development experience.

These issues – which messages to send and which alliances should be pursued – are being discussed by development NGOs, but there seems to be no consensus on whether and how NGOs should collaborate with the private sector, on whether exploiting fear (the spread of disease or migration, for example) or anger (the obscenity of global poverty) is a legitimate approach to public engagement, or on how to develop alliances around shared Canadian and global problems (jobs, trade, the environment). The media form a key constituency. Drawing a parallel, NGOs in Pakistan made a concerted and largely successful effort to educate the media about environmental issues and the media became one of the constituencies in the development of the National Conservation Strategy.

It seems clear that there is a strong need to build public understanding of international co-operation through more deliberative, participatory, and public dialogues, such as those developed by the Public Agenda Foundation and the Kettering Foundation in the United States and The Society We Want forums of the Canadian Policy Research Network.

FUTURE POSITIVE?

Several strategic issues must be addressed if the global non-profit sector is to fulfil its promise to deliver public goods effectively and to help buttress democratic governance by a socially engaged citizenry. The key issues include: (1) improving the sector's visibility and knowledge base; (2) promoting a more enabling environment for national philanthropy by expanding charitable support; (3) enhancing collaboration with government as well as institutional professionalism and performance; and (4) coming to terms with globalization (Salamon & Anheier 1994).

Like it or not, NGOs are the main boosters for international co-operation. They are an increasingly important part of the political process and are the best placed to make the case that Canada's aid programmes should focus on the alleviation of poverty. Canadian NGOs have a valuable role to play in building support for a vision of international co-operation focused on poverty reduction and the construction of durable civil societies. They can take a cue from the comparative polling experience in many other OECD countries, which in aggregate suggests that while citizens have very little faith in the efficacy of governments, they are more confident about the capacity of the non-profit sector to deliver development.

What will Canada's development NGO sector look like in the next century? While prediction is a hazardous business, some trends do seem likely. If ODA funding continues to be squeezed, competition and scarcity will, with Darwinian ruthlessness, push more NGOs to the wall. Such trends in the private sector have prompted mergers, but such a solution seems unlikely in the fiercely autonomous development sector. However, there may also be a change in the framework for the engagement of Canadian civil society in the wider world. The future may lie not with organizations that focus entirely on individual projects of international co-operation, but with NGOs that pursue their objectives through strengthened links with a wider array of domestic institutions that have an international component to their work (trade unions, professional associations, women's and environmental organizations, universities, co-operatives, local governments). This conceptual leap has already been taken by government but may not yet have been adequately considered by many development NGOs.

The larger NGOs may command increasing state resources and fare better than their smaller counterparts in competitive bidding processes, though not necessarily when up against the private sector. NGOs with strong programming portfolios could play a more substantial role in development education. There may also be increasing pressures towards specialization which will enhance operational impact and ensure that some smaller NGOs occupy a relatively stable niche. Current examples of small but successful "niche" NGOs include RAFI, Street Kids International, and – in micro-credit – Développement International, Desjardins, and Calmeadow. Finally, Canadian development organizations face a greying of their human resources, and NGOs will need a new cadre of young professionals that draws more effectively on the resources of Canada's multicultural population.

It remains to be seen whether development NGOs can more systematically engage the private sector. Childfind, a small domestic NGO, shows what can be done. This agency, whose mission is to locate missing children, persuaded major milk manufacturers to put pictures and basic information about some missing children on milk cartons. While some NGOs continue to see profit as a dirty word, corporate social philanthropy will be a major issue in the twenty-first century, whether addressed from the perspective of global labour standards and trade or investment decisions or through the perspective of affirmative action as companies invest in community economic development or provide cash or in-kind giving. Development NGOs have an opportunity to be creative in engaging firms committed to the principle of good corporate citizenship. Fair trade, ecotourism, and ethical investment are three arenas where development NGOs have the potential to develop know-how.

One way out of the impasse of the voluntary sector's current role confusion is for Northern NGOs to move beyond control-oriented, project-driven relations with Southern NGOs, to reframe the mantra of "partnership" to focus on people-to-people or twinning arrangements and to become facilitators between groups and communities trying to build a global civil society. However, there is no consensus on whether or how the Northern development community should "deprofessionalize" in order to deepen its organic roots with civil societies. Professionalization is also part of the NGO sector's solution to its sustainability and credibility with both political élites and mass publics.

Pollsters like Angus Reid and Frank Graves confirm a widening disconnect between the fundamental values and preoccupations of the governing élites and the public in Canada (Ekos 1996; Reid 1996). They say that Canadians seek "a moral community from government as much as an economic association" (Ekos 1995: 20). This public mood offers an opportunity to promote international co-operation as a vital part of our collective experience as Canadians; a vehicle to unite Canadians from coast to coast and a means through which we put into action some of our most fundamental shared beliefs, such as fairness, self-reliance, equity, and freedom. The public engagement strategy of the development community must drive home the message that decisions about Canada's support for international co-operation will play a significant part in defining Canadians' overall social vision of their country in the twenty-first century.

REFERENCES

Axworthy, L. 1996. "Foreign Policy at a Crossroad." Address by the Minister of Foreign Affairs to the Standing Committee on Foreign Affairs and International Trade. Ottawa: DFAIT, statement 96/12. 16 April.

Ekos Research Associates. 1995. *Rethinking Government '94: An Overview and Synthesis.* Ottawa: Ekos.

– 1996. *Rethinking Government: Overview Comparing Elite and Mass Perspectives on Government.* Ottawa: Ekos.
Gordon, David, Catherine Gwin, & Steven W. Sinding. 1996, *What Future Foreign Aid?* Washington: Overseas Development Council and Henry J. Stinson Center.
Reid, A. 1996. *Shakedown.* Toronto: Doubleday.
Salamon, L.M., & H.K. Anheier. 1994. *The Emerging Sector: An Overview.* Baltimore MD: Johns Hopkins University Press.
SCFAIT (House of Commons Standing Committee on Foreign Affairs and International Trade, Canada). 1996. "Forum on Promoting Greater Public Understanding of International Development Issues." *Minutes of Proceedings and Evidence,* Issue 9 (18 April).
Smillie, I. 1995. *The Alms Bazaar: Altruism under Fire – Non-Profit Organizations and International Development.* London: Intermediate Technology Publications.
Winter, A. 1996. *Is Anyone Listening? Communicating Development in Donor Countries.* Geneva: United Nations Non-Governmental Liaison Service.

APPENDIX ONE

Canadian Voluntary Organizations and CIDA: Framework for a Renewed Relationship

INTRODUCTION

The Canadian International Development Agency (CIDA) and the voluntary sector go back a long way – to the days when CIDA, or the External Aid Office (EAO), as it was known then, was still a part of the Department of External Affairs. Since the formation of the Voluntary Agencies Division in the EAO in 1967, the Government of Canada has been supporting the development work of a wide range of Canadian organizations by enhancing their ability to put their experience and expertise at the service of a wide range of developing countries. Canadian Voluntary Organizations (CVOs) and CIDA have grown up together, worked together, and learned together, and there are many victories to celebrate together, with our partners from the South.

Why a new framework? Because times and relationships change. At the turn of the millennium, the roles of government, the private sector and voluntary sector are changing; boundaries are dissolving, new partnerships are forming, new ways of working together are evolving. We serve a common purpose – sustainable development – and we need to find new ways to build on each other's efforts in pursuit of that goal. At the same time, resources are shrinking and new challenges are facing us all, North and South: rapidly evolving technology, globalization,

---

This document was issued by the Canadian International Development Agency in November 1996 and is reprinted here with the permission of the Agency.

the growth of an international civil society, the upsurge of democracy and free markets – all these affect our work and our relationships with our partners in the South.

Over the last two years, CIDA has embarked on a wide-ranging consultation process to renew its relationships with Canadian voluntary organizations. Over 500 organizations across the country have contributed to the drafting of this new framework, a living document which sets out the basic principles that guide the relationship and underscores the common purpose that animates and sustains it. It outlines the ways and means required to meet the challenges of the Fifth Development Decade; and its goal – and the results by which it will be judged – is to support the high-quality work that CIDA and CVOs will do together to promote sustainable development.

1 A COMMON PURPOSE

This framework fulfils a commitment made by the Government of Canada in the foreign policy statement *Canada in the World* (February 1995): "In consultation with Canadian partners the Government will develop a framework for a renewed relationship between CIDA and Canadian voluntary organizations based on the principle of complementarity of action." (p. 44)

In that document, the Government recognized that Canadian partners are a key source of the skills, know-how and technology needed to promote sustainable development. Collaboration with Canadian partners, including those of the voluntary sector, is one of the ways the Government works to fulfil the mandate of the Official Development Assistance (ODA) program.

This framework states CIDA's purpose in its relationship with Canadian voluntary organizations. It identifies principles which guide the relationship, and outlines implementation strategies. Finally, it identifies a number of issues on which work continues. Underlying the framework is the mutual recognition by CIDA and Canadian voluntary organizations that a strong relationship is important for fulfilling the mandate of Canada's ODA program and for meeting voluntary organizations' own goals. It also contributes to the strength of the overall Canadian international development effort.

The process itself of preparing this framework has contributed to renewal. The Agency has been open and participatory in its approach, consulting at all stages of its work over a two-year period. National consultations were held in November 1995 followed by regional meetings involving more than 500 organizations from all parts of the country. Voluntary organizations themselves made important contributions to

> The "voluntary sector" encompasses a wide range of community, grassroots and peoples' organizations, development and environmental organizations, churches, labour unions, professional associations and cooperatives. All are accountable to constituencies or memberships through governing structures. Most maintain a financial relationship with government, but all are autonomous. Equally important, all consider themselves part of a broader civil society and are driven by values such as justice, equity and solidarity in their international work.

the process. Small focus group discussions also took place and CIDA consulted its own staff. Throughout, informal dialogue continued with umbrella groups and individual organizations.

This dialogue has highlighted the diversity of voluntary organizations, the range of roles they play in sustainable development, and the many facets of their relationship with CIDA. It has also served as a reminder of the extent to which the Government and the voluntary sector have a common purpose in development assistance activities: the promotion of sustainable development.

2 SUSTAINABLE DEVELOPMENT, CIVIL SOCIETY AND CANADIAN VOLUNTARY ORGANIZATIONS

A key dimension of sustainable development is building strong civil societies. Strengthening civil society, and the voice and capacity of marginalized actors within it, has become an important element in CIDA's development policies and in the work of Canadian voluntary organizations. Views about its definition vary, and our understanding of its role in sustainable development continues to evolve. For these reasons, it is an important concept for CIDA and its partners to explore further.

Community-based organizations operating in open and active civil societies – the arena of organized activity distinct from the private sphere (the household and the private firm) and the formal institutions of governance (legislatures, political parties, the army, the judiciary among others) – enable people to define, shape and negotiate their own development. Private sector entities are important for efforts to accelerate economic growth through the market. Government institutions facilitate and manage the democratic processes and structures of society, permitting sometimes contending actors to resolve conflicts and seeking to allocate the costs and benefits of development equitably and peacefully.

The three are not separate and distinct sectors, but rather, dynamic and fluid spheres of activity that continuously interact and change, a complex system that varies enormously from country to country. A better understanding of this interaction is important for improving our approach to development work, as well as the ability of each sector to relate to the others more effectively. Powerful, well-resourced and articulate groups often dominate civic space in society. Governments play a critical role in ensuring the accountability of state institutions to all citizens, including those who are excluded.

The Canadian voluntary sector contributes to sustainable development in many ways, for example, by working at the household level to reduce poverty, by acting in the market through micro-enterprise programming, by building the program delivery capacity of governments, and by providing emergency and humanitarian assistance in response to disasters. Many have placed particular emphasis on social sustainability and the equitable impact of development programming. Their experience and concerns have contributed to the evolution of Canadian development thinking and practice.

As well, Canadian voluntary organizations promote sustainable development through efforts to strengthen developing country civil societies, both working alone and in partnership with the private sector and government. Canadian organizations provide direct support to partners, transferring resources to disadvantaged groups, enabling them to improve their social and economic condition and position, and building the capacity of partner organizations to mobilize resources and manage processes of change. Also important are efforts to work with developing country partners to engage local and national policy actors in policy dialogue and to advocate for equitable and sustainable development policies.

Canadian voluntary organizations engage Canadians in the global challenge of development by seeking to build their understanding and providing channels for their responses. They support Canadians' efforts to define themselves as global as well as local citizens with all the rights and responsibilities this entails, and facilitate connections between individuals and between civil society organizations for the purpose of mutual learning.

Canada's development assistance program supports the Canadian voluntary sector in its work, in addition to taking other measures to strengthen developing country civil societies. Approaches include providing direct support to developing country organizations working at the grassroots and intermediary levels, as well as through networks, and assisting these organizations to engage in policy dialogue in national and international fora. CIDA supports capacity-building initiatives implemented by the full range of CIDA partners, in addition to those of Canadian voluntary organizations.

CIDA seeks to foster an environment for mutual learning through which CIDA and its partners can strengthen effective interactions between state, market and civil society actors, as well as between those within civil society. The Canadian voluntary sector is a valuable partner in this process.

3 THE EVOLVING RELATIONSHIP BETWEEN CIDA AND CANADIAN VOLUNTARY ORGANIZATIONS

Voluntary organizations are a significant part of Canada's presence in the world, and make important contributions to Canada's international development effort. For many years, they have played an active international role, working closely with partners in developing countries, implementing projects on behalf of donor agencies, delivering assistance in times of crisis, and contributing to the development of foreign and ODA policy. In so doing, they have built awareness, raised funds from the public, and mobilized the talents and energies of many thousands of Canadian men, women and children for the global challenge of sustainable development. From the outset of Canada's development assistance program, the Government has worked closely with Canadian voluntary organizations.

Like CIDA, Canadian voluntary organizations face many pressures for change.

- *Changing roles*: Governments are downsizing throughout the world and changing the nature of their activities. Some long-standing governmental functions are being eliminated or turned over to other sectors. Meanwhile, voluntary organizations are taking on new roles, often with insecure funding and at risk of compromising their original mandates. In some instances, distinctions between government, non-governmental and private sectors are blurring as new alliances are created and hybrid organizations emerge.
- *New challenges in development*: The changing realities in developing countries have demonstrated the important roles of government, the private sector and civil society in sustainable development. In many countries, strengthening civil society is particularly important. Lessons learned from development experience, such as the need to include women as full participants and decision makers, and the importance of environmental sustainability, have underlined the need to support new sectors, activities and strategies. Other factors,

such as deep-rooted conflict, challenge many long-standing assumptions about the development process and our roles.
- *New relationships with developing country organizations*: As they become more capable and more global in their outlook, developing country organizations seek a different kind of support from Canadian partners. While traditional requests for project support and emergency assistance continue, many also emphasize the importance of educating the Canadian public, changing government policy and addressing development issues at a global level.
- *The need to find new sources of funding*: Government funds for international development have shrunk and will continue to be under pressure in the immediate future, making heavy dependence on government funding no longer realistic. Some Canadian organizations have been able to tap new sources of financial, in-kind and volunteer support, but a number have found traditional approaches less and less successful in generating the resources required.
- *Public attitudes are changing*: Support for development assistance remains strong, but scepticism is growing. Many Canadians accord low priority to development assistance in government spending; and, on a personal level, they face competing demands for their private donations. Many now seek assurances not just that funds are well spent, but that development results are achieved. At the same time, more Canadians want to become involved in international development work, many for the first time, and new organizations are seeking to work with the ODA program. Such groups include ethnic communities, aboriginal peoples and youth.

Voluntary organizations are responding in diverse ways to these pressures. Many have shifted emphasis away from direct delivery of projects toward long-term institutional development of partner organizations. Some have placed new emphasis on addressing development issues at a global level and working through networks. All are seeking to strengthen their constituency base and to involve new sectors of the public in international development.

For its part, the Government has sharpened the focus of Canada's ODA program. Following an extensive review of foreign policy in 1994 and 1995, with important contributions from Canadian voluntary organizations, the Government clearly identified the mandate and priorities for development assistance within the framework of foreign policy objectives. New emphasis has been placed on achieving development results, increasing program effectiveness based on the lessons of experience, and reporting to Parliament and the public. At CIDA, work has continued to establish development policies to guide Agency efforts in addressing the ODA mandate and priorities.

In the 1995 foreign policy statement *Canada in the World*, the Government outlines three objectives to guide its international actions in the years to come:

- the promotion of prosperity and employment;
- the promotion of global peace as the key to protecting our security; and
- the projection of Canadian values and culture.

Further to these objectives, the Government specifies the purpose of Canada's ODA program: "... to support sustainable development in developing countries, in order to reduce poverty and to contribute to a more secure, equitable and prosperous world." (p. 42)

Canadian ODA will be concentrated on six program priorities, each supported by a development policy statement:

- basic human needs, including support for efforts to provide primary health care, basic education, family planning, nutrition, water and sanitation, shelter, and humanitarian assistance in response to emergencies;
- women in development, to support the full participation of women as equal partners in the sustainable development of their societies;
- infrastructure services, to help developing countries to deliver environmentally sound infrastructure services, with an emphasis on poorer groups and on capacity building;
- human rights, democracy and good governance, to increase respect for rights, promote democracy and better governance, and strengthen both civil society and the security of the individual;
- private sector development, to promote sustained and equitable economic growth by supporting private sector development in developing countries; and
- the environment, to help developing countries to protect their environment and to contribute to addressing global and regional environmental issues.

CIDA works with Canadian voluntary organizations because of the diverse contributions they can make to meeting the ODA mandate and priorities. The sector has shown itself capable of developing and implementing effective programs, with emphasis on building the capacity of developing country organizations through long-term partnerships. It plays an important role in building developing country civil society, an explicit element of the *Government of Canada's Policy for CIDA on Human Rights, Democratization and Good Governance,* and an important element of all of CIDA's development policy statements. Canadian organizations are innovative and flexible in seeking to address new development challenges. Many have developed specialized expertise and a unique capacity in particular areas. In Canada, they are an important channel for engaging the public in the challenge of international development.

Although faced by many pressures for change, Canadian voluntary organizations and CIDA are in a position to strengthen their relationship, based on their unique capacities, expertise and resources. Through improved collaboration, each will be better able to serve their mandate and priorities and contribute to the Canadian international development effort.

4 CIDA PRINCIPLES FOR ITS RELATIONSHIP WITH CANADIAN VOLUNTARY ORGANIZATIONS

The principles below have grown out of the lessons of many years of collaboration between CIDA and Canadian voluntary organizations, and have been shaped by the dialogue that took place in preparing this framework. They both guide CIDA in its relationship with voluntary organizations, and stand behind CIDA's expectations of the relationship.

Fundamental to the Agency's relationship with Canadian voluntary organizations, as with all partners, is the principle of *development impact*: CIDA seeks to maximize the development results of its development assistance program and of the Canadian voluntary sector initiatives it supports.

Specific to its relationship with the Canadian voluntary sector, the Agency abides by the following principles:

- *Mutual respect.* CIDA respects the diverse roles of Canadian voluntary organizations: they formulate and implement programs together with developing country partners; mobilize the Canadian public; work globally to address global issues; and engage in dialogue on policy issues. The voluntary sector initiatives CIDA supports complement other Agency programs serving the mandate and priorities of the ODA program. The Agency recognizes that the sector's roles in society are broader than those which CIDA funds.
- *Accountability.* CIDA is accountable to Parliament and the Canadian public to report on the results of its development efforts. CIDA requires similar accountability from Canadian voluntary organizations to the Agency concerning the initiatives it supports, and to organizations' memberships and constituencies through sound governance

structures. Together, CIDA and voluntary organizations recognize that they are accountable to the Canadian public for reporting on initiatives on which they collaborate.

- *Participation.* CIDA seeks to collaborate with voluntary organizations from all parts of the country and all sectors of society in delivering the ODA program. The Agency seeks to work with organizations that effectively engage the Canadian public in Canada's international development effort.
- *Dialogue.* CIDA seeks an open, transparent and ongoing dialogue with Canadian voluntary organizations on development policy and practice. Mutual learning is important for the efforts of all parties to improve the development impact of their initiatives.
- *Simplification.* CIDA seeks to streamline the processes and requirements on which its decisions are based, and to support cost-effective initiatives that avoid unnecessary layers of administration and decision making in Canada.

5 STRATEGIES FOR CIDA ACTION

Collaborate to Implement Programs

There are many areas in which the development priorities of CIDA and voluntary organizations converge. Voluntary organizations also have specific expertise in themes, sectors and countries which are important to the Agency in meeting the Government's ODA priorities. Within the limits of available funding, CIDA will collaborate with Canadian voluntary organizations to implement programs in these areas.

- *Responsive programming.* CIDA will provide financial support on a responsive and cost-shared basis for programs and projects conceived and implemented by Canadian voluntary organizations. CIDA funding will fall within the mandate and priorities set for the ODA program, and will be guided by criteria established by CIDA. These criteria currently include the extent to which initiatives build the capacity of developing country partners, are strategic, support ODA priorities, mobilize resources beyond CIDA, and build public support and understanding in Canada. The strength of the organization's governance and management is also a factor in decisions.
- *Delivery of CIDA programming.* CIDA will work with Canadian voluntary organizations to implement programs funded through the geographic branches and to deliver food aid and humanitarian assistance in areas of particular priority to CIDA where voluntary organizations have demonstrated expertise.

Strengthen Policy and Practice

CIDA and voluntary organizations have an important relationship as development colleagues. Both seek to understand and meet the many challenges of sustainable development in keeping with their respective mandates, and face a range of common issues. Through the relationship, CIDA and voluntary organizations can learn together from the experience of both, and use these lessons to reach development goals more effectively. CIDA seeks to build a stronger and more collegial relationship with voluntary organizations so that all parties can strengthen their development policy and practice.

- *Consultation.* CIDA will seek to further improve how it consults Canadian voluntary organizations. The Agency will consult in preparing development policies and Programming Framework documents for its country, regional and institutional programs. The Agency will also consult in making changes to funding criteria and processes, and will seek to improve mechanisms for liaison on operational issues.
- *Institutional knowledge, analysis and coordination at CIDA.* CIDA will build a stronger base of knowledge within the Agency concerning Canadian voluntary organizations and will improve communication and coordination among branches concerning initiatives that affect particular voluntary organizations. Through the Agency Information Framework, CIDA will identify cost-effective ways of sharing data and improving communications both inside and outside the Agency.
- *Simplification.* CIDA will continue efforts to streamline administrative and reporting requirements that affect Canadian voluntary organizations. The Agency will continue to improve its contracting process to ensure greater transparency, fairness and accessibility.

Build Global Roles

Canadian voluntary organizations play important roles at the international level, at UN [United Nations] conferences, in other intergovernmental fora, and through non-governmental networks. A number also undertake project work under contract to the UN, multilateral development banks and other international agencies. By advocating for development issues, pressing for better governance and accountability, delivering project services, and working with developing country partners to do the same, they support the purpose of the ODA program. CIDA will continue its efforts to enhance the global presence and role of Canadian voluntary organizations and their partners within the limits of available resources.

- *Access to key fora.* CIDA will seek to develop Canadian positions in favour of strengthening NGO [non-governmental organization] access to UN and other international fora.
- *Participation at key events.* CIDA will promote the participation of Canadian and developing country voluntary organizations in key UN conferences and other important intergovernmental and non-governmental fora. CIDA will facilitate their involvement in the preparation for and follow-up to these key events.
- *Support for Canadian delegations.* CIDA will draw on the expertise of Canadian voluntary organizations to support Canadian delegations to key international events. Where appropriate, voluntary organization representatives will be included as delegation advisors or members.
- *Delivering project services.* With the assistance of Canadian representatives at international organizations, CIDA will seek to provide information about project opportunities and advice concerning the bidding and contracting process.

Engage the Canadian Public

CIDA and Canadian voluntary organizations have a common concern for engaging the Canadian public in international development. The shared challenge has several facets: building public knowledge and understanding of development, mobilizing the energies of a broad spectrum of Canadians for development activities, and better informing the public about the development results achieved through their contributions and tax dollars. CIDA will work with Canadian voluntary organizations to better engage the Canadian public in international development.

- *Global awareness.* CIDA will continue to work with voluntary organizations to reassess approaches to building global awareness in Canada.
- *New constituencies.* CIDA will seek to involve a broad cross-section of the Canadian public in the ODA program.
- *Regional presence.* CIDA will ensure that all regions of Canada participate in the ODA program, and that development assistance activities are visible in all parts of the country.
- *Improved information.* CIDA will encourage the efforts of voluntary organizations to inform the public about their activities and the development results achieved. CIDA will collaborate with voluntary organizations to develop public information strategies.

6 NEXT STEPS

This framework is a living document. It will be updated regularly to reflect important decisions and the conclusions of ongoing work that have a bearing on the relationship. CIDA will report regularly on actions it is taking in light of the principles and strategies outlined above.

The success of this framework will be apparent in several ways. All involved should gain a better understanding and appreciation of the ways in which they relate and their respective roles in development programming. Transparency should increase and mutual expectations should become more realistic and clearly defined.

Possibly the most important measure of the relationship will be the strength of the development work supported by CIDA and Canadian voluntary organizations, and the quality of the dialogue and collaboration that supports it. Meeting the many challenges of development that we face will require the best efforts of our respective organizations over the coming years.

APPENDIX TWO

Global Citizenship: A New Way Forward

SUMMARY OF KEY RECOMMENDATIONS

1 Global citizenship should be the organizing concept used to build public support for Sustainable Human Development. As such, it must become the principal driver in NGOs'[non-governmental organizations'] relationships with the public.
2 The three relationships: with the Canadian Public, with Southern partners and among NGOs must be integrated and mutually compatible; NGOs should increasingly become bridge-builders.
3 NGOs should abandon the conversion model of interacting with the public in favour of an engagement model.
4 NGOs should accelerate the development of a culture which values diversity and expand their organizational boundaries in order to

---

This document was endorsed by the board of directors of the Canadian Council for International Co-operation (CCIC) in September 1996 and is reprinted here with the permission of the Council. The members of the Task Force on Building Public Support for Sustainable Development were: Anne-Marie Stewart (chairperson), organizational change consultant; Zack Gross, The Marquis Project; Larry Kuehn, British Columbia Teachers Federation; Waldo Neufeld, Mennonite Central Committee; Jean Perras, Learning for a Sustainable Future; Johanne Perron, Atlantic Council for International Co-operation; Gail Picco, fundraising consultant; Susan Reisler, radio producer; Dr. William Ryan, Jesuit economist and specialist in the ethical and spiritual dimensions of development; Eric Young, president, E·Y·E Inc., a social marketing firm; Ken Theobald, Ontario Council for International Co-operation and Linda Tripp, World Vision Canada – CCIC board liaison; Ronald Bisson, consultant to the Task Force.

develop strategic alliances that are sector-based, deliberate, and coordinated.

5 The NGO community must increasingly work sectorally to meet the challenge of building public support for Sustainable Human Development.

INTRODUCTION

CCIC's 1995 Annual General Meeting mandated a Task Force on Building Public Support for Sustainable Human Development (SHD) to develop a framework through which NGOs could engage and mobilize Canadians in support of sustainable human development. The Task Force was seen as a nine-month initiative within a longer one to two year process.

Soon after it began its work in November 1995, the Task Force realized that it would not fulfill its mission by masterminding a new communications strategy. Rather, what was needed was a clear, long-term vision based on a fresh look at the nature of NGOs, how they work, and their relationships with groups in the South and with Canadians.

While many people involved in international cooperation feel that public support is declining, the results of recent public opinion polls are ambiguous. On the one hand, a large majority of the public say they *support* development assistance. On the other hand, the percentage of those who believe Canada *spends* too much on development assistance has risen significantly and is now 44 percent. In one poll ranking 19 areas of public spending by perceived importance foreign aid ranked last.

Government decision making is currently deficit-driven and Canadians are required to make difficult public policy trade-offs. Most Canadians have become sceptical of all institutions that purport to act on their behalf – including governments.

It is clear that the 20-year-long push to inform Canadians about the need for development and development support did not build a bedrock of public understanding and commitment. We are encouraged, however, by recent studies and articles suggesting that Canadians share basic values consonant with international cooperation.

WHAT IS GOING ON TODAY: KEY FACTORS

In the World

Today we live in an increasingly integrated world. The market, civil society[1] and the state[2] are all in flux, and they are integrally woven into people's lives. Citizens work in the market, buy in the market, live in society, elect the government, pay their taxes, etc. Ideally, all three spheres should work in tandem for the benefit of society.

Economic globalization – the integration of markets for goods, services and capital – has had devastating consequences for many individuals and communities. As capital moves unregulated across national borders, individual governments lose the power to regulate and define domestic policies. The rush to minimize costs of production and services in order to compete in the global market results in the loss of jobs to areas where labour is cheap and environmental standards not enforced.

Globalization and the growing complexity of its related issues leave many people feeling powerless to influence decisions that affect their lives, the communities in which they live, and the environment. Among the three spheres the market is now the most influential. Meanwhile, civil society is the principal vehicle through which individuals, acting in groups, are combining their energies to work on social issues. For example, they are coming together around education, peace, human rights, environmental protection, community economic development, access and diversity. They are participating in a range of activities that place people before markets. By sharing visions and values they seek to infuse social justice into the prevailing market economy.

For many individuals, involvement in civil society springs from an energy grounded in the rich interaction of reason, values, emotions and spirituality. These all play a role in people's decision-making and actions. In recognition of the growing public awareness of this interaction, both the World Bank and CIDA [Canadian International Development Agency] have recently held conferences on spirituality and sustainable human development.

The state also has a duty to work for the social good of all. Once, the state in many countries was overly dominant. Today economic globalization has eroded this role. Yet citizens continue to hold governments accountable for their overall quality of life. They expect governments, individually and multilaterally, to safeguard the interests of all citizens, especially the most marginalized. The government cannot simply absent itself and expect the market and civil society to pick up the pieces.

The government must play a role in fostering civil society. It should create the appropriate conditions for vibrant, diverse, and autonomous civic organizations to act in the interests of a variety of groups towards a common good. It should do so through both formal means (laws, rules and regulations, structures, co-ordination, dialogue/negotiation) and informal means (creating a climate that encourages decency, mutual respect, citizen participation, cooperation, tolerance etc.).

Rajesh Tandon of the Society for Participatory Research in New Delhi, India argues that this scenario has implications for NGOs: "NGOs need to be seen as institutions of civil society engaged in the process of strengthening civil society in its relationship vis-à-vis the state ... this implies strengthening 'citizenship'." Tandon identifies strategies that NGOs can pursue to fulfill this mandate; they can provide resources; they can help local communities and people's organizations gain greater access to and control over resources; they can help generate informed public judgement and build capacity in civil society organizations so that alternative, people-centred, community-based, and citizen-governed development models emerge. He argues for the promotion of better citizen access to and engagement with public policy issues.

For NGOs

Through community-wide dialogue, workshops, focus groups, and interviews, the Task Force met with over 400 people involved in the NGO community across Canada. We got a sense of where realistically to start the work to implement the framework. We assessed the strengths, energy level, and motivation of the community.

In summary
- After the federal government funding cutbacks in early 1995, some NGOs were forced to close. Many small NGOs are struggling to survive, while larger NGOs are struggling with downsizing issues. Cutbacks will continue in '97 and '98.
- The 1995 federal budget cuts had the greatest impact outside this central Canada corridor. NGOs based outside the Toronto-Montreal-Ottawa corridor, provincial councils, and local committees of national NGOs are very concerned about their ability to continue locally-based programming. Smaller, locally-based NGOs, valued for their strong community roots and creativity are seen as an essential part of the Canadian NGO community.
- There is an aversion to leadership, based on conventional ideas and models. Many see individual leadership as contradicting NGO values of consensus and open decision-making. Most current NGO leaders focus their role only on their individual organization. They do not usually consider how their decisions impact, or could benefit, the community as a whole.
- There is some resistance to collective fundraising efforts. Some church-based NGOs and members of CCIC say the disparity of values, missions and approaches will make collective fundraising difficult. Others believe there is more inter-connectedness and potential for engagement possible through one-on-one organizational relation-

ships. Smaller NGOs and global education centers are most open to the idea of collective fundraising.
- Fundraising is attracting greater institutional and strategic focus. This generates anxiety that too much focus will be given to fundraising at the expense of programming.
- There is a commitment to preserving individual identity. Many people worry that working as a sector and increased collaboration will result in the homogenization of NGOs and will discourage experimentation and hinder community learning.
- Most NGOs recognize the need to change to meet today's new challenges, but they are unsure about how to change or where to start. Much energy has gone into implementing organizational efficiencies and program innovation, but there is a sense that more fundamental changes are still needed.
- Within the NGO community, the preferred approach to change is to undertake a thoughtful analysis of all issues, guided by clearly defined concepts and principles. This approach can also be used to resist or avoid change. It can become an excuse for not taking action.
- There is growing collaboration among "clusters" of NGOs (e.g. volunteer-sending, child sponsorship etc.) This increases trust and builds models for sharing effectively.
- There is a strong sense of determination in the community; there are dynamic "pockets" of energy and innovation. Many NGOs have adjusted to lower levels of government funding and lower staffing levels and have begun new programming. Several have built a base of support in a community or with a constituency, decreasing dependency on government funding.
- People enjoy being able to put aside their daily organizational worries to come together to explore creatively new ideas. They want to be part of something greater. Fora and processes such as those used by the Task Force are stimulating and energizing.
- Many people see the need for new alliances in order to increase the relevance of NGOs to new publics, increase the impact of NGO work, and find new ways to understand changes needed in the world today. The potential for alliances with other social sector groups such as unions, the women's movement, environment groups, etc. are [sic] welcomed. There is a growing openness to exploring potential areas of collaboration with the private sector.

THE ORGANIZING CONCEPT — GLOBAL CITIZENSHIP

The Task Force sought views from more than 400 people across Canada, including representatives from the membership of CCIC and the

Provincial/Regional Councils. We also spoke with representatives from outside the NGO sector: media, youth, local community leaders, ethno-racial groups, etc.

The NGO community strongly supported the concept of sustainable human development and the values it represents. As an idea, however, global citizenship seemed to resonate much more with people outside the NGO community; it also had broad support from within our community. The Task Force believes the two concepts of sustainable human development and global citizenship are linked.

Sustainable human development is a process that enhances the capacity of people to share visions and values, to deliberate together on the common good, to define goals collectively, and to build strategies to reach them. At its heart is the belief that human beings are the agents of change – that people must define their own development.

Sustainable human development is thus rooted in people's active participation – not just to fulfill their economic and social needs, but to voice their concerns and perspectives on their society and government, to contribute to shaping their destinies. Our development experience says that it is impossible to promote sustainable human development by working only in the South, or by working only with the poor. Building sustainable human development will require considerable changes within our own Northern societies and governments. We must affect trade and finance flows, consumption patterns, regulation of transnational companies, immigration and refugee policies, and our own use of the global commons.

Global citizenship nurtures *collective action for the good of the planet* and promotes equity. As citizens each person has equal rights. Global citizenship hinges on Canadians recognizing that they are members of a community of peoples who share a single planet. The challenge is to build Canadians' understanding that they have a stake in the well-being of that planet and its people. Opportunities must be taken to debate issues of collective concern and to participate in meaningful action. People can do this in informal groups; but opportunities for discussion and action should also exist through such organizations as unions, consumer groups, and teachers associations.

As global citizens Canadians would be prepared to take action in multilateral fora. Moreover, their views and actions on local or domestic issues would be informed and tempered by an awareness of the impact that local action can have on the quality of life in the world at large. As NGOs, we would approach this from the perspective of our values of justice, fairness, equity and a profound belief in the inherent dignity and rights of every human being.

The Task Force believes that building global citizenship should be the goal of NGOs' engagement with their publics. The current reality is very different; NGO messages often promote the idea that Canadians (and Northerners in general) "provide for" Southerners, rather than the idea of interdependence and connected destinies.

The assumptions about Northern benevolence are reflected in Public Service Announcements, development education materials, and fund-raising messages; these stress the transfer of money (from rich to poor), the use of international volunteers and the transfer of technology or knowledge.

One of the many negative impacts of "North gives, South receives" messages is that they hammer home a single message – the endless need of the South. No wonder so many donors consider the situation hopeless. Despite years of giving, they continue to receive the same appeals they've heard since 1980.

The Task Force believes that the "North gives, South receives" message will support neither Sustainable Human Development, nor a social movement broadly focused on an active, engaged citizenry. Nor will it enable Canadians to become global citizens involved in both domestic and global issues.

This does not mean that fund-raising and donors will cease to play a central role in the life of NGOs; but fund-raising should be done within the broader frame of global citizenship. The changed framework and focus will affect how NGOs fund-raise. It will affect the messages they send and their relationships with and obligations towards their donors.

APPLYING THE ORGANIZING CONCEPT TO THE KEY RELATIONSHIPS

In light of the context in which NGOs operate, the priorities of their partners in the South and our belief that NGOs must communicate with the public more forcefully and collectively, the Task Force proposes a rethinking of NGOs' relationships with three key constituencies:

- the Canadian public;
- Southern Partners;
- other NGOs.

While currently these relationships are all part of an NGO's operating reality, they often compete for resources and energy. In fact, their goals are sometimes contradictory.

For example, an organization seeking Canadian donations may say "$5 will buy seeds, $10 will buy a shovel, etc." While using the funds in this way, the organization may also be helping peasants organize or lobby for land reform. But these aspects of the work do not always get communicated to the donors. The public is left with the impression that development work is primarily welfare-oriented. This idea is often at odds with the reality of development work in the South. Misconceptions prevail because the message is often one-dimensional.

Further, the Task Force believes that NGOs have tended to play the role of "gatekeepers," guarding their relationships with Southerners by setting the terms and conditions for access to them. If people North and South are to connect, however, NGOs should instead assume the role of "bridge builders." Precedents exist. For example, NGOs have helped groups in the South develop links with an NGO's constituency or with other groups in Canada.

When a particular NGO gives up its monopoly over its relationship with a Southern partner, the benefits of that relationship are more widely shared; information and learning reaches more and different people. NGOs may act as interpreters of cultural differences, but this role is facilitative and catalytic, rather than restrictive.

Integrating these three significant relationships around the themes of sustainable human development and global citizenship serves many goals; it

- focuses energy;
- improves the ability of NGOs to operate with authenticity and professionalism;
- allows NGOs to achieve outcomes that are mutually beneficial; and
- fosters public trust.

By integrating these relationships NGOs are more accurately reflecting the reality of their work and encouraging the public to view NGO work with optimism.

STRATEGIC LEVERS FOR CHANGE

The Engagement Model

Global citizenship means an active, engaged citizenry who will want to have a role in shaping the world they live in, the world their children will inherit.

Many recent studies on how public opinion is formed indicate that people want to be involved in two-way dialogue on public concerns. People want to debate issues. They resent being preached at, persuaded, or presented with simplistic views of the world. They resist polarization of ideas and instead seek room for ambivalence. They look for a grey area in the public debate in which to question, discuss, test ideas, and gain confidence about their views.[3]

This is at odds with the way many NGOs have tackled public education. At one end of the spectrum, development education has been a one-way dissertation that seeks to impart information in the hope that, once people know what we know, they will think what we think. The Task Force has called this the "conversion model" – seeking to convert others to our view of the world. Recent thinking and reflection from communicators, educators and social marketers says that this will not work if the goal is to create engagement, a commitment to action, and the formation of new public ideas – that is, ideas that have currency in the society, that have a shaping force on collective decisions and action.

The Task Force believes that the CCIC and its membership must move from a "conversion model" of relating to the public to an "engagement model."

Valuing Diversity

Engaging people on issues which are important to them and finding common cause and relevance are important aspects of building public support. Yet across Canada, we received harsh messages from Canadians who were not "white." They said that NGOs excluded them. They said that while NGOs were active in their countries of origin, they themselves could not find a place in the NGO community. They said that NGOs have little relevance for them.

This culture of exclusion, as they named it, also extends to others such as youth and people who are not among the fortunate veterans of overseas work.

Building diversity involves going beyond outreach and inclusive language. What is needed is an analysis of the systemic barriers and structures that impede access.

What is needed is an explicit commitment by NGOs to change, and an action plan to implement that commitment within a reasonable time. NGOs should become more diverse. The rationale for such changes is not mere altruism. There are pragmatic reasons.

Diversity will improve NGOs' ability to connect with and engage a wider range of people. For example, by the year 2001 the number of visible minorities in Canada is projected to be about 5.7 million, or 17.7 percent of the population (an increase of over 350 percent in 15 years).[4] In addition, NGO staff, like the rest of the population is aging. NGOs need to attract youth.

There are also financial considerations. By the year 2001 a fifth of the labour force will be visible minorities. They will control a fifth of the GDP [gross domestic product] of the country in 2001, about $311 billion, compared to $76 billion in 1991.

Another element of diversity is that NGOs must become more "permeable." They must loosen their organizational boundaries in order to develop new kinds of alliances and relationships. To build effective alliances, NGOs must first identify the issues on which they wish to work and then find groups or organizations that share those concerns. This does not mean that NGOs will always take the lead; often they will join others.

Strategic alliances will be crucial for building public support. They should:

- be sectorally-based;
- reach beyond traditional networks to engage new actors; and
- be chosen deliberately and be coordinated to link local, national and international issues.

Working as a Community: A Sectoral Approach

The NGO community has already demonstrated capacity and success in working sectorally, for example, through the Foreign Policy Review Process, the CCIC Code of Ethics and the annual Parliamentary Days. It has also demonstrated its ability to work as a sector in alliance with other sectors through structures such as the NGO Organizing Committee for the World Summit for Social Development and the Canadian Participatory Committee for the UN Conference on Environment and Development. Clusters or families of NGOs are already working as "subsectors": church groups, child-sponsorship groups, development education groups etc.

In relation to the Canadian public, working sectorally means that:

- individual NGOs or groupings of NGOs do their own programming, but within a common framework;
- NGOs agree on the broad strategies and collective alliances that can be developed with other sectors; and
- brand recognition is developed, reinforcing a set of values and images which position the NGO community in the public's mind.

ACTION PLAN

Model of Change

It is the Task Force's belief that a few strategically-chosen, well-planned, and successful initiatives can create momentum for change. They can develop profile and energy sufficient to attract the interest of other organizations to participate in the changes. This interest will encourage others to find approaches and programmes which fit within the overall strategic framework. The Task Force calls this the "slipstream model."

While the first projects may be relatively small, they will be chosen for maximum impact. The projects would be designed to excite the imagination and promote the concept of global citizenship and sustainable human development. These efforts will be fully supported by research and media strategies. Guideposts which provide visible measures of success would enable people to see the impact being made.

The initiatives will demonstrate that effective change is possible. They will stress two-way dialogue with the public and be made accessible to others. Success will be measured not by whether all NGOs are involved, but rather by whether their momentum is enough to bring other NGOs and publics in, generating an ever-increasing cast of players over time.

A process of change requires ongoing monitoring and evaluation. Effective communications are constantly needed as those involved move back and forth through several phases. The principal phases are:

- *Readiness for Change* – recognizing the need to change and opening up to the possibilities, challenges, opportunities and approaches to effective change, etc.;
- *Re-focusing* – clarifying desirable, achievable goals, outcomes, messages, possible alliances and partners, measures, learnings, etc.;
- *Task Implementation* – small concrete tasks that remain central to the organization, involve as many people as possible, staff and volunteers, and, above all, make possible new learning and new insights; and
- *Data Gathering, Evaluation and Feedback* – essential mechanisms for change.

The "readiness for change" phase requires initial processes that lay the ground for new ideas and experiences, ones that shake up the underlying assumptions that attitudes, behaviours and structures are based on. One way to think of this is that people "unfreeze" when there is a significant change in behaviours, structures and attitudes that surround them. This change must occur in at least two of these parameters at once. If it occurs in only one, the other two pull people back into their old patterns. This is one reason why experiences overseas are often transformative; the salient structures, behaviours and attitudes in Honduras or Ethiopia can be very different from those in Canada.

The success of recycling can also be understood in this way. Accompanied by strong environmental messages at a variety of levels in the society, the recycling "blue box"[5] provided a very tangible and practical way to change one's behaviour. The method of garbage collection also changed, making it easy for people to recycle; they had only to deliver the recyclables to the curb on garbage day. The visibility of the blue boxes turned neighbours into role models and promoters of the change in attitude toward recycling. People began to participate. New behaviours, structures and attitudes combined to create fertile ground for new types of initiatives. The NGO community must find the global citizenship's "blue box."

Specific Actions

Within the overall frame of Sustainable Human Development and global citizenship, transformative strategies and actions must be developed in all three key relationships: with the Canadian public, with Southern partners,[6] and among NGOs.

NGO COMMUNITY ENGAGEMENT
Valuing Diversity
The Task Force concludes that this is one of the most urgent areas requiring action. NGOs must begin to adapt to the changing demographic reality of Canada in real and significant ways. The community must recognize that the issue is one of power, not of token representivity. Negotiated and shared values and goals are pre-requisites for effective interaction. Competency, whether as staff, volunteers, or in joint action is crucial.

An organization or community that values diversity would have the following profile:

- Joint projects with groups representing minority communities.
- Diversity present at every level in organization, including the Board.
- Reliance on non-traditional networks.
- Forums for exchanges of diverse opinions and perspectives.
- Explicit policy statement re diversity that ensures representivity beyond tokenism.
- Action plan to recruit people of colour, youth etc.
- Ongoing review of organizational policies/practices to reduce/remove barriers to inclusiveness.
- Close, two-way links with diverse local communities, based on trust and strong credibility.

How to begin
- Use the guidance document of the Code of Ethics as a vehicle for focusing members' attention on this issue. Conduct a workshop for members on the policies and practices necessary to meet the requirements of the Code.
- Include representatives from target communities in the planning and design of actions.
- Hold forums for direct engagement with communities of interest.

Funding
NGOs communicate with the public primarily through fund-raising. Canadians are either donors or prospective donors. At present, most organizations raise funds for their work individually, mainly through direct mail. A few raise considerable funds through TV appeals. For many church-based organizations, the majority of funds come from collections in the church. Overall, fund-raising by international development charities has been highly successful, generating an estimated $300 million each year. However, the Task Force heard that maintaining these levels is getting harder as the donor base ages. Organizations are spending more and more to get those last dollars in.

Despite attempts to develop new messages and approaches, most fund-raising appeals today are based on the "North gives, South receives" model. This will not change overnight. The Task Force anticipates that the "bread and butter" fundraising will remain for some time to come. However, it is the Task Force's firm belief that fund-raising messages and approaches should also build public support for sustainable human development. The NGO sector must put concerted energy into developing such alternatives. Fund-raising communications and activities must relate to Canadians as global citizens who share common concerns with people in the South. At the same time they must be able to meet the fundraisers' goal of raising considerable funds for their organizations. NGOs must take the most successful fund-raising approaches, adapt them, test them, and share the results.

The Task Force believes that the goals of fund-raising and building public support for sustainable human development can be successfully combined and will be best served by:

- incorporating the spirit and concept of global citizenship into fund-raising concepts from the outset;
- developing creative and dynamic messages that are an authentic reflection of NGO work and of the spirit in which it is carried out, messages that convey how NGOs are attacking the root causes of poverty, not just alleviating the symptoms;

- building a relationship between donors and global issues that promotes a transformative view of development;
- collaborating to become more accessible to the public and present a more common face to the public. This could start with collective work around messages, imaging, market-testing, etc.; and
- developing a more diversified fund raising base including partnerships with other sectors.

How to begin
- Develop a "learning circle/peer support" forum for NGO fundraisers, which explores lessons learned, constructively provides feedback on each others' work, and is supported by a research initiative on new forms of fund-raising, alternative sources of financing, and messages.
- Collaborate on the research mentioned above, including developing new images, messages and processes which support the global citizenship concept.
- Collaborate on a relationship-building program with donors, one that provides opportunities for donors to identify themselves as actors in the broader initiative of Sustainable Human Development.
- Consciously and deliberately use new initiatives, such as alternative revenue generation, the One World Fund or Development Makes Cents, as pilot vehicles to begin using global citizenship as the organizing concept through messaging, imaging and programming with donors.

Readiness for Change
Over the last several years, the CCIC membership has launched itself on a transformative path. Not only will change be necessary by NGOs individually; the NGO community must change how it functions collectively, its peer accountability mechanisms and its coherency of vision.

While the idea of global citizenship has been roughly sketched out, it will be up to NGOs to work it through. Greater clarity can be sought at an intellectual level, but action is essential immediately.

How to begin
- Support NGOs to bring the work of the Task Force to their senior staff and Boards.
- Document more systematically (from an action-research perspective) innovative programming already underway that reflects the recommendations of the Task Force.
- Encourage further analysis of the concept of global citizenship.
- Put in place a deliberate system for monitoring changes taking place and share the learnings resulting from these across the community.

PUBLIC ENGAGEMENT

There are two main ways to engage the public.

1 Create public ideas.
2 Get people talking and acting.

Creating Public Ideas

"Individuals hold private ideas. But we are held together as a public by shared ideas ... A public idea takes time to form. Its genesis may be rooted in the expertise and/or conviction of a small number of people, but it passes through gateways into the broader social arena where it is shared and shaped by many others. The process is not so much one of consensus as of convergence. What wasn't important becomes important; what was marginal becomes mainstream. Our collective perspective shifts; our collective priorities become realigned. A public idea is a social construct, and it has social consequences."[7]

The environment, gender equality, down-sizing, and deficit reduction are all examples of ideas that have become public ideas and have had the power to shape our society, its policies and practices. Not everyone has to be in agreement or even informed in order for public ideas to be effective. An example is the creation by a think-tank of the tax-free day. This simple communications vehicle carries a huge impact, reinforcing, year after year, the message that one spends half the year working just to pay taxes. This helps nourish the set of public ideas related to a belief in over-taxation, the necessity for government down-sizing, the individualism of the new economy, etc.

How do certain ideas come to have this force? No one really knows, but everyone participates. Some ideas catch like wild fire. Others limp along to extinction. Certainly, timing and context are part of it. The Task Force believes that the time is ripe for global citizenship. However, timing is not enough. The ideas must be nurtured; they must be framed in ways accessible to others. The NGO community will need to test the concept of global citizenship with Canadians and to find creative ways in which to make it meaningful and accessible to them.

Historically, think tanks have played a powerful role in the creation, dissemination, and legitimization of ideas. Some of them have been quite small but have still had a major impact. Often think tanks work not only on initiatives aimed at the public, but also on sustained communications targeted at influencers. These might be described as people who can "command some degree of public attention and who have some effect on public thinking." They help to give credibility and urgency to an idea as an issue worthy of public concern. They can help transform "a marginal idea into a mainstream priority."[8]

How to begin
- Talk to Canadians to test and further explore the idea of global citizenship and its resonance for and accessibility to the public.
- Work with existing organizations and institutions to add a global citizenship component to existing programs and processes; e.g. encourage the Boy Scout and Girl Guide movements to award a badge for good global citizenship.
- Over time create a global citizenship think tank (virtual or otherwise) in collaboration with other sectors. Its purpose would be to develop, promote, and coordinate the work on global citizenship, creating public ideas around the roles and responsibilities of global citizens, engaging influencers and stimulating their capacity to help carry these ideas into the public sphere. As a starting point, CCIC could be the locus for this effort.

Engaging the public in dialogue and action
What is the public? We've used the term as if there is a tangible, homogeneous entity somewhere called "the public." This is of course not the reality. The public comprises many individuals, anyone of whom wears a number of different hats. He/she may be a civil servant from 9 to 5, a church-goer, parent or daughter, a donor, a taxpayer, etc. We all have multiple roles and allegiances, and juggle a variety of interests and values (including the tension between altruism and self-interest).

How these play out for us on any one day, at any one time, will vary. Whether we become engaged in an issue will depend on how urgent an issue seems to be, how well it connects to where we are, and how others are reacting to it.

The authors of *Meaningful Chaos*[9] argue that people do not form judgements or relationships with public concerns in isolation. Sometimes people in their daily lives become the catalysts who discuss and act on public concerns. Sometimes institutions – schools, churches, NGOs – provide places for people to come together to talk about, learn, and act on public concerns. For an NGO, engaging the public might involve starting with its current constituency, e.g. a union, a school class or donors, but working with them in a different way.

Engagement means two-way dialogue, a discussion and working through of real (not contrived or biased) options. There are models for this that we can learn from. For example, work in the United States by the Kettering Foundation and by pollster Daniel Yankelovich on public judgement. In Canada, there is a very recent initiative called *The Society We Want*. New forms of engagement are possible.

A key challenge for the NGO community will be to find the harmony between these new forms of engagement and the strong value base of social justice and equity which the NGO community stands for. While the Task Force believes strongly that the NGO community must move away from the conversion model, it is not suggesting that NGOs become neutral in their values or vision.

The work of the Harwood Group suggests that people seek the opportunity to have personal influence on issues of public concern. A complete victory does not seem to be the goal, merely the possibility of progress and some discernible movement.[10]

We need to answer the questions, "how can people become engaged in global citizenship?" and "what would good global citizens actually do?" We need to find ways to tie action to people's daily lives – to see good global citizenship as actions that might include campaigning for a reduction in pesticide use in a local community, linking that to pesticide use in other parts of the world, being concerned about the working conditions under which one's clothing or carpets were produced, and urging the Canadian government to take a stronger stand on human rights in Nigeria. There are already many positive experiences with this in the NGO community that can be built upon.

However, it is not a simple matter of providing people with laundry lists of activities. Nor do we need bottled prescriptions for the globe's ailments. Part of the work will involve helping people discover roles for themselves as global citizens and implementors of change.

How to begin
- Create the "blue box" of global citizenship. Begin by holding a "find the blue box" workshop to brainstorm ideas.
- Develop demonstration projects within the framework of global citizenship as activated through selected issues. Choose an issue around which the first demonstration projects can be established. Parameters which should be considered in selecting a theme are its urgency in the eyes of Canadians; its ability to serve as a test case for NGO bridge-building between Canadians and people in the South; the potential for real change and positive solutions (outcome is not a foregone conclusion); its ability to engage influencers.

THE ROLE OF CCIC
In the short term (the next 5 years), CCIC must be prepared to take a leadership role in acting on the recommendations of the Task Force. It must do this at three levels: transforming individual organizations (including itself), stimulating and monitoring change in the NGO community, and stimulating and monitoring the process vis-à-vis the public.

How to begin
- Support NGOs in bringing the work of the Task Force into their organizations. Set up a support team and develop the tools necessary to

do this. This team would meet every Board and senior staff team in the membership at least once over the next two years.
- Foster further community debate and dialogue concerning the Task Force's work and its implementation among NGO groupings (e.g. volunteer-sending, child-sponsorship, development education). This could grow into the development of a global citizenship think tank.
- Take responsibility for the Task Force follow-up, including searching out the members willing to take leadership roles on specific actions, determining its own leadership role, setting up and implementing a monitoring and evaluation system.

Measuring Success

There are several criteria that are fundamental to the success of the global citizenship approach. Turned into questions, these could be used as filters to choose between a range of strategies, tactics and actions. It is not anticipated that any single initiative will meet all the criteria; but they will help to provide guidance and allow one to be clear about which success criteria a particular initiative is addressing.

Some of the following criteria pertain to the public sphere, while others address NGO work. Some relate equally well to both. The criteria are not listed by order of priority.

1. Enhances public engagement.
2. Broadens the base of the NGO community and builds alliances.
3. Presents a variety of ways for people or groups to participate.
4. Engages the public with some aspect of global citizenship.
5. Enables Canadians to deliberate on the issues – to work them through themselves, rather than being preached at.
6. Works towards autonomous, core funding.
7. Builds momentum and synergy inside and outside the community.
8. Focus of action is closest to the public(s) to be engaged (eg. community-based programming).
9. Makes people and communities (not documents or institutions) the priority.
10. Promotes diversity.
11. Fosters systemic learning within the sector.
12. Impacts on Canadian public policy in support of sustainable human development.

CONCLUSIONS

The time for change is now. To create the momentum needed to accomplish the Task Force's recommendations requires action by NGOs individually and collectively. The recommendations found throughout this document delineate a major shift in the way NGOs work. This is not to undermine the work already in progress, but to emphasize the need to reexamine *how* it is being done. We recognize that the degree of change will vary from one organization to the next, but we cannot overstate the urgency of the need for all organizations to act now.

NOTES

1 Civil society has been defined as the arena of organized citizen activity outside of the state and the market. It is people coming together to define, articulate, and act on their concerns through various forms of organization and expression.
2 In abstraction, these three spheres are not linked to a pre-determined set of interests or values. All three produce both good and bad human results, depending on the people and powers active in them.
3 The Harwood Group, *Meaningful Chaos: How People Form Relationships with Public Concerns.* A Report Prepared for the Kettering Foundation 1993.
4 John Samuel, *Visible Minorities in Canada: A Projection* (Ottawa: Carleton University, June 1992).
5 We recognize that the "blue box" takes on many colours and forms throughout the country. It is the concept of a tangible symbol accompanied by action that we are emphasizing here.
6 The Task Force did not have the time or capacity to develop actions or strategies in regard to the NGO relationship with the South, except to insist that the present one-way "north to south" emphasis be changed, and that the partnership relationship be further developed and strengthened to become more genuine. This remains a crucial task for the future.
7 Eric Young, "Strategies of Public Engagement," paper prepared for the Aga Khan Foundation Canada Roundtable on Systematic Learning, June 1996, 10.
8 Ibid., 11, 12.
9 The Harwood Group, *Meaningful Chaos: How People Form Relationships with Public Concerns.* A Report Prepared for the Kettering Foundation 1993.
10 Ibid., 31, 34.

Contributors

TIM DRAIMIN is a consultant specializing in international co-operation, non-governmental organizations (NGOs), and public policy. He has worked with Canadian NGOs, both in Canada and abroad, for over twenty years, most recently as director of policy with the Canadian Council for International Co-operation. In addition to his practical experience in foreign policy dialogue, he has written widely on development and foreign policy making. Recent publications include: "Sustainable Human Development as a Global Framework," *International Journal* (spring 1996); "Civil Society and the Democratization of Foreign Policy," in *Canada among Nations 1995: Democracy and Foreign Policy* (1996); *Potential for Partnership: International Co-operation Institutions and Canadian and Latin American NGOs* (1994); "Public Policy Dialogue and Canadian Aid," in *Canadian International Development Assistance Policies: An Appraisal* (1994).

MICHAEL A. EDWARDS was until recently Head, Information and Research, Save the Children Fund-UK. At SCF he pioneered the application of organizational learning to the non-profit development sector and has overseen a ground-breaking series of studies on non-governmental organizations (NGOs). He has fourteen years of direct NGO experience, including four years as Oxfam-UK's representative in Lusaka and two years as director of the PRASAD Foundation in India. He has also been a Leverhulme Fellow at the University of Manchester's Institute for Development Policy and Management. He has co-edited a series of books with David Hulme: *Beyond the Magic Bullet: NGO Performance and Accountability in the Post–Cold War World* (1996); *Too*

Close for Comfort? NGOs, States and Donors (1997); and *Making a Difference: NGOs and Development in a Changing World* (1992).

DAVID GILLIES is Manager, Development Policy & Research, Aga Khan Foundation Canada, and has responsibility for co-ordinating a research programme on challenges facing South Asian non-governmental organizations. Previously policy coordinator at the International Centre for Human Rights and Democratic Development, he has also been a consultant for the Canadian International Development Agency, the North-South Institute, the Canadian Council for International Co-operation, and the Department of Foreign Affairs and International Trade. Recent publications include *Between Principle and Practice: Human Rights in North-South Relations* (1996) and (with Gerald J. Schmitz) *The Challenge of Democratic Development* (1992).

ABAN MARKER KABRAJI is Country Representative and Regional Director for South and South East Asia, World Conservation Union (IUCN), Pakistan. She is responsible for the overall management of the three IUCN offices in Karachi, Islamabad, and Peshawar and for all IUCN programme activities in the country. These responsibilities include the overall supervision of the implementation of the National Conservation Strategy (NCS). Under her leadership, the IUCN has emerged as a key player in Pakistan's sustainable development agenda. Mrs Kabraji was instrumental in the development of Pakistan's National Conservation Strategy and played a key role in collaborating with the Ministry of Environment in the conceptual development and political and staff management of the NCS. She is a member of the board of the Sustainable Development Policy Institute (Pakistan) and of the board of the International Institute for Sustainable Development (Canada), and a member of the President's Round-Table, International Development Research Centre (Canada).

ROGER C. RIDDELL is a Research Fellow at the Overseas Development Institute, London, England. He has undertaken major evaluations on the impact of non-governmental organizations (NGOs) for the British Overseas Development Administration and the governments of Finland and Sweden. His work on official development assistance includes a major study on "Linking Costs and Benefits in NGO Development Projects," and he is the main author of a European consortium study on Northern NGOs in the post–Cold War era (*Discerning the Way Together*). Recent publications include: *The Future of Aid* (1996); *Non-governmental Organizations and Rural Poverty Alleviation* (1995); and *Foreign Direct Investment in Sub-Saharan Africa* (1991).

GERALD J. SCHMITZ is with the Research Branch of the Library of Parliament in Ottawa, Canada. He is currently Research Director of the House of Commons Standing Committee on Foreign Affairs and International Trade and also an adviser to the Canada-Europe Parliamentary Association. As well as numerous journal articles, he has co-authored two books: *The Challenge of Democratic Development* (1992) and *Debating Development Discourse* (1995).

ERIC YOUNG is President of E·Y·E Inc., a communications agency he founded in 1993 which specializes in the creation of strategies, campaigns, and partnerships to influence social change. He has consulted to senior executives of some of the most progressive government, non-profit, and private sector organizations, helping them to manage repositioning and change strategies. His clients have included the Bank of Montreal, the Lung Association, Social Investment Organization, National AIDS Secretariat, and the International Centre for Human Rights and Democratic Development. He is a director of the Canadian Centre for Philanthropy and Calmeadow, an adviser to the Media Analysis Lab at Simon Fraser University, and serves/has served on advisory committees to the Art Gallery of Ontario, the National Capital Commission, PEN Canada, and the Canadian Council for International Co-operation. He was elected a Fellow of the Royal Society for the Encouragement of Arts, Manufacturers, and Commerce in 1992.